The Hidden Reader

The

HIDDEN READER

Stendhal, Balzac, Hugo, Baudelaire, Flaubert

VICTOR BROMBERT

HARVARD UNIVERSITY PRESS

Cambridge, Massachusetts, and London, England 1988

Library of Congress Cataloging-in-Publication Data

Brombert, Victor H.
   The hidden reader: Stendhal, Balzac, Hugo, Baudelaire,
Flaubert / Victor Brombert.
      p.   cm.
   Includes index.
   ISBN 0-674-39012-1 (alk. paper)
   1. French literature—19th century—History and criticism.
2. Reader-response criticism.   3. Authors and readers—France—
History—19th century.   I. Title.
PQ282.B75   1988   87-26115
840'.9'007—dc19   CIP

To Beth

Lauren

Marc

and to James Gill

Acknowledgments

I OWE a great deal to many friends, students, and mentors whose intellectual and human presence inspired me. High on this list are Henri Peyre, Jean Boorsch, René Wellek, Georges Poulet, Jean Starobinski, Jean Rousset, Jean-Pierre Richard, and the late Erich Auerbach. But my greatest debt by far is to my wife Beth, who has been my most generous and my most demanding reader. Her critical comments were unfailingly perceptive and helpful.

Special thanks are due Timothy J. Clark for valuable perspectives on nineteenth-century "readers" in art; to Joseph Frank for encouraging me in conversations and through his example to keep love of literature and love of ideas in proper balance; to James Gill for reminding me, also through his example, that critical insight is by no means the exclusive privilege of academic critics.

Further thanks go to Carol Szymanski, Linda Torbert, and Rosalinde Core, who in so many ways have provided much-valued assistance.

Finally, I wish to express my warm appreciation to Maria Ascher, who, once again, has given a manuscript of mine her expert and sensitive editorial care.

Contents

The Hidden Reader

Approaches

The title of this book is meant to be a suggestive signal, not a threat of a systematic approach. It echoes the title of an essay included here, on Balzac, in which the image of the hidden reader has fairly broad implications regarding literary mediation and the gap between text and event.

Two specific literary activities are brought together in that title: the act of reading made manifest at a number of levels; and the strategies of concealment, conscious and unconscious, which in the writing / reading process remain inseparable from the desire to reveal. A variety of "readers"—real, fictional, metaphoric—may indeed be involved in the act of literary communication: the actual reader, facing the text, whose presence in time may or may not coincide with the time of the writing; the imagined or putative reader, that is, the one explicitly or implicitly (at times polemically) projected by the work, who may in some ways resemble yet is radically different from the real reader; the fictional reader embedded in the text, namely any figure within the literary construct who reads a part or the whole of the written substance (this can be an invisible figure, like Natalie in Balzac's *Le Lys dans la vallée,* to whom the entire story is in fact addressed as a form of confession); and of course the author himself, whether in the act of writing, revising, judging (and misjudging) his work and that of others. Stendhal by his own admission enjoyed reading himself *pour se désennuyer;* but more significant than this recourse against boredom is the exemplary mobility, improvisational verve, and sense of vibrato which in his case are demonstrably engendered by his reactions to the very activity of writing.

What is true of Stendhal's indirections, improvisations, spontaneous reactions to his own compositional thrusts, games of dissimulation, and camouflaged self-revelations is basically true of all writers, though perhaps in a less consciously provocative manner. It is these paradoxes of creation, these private theatricals pointing to a hidden "inner" text, that make literary interpretation such a fascinating and elusive activity. The obliquities of literary discourse are linked not only to ironic strategies, to the eros of observation and self-observation, to shifts and conflicts involving different levels of language and concealed meanings, but also to impulses of deceit and self-deceit which ultimately induce both writer and reader (at times they are one and the same) to "read" themselves.

According to Proust, every reader of a literary work is first and foremost a reader of himself, "le propre lecteur de soi-même." The statement, which can be extended to the act of writing, should not be attributed to narcissistic self-indulgence. Self-knowledge and self-creation go hand in hand. This presumably is what Montaigne had in mind when he declared that he and his book were "cosubstantial" ("livre consubstantiel à son autheur . . .").[1]

Writing an introduction to one's own essays poses some special problems. It unavoidably means reading oneself, quite literally so—a sobering experience at best. Even if one tries to remain as unassuming as possible, one is bound to raise some fundamental questions. The backward glance at one's own critical efforts raises for instance the vexing question of unity and intent. Are the suggested order, unity, and purpose merely contrived afterthoughts, or do they represent a credible reading of an underlying project? Coming as it does at the beginning, but having in fact been written last, this introductory essay thus exemplifies any number of textual overtures, reenacting the enigma and artifice of opening signals. To what extent is any textual beginning determined by what is known to follow? To what extent does it impose a more or less conscious intentionality?

"Opening signals" are the specific subject of the next essay in this collection, but the problem of beginnings, or *incipits,* informs a number of other essays. For textual overtures are intimately related to writing / reading strategies and interpretive provocations. Opening sentences, as for instance in Diderot's *Jacques le Fataliste,* can establish from the outset a dialogic tension between narrator and reader, thus questioning the act of communication. Beyond the self-consciousness about literary technique and genre tradition, large issues are at stake at the threshold of any literary construct: the articulations of freedom and necessity, the links between metonymy and metaphor, the "memory" of the text capable of transforming a sequential into a simultaneous experience.

Paying close attention to opening signals is only one of the forms of close reading, and should be a basic rule of good criticism, whether old or new. Such criticism implies that every detail in a literary work is significant, even when aggressively "nonsensical"; that poetic and ironic effects, as well as the production of meaning, are dependent on more or less deliberate and more or less complex linguistic interplays and tensions. From that point of view, the reading of prose fiction is not an essentially different experience from the reading of poetry, and the most rewarding way of dealing with a novel may well be to approach it as a poetic construct. Such an approach does not always come easily. The sheer length, the complexities, the apparent digressions, the seductions of the plot (or its disturbing absence), and the hybridities of the novel as a genre may seem to deny the possibility of treating fiction as a tightly woven verbal texture and structure. It is significant that the so-called New Critics preferred on the whole to concern themselves with poems—and short poems at that. There were of course other reasons behind this predilection for the concentrated lyric poem. But the fact is that the attentive and rigorous reading of fiction calls for a patiently acquired intimacy which can come only from repeated contact with the work, from a long-standing and demanding relation into which many readers—even sophisticated ones—are not always willing to enter. Yet modern fiction, especially to the extent that it uses a narrative mode to subvert narrativity, would seem to require precisely such an approach: one that looks beyond plot, concatenation, and sequentiality to the poetic artifices of spatial form.

What kind of reader am I? This question, which no self-critical critic can avoid, points to another aspect of reader-concealment. The underlying quest for self-knowledge can be neither satisfied nor eluded. Hiding and even dissimulating may well be necessary features of the difficult enterprise of finding oneself. The problem of language is central to this paradox. Max Frisch, in his novel *Stiller,* which plays any number of variations on the nettling question of identity, maintains that we possess language only to know what we are not. He posits this as the obverse of a utopian wisdom of silence: "Wer schweigt, ist nicht dumm" ("He who is silent is not dumb").[2] But the mendacity of language, even if it leads us through the most scabrous fictions, ultimately may lead us to our inner center. The playful obliquities of literature are hardly ever frivolous, for they allow us to come closer to ourselves. In that sense, one might say that all writing, including criticism, is and should be autobiographical. Which is not to suggest that it should be self-indulgent, or that it comes without discipline. Individuals, as well as groups and

3

entire cultures, must work hard and long to gain what is quite properly called *insight*.

After years of teaching and writing about literature, it would indeed be surprising if I had not asked myself some basic questions about my preferences and beliefs. *Credo* is no doubt too pretentious and dogmatic a word to account for what is essentially a suspicion of all doctrinaire stances, an instinctive distaste for presumptuous critical absolutism. As long as I can remember, I have suspected that precision and rigor were not to be confused with pseudoscientific arrogance and theoretical terrorism. Above all, ever since my student days, I have felt an aversion for all critical discourses that forced an arbitrary reading on a text without regard for how that text asked to be read. Even more appalling seemed to me the dogmatic self-assurance of critics more interested in hearing themselves, and each other, than in tuning in to the special music of a work and the unique voice of an author. The lack of humility before a work of art and the refusal to accept the role of attentive interpreter seemed to me something of a heresy—if this word did not also smack of dogmatism and intolerance. Such an attitude, which was nothing but a determination to treat the work as a mere pretext for the critic's intellectual prowess, seemed to place the practitioner above, or rather outside, the central purpose of his practice. I kept thinking of musicologists who preferred to discuss musical structure rather than hear music performed, doctors more interested in pathology than in patients, theologians more concerned with doctrine and with excommunicating one another than with faith and the spiritual life. It did not take much imagination to see the link between all perverse excesses of abstraction.

The sad truth is that literary studies have been in increasing danger of losing touch with the general cultivated public by locking themselves up in a number of hermetic discourses. Even colleagues specializing in the field readily admit—in moments of lucid despondency—that they can no longer understand one another. Yet it remains the passionate conviction of some that literature can be a revelatory communication, that its complexities and difficulties need not be a proof of nonmeaning or "undecidability," and that linguistic games do not exclude intellectual and moral substance. In this perspective, the critic's function, both as reader and as interpreter, is to relate the detail to the larger pattern, tracing the subtle and often paradoxical connections between language and ideas, constantly engaging in a shuttle between minimal and maximal readings. Such readings, whether for instance of the contradictory signals in a title such as *Germinal*, or of the conflicting temporalities implicit in the first sentence of *L'Education sentimentale,* are never sheer displays of the critic's cleverness and virtuosity. They raise questions having to do with the tensions between history and individual destiny, between the ideologies of progress and the longing for a mythical order, between commitment to life and commitment to an artistic, posthumous order. For ultimately literature speaks to us of life and death.

Along the way, even the least theoretically inclined critic with a genuine sense of discrimination will of course be sensitive to questions of method. But being alert to methodological problems is not the same as being crushed or blinded by them. It may help to remember that the word "method" (from the Greek *meta* = "along," and *odos* = "road") suggests just that: an ordering process that occurs "along the way," a process that accompanies and follows an activity rather than precedes it. Method should thus never be a tyrannical prescription, but be a supple way of using available approaches and of testing them in an almost experimental way. Some might be quick to denounce such a view as hopelessly eclectic. But who is to say that eclecticism is bad? Although in practice all criticism is partially blind and biased, should not the ideal aim be a totalization of all possible approaches? Such a totalization is of course beyond the grasp or scope of any single individual. Still, the ability to combine perspectives—the blending, for instance, of thematic, structural, and deconstructive approaches—is likely to be more reasonable and productive than locking oneself up in a single-minded, abstractly rigorous, largely rigid and myopic system.

Perhaps the trouble is that so few of the practicing critics aiming at theoretical sophistication have retained a sense of a personal voice. Influenced and awed by masters who strive for originality yet demand strict obedience, academic critics in particular often write as though they were engaged in parody. Rarely in the past has the critic's discourse been so conformist and predictable within the confines of various overspecialized idioms. After the first paragraph, sometimes earlier, one can usually foretell the references, the footnotes, the conclusions.

It may therefore be more important than ever to expect that sound criticism, while attuned to texts and sharply focused on issues, be an intensely personal affair. But being personal, and even autobiographical in a deep sense, is not the same as being self-serving and arrogantly subjective. Of the critic, one might say what T. S. Eliot said of the poet: that he is a medium, not the affirmation of a "personality."[3] Personal yet unassuming, the self of the critic, unveiling and producing meaning, is actively engaged in a drama of forms and ideas.

To paraphrase Virginia Woolf, who was writing about literature in general, criticism is an art, not a method of self-expression.[4] And an art it is, or should be. The good critic or literary interpreter, much like the musical interpreter, knows how to perform at the same time faithfully and inventively. The musical metaphor is of course only approximate, and does not stand up under close inspection. Literary criticism is not a performance, and literary interpretation cannot be reduced to a reading—though a good public reading of, say, Dante or Rilke, can in itself be a masterful act of criticism. And the practice of reading aloud should perhaps be a prerequisite for all those who claim to be serious students of literature. But talking intelligently about literature evidently requires other skills too. For the specific challenge of literary criticism is that it necessarily involves a problematic discourse of words about words, and a construct of meanings to the second degree—that is, an elaboration of meanings about meanings.

The musical metaphor may nonetheless be valid because it lays stress on *interpretation*—another word that has fallen into disrepute in some quarters. Nothing, of course, could be less justified than such theoretical hostility to interpretation, for interpretation is a fundamental human activity ("the normal respiration of the intelligence," to use Borges's expression)[5] and corresponds to the permanent need to account for experience. It is precisely such a need that impels Baudelaire to write, upon hearing Wagner's music, that he would like to *transform* his aesthetic pleasure into knowledge ("transformer ma volupté en connaissance"). But the knowledge in question clearly transcends aesthetic gratification. Malraux perhaps put it most tersely when he had one of his intellectual heroes assert that a human being's noblest effort is to transform the widest possible range of experience into understanding or knowledge ("transformer en conscience une expérience aussi large que possible").[6]

Needless to say, such translation or interpretation does not go without the risk of intellectualization or betrayal. And there is the further risk, especially for the critic who also happens to be a teacher, of usurping authority. For ultimately, no matter how useful the function of the literary specialist may be, interpretation should be each individual's responsibility; it is a fiercely private affair which must not and cannot be delegated. What this means is that the critic must not impose his reading by interpreting for others, or suggest that interpretation is the monopoly of literary mandarins. Respect for the reader's integrity and responsibility goes hand in hand with respect for the text.

What good criticism, attentive to literary and metaliterary signals, can reveal is the relation between the never insignificant detail and the reasonable parameters of a literary work. This still leaves considerable freedom and a wide range for further critical maneuvers. Playfulness is of the literary essence. And respect for the work is not to be confused with pious literalism. The interplay of metaphoricity, symbolic language, and thematic structures—the proper subject of criticism—calls for mobility, especially as neither language nor symbols and themes are ever stable. Words slip and slide, as Eliot puts it; they will not stay in place.[7] The same could be said of themes, which are not inert, pre-existent realities, but—like meanings—are elaborated, or rather woven, within and by the text. Decipherment of linguistic and figural patterns thus remains provocative and frustrating. This intellectual and emotional provocation is at the heart of any artistic "order," specifically in those fictions created with language. As Borges said with true humanistic pride, referring to the imaginary region of Tlön and the intrusion of the world of fantasy into the world of reality: "Tlön is surely a labyrinth, but it is a labyrinth devised by men, a labyrinth destined to be deciphered by men."[8]

These challenging indirections and elusive readings are further complicated by the intertextual nature of all literary endeavors. For texts feed on texts, and writing depends not only on reading but on unreading and unwriting other works. Thus, Italo Svevo's *Una Vita* is not merely the story of a sensitive but somewhat inept young provincial asphyxiated by the bureaucratic banking world of Trieste; it is a reworking in specifically Svevian terms of Balzac's Rastignac, Stendhal's Julien Sorel, and Flaubert's Frédéric Moreau. A conscious and partly unconscious dialogue, or rather polylogue, is established, implying a succession of more or less hidden readings. This dialogic nature of literary creation and literary communication obviously involves the author in a dramatic tension with himself, and transforms his consciousness into a multi-voiced stage. It also means that the reader cannot merely be the passive receiver of an unequivocal written message. He too is compelled to enter into a conflictual relation with the text (and with himself), and must experience in the process of reading a series of fluctuations, hesitations, changes of mind, inner contradictions, doubts, and uncertainties. For the passionate lover of literature, these doubts include doubts concerning literature itself and the possibility of any reliable discourse about it.

Perhaps it is these doubts and uncertainties which ultimately provide the most stimulating challenge to the student of literature. "What is literature?"—the title of Sartre's important essay surely corresponds to the disturbing question every literary scholar worth his salt must have asked himself. And that question leads to other equally troubling questions. What is the purpose of literary studies and literary analysis? Why not just enjoy the experience of reading? What is it that can justify the existence of teachers of literature and literary critics? What exactly is the purview of that academic subject called Literature, and what accounts for the formation of literary canons and the institutionalized reverence for masterpieces?

The truth is that these apparently irreverent questions are not at all dismissive; they go to the heart of literary studies, and sustain them in a probing and fecund manner. Attempting to define the specifically literary nature of literature—its literariness—is also a way of assessing its relation to, and distance from, the world it claims to represent and the wide range of problems it faces. Tracing the tenuous and often mobile frontiers between "literature" and "reality" is also a way of examining the relation between poesis and mimesis, between fiction and life, between all ludic enterprises and the human search for meanings. For even the Knights of Nothingness, as Sartre calls them, were highly dependent on the referential reality they despised or denied. Flaubert's love-hate relation with this so-called reality is a case in point, and constitutes as it were the central subject of his entire work, which proclaims the superiority of art over experience and at the same time the inability of language ever to account for an experience that remains ineffable.

This implicitly tragic paradox, capable of producing hidden meanings at a variety of levels, is in the final analysis what the reader of literature is privileged to confront. Such a "hidden" participation no doubt requires agility, nimbleness, an ironic bent, a sense of joy, love of language and ideas (as well as a distrust of them), a need for communication and communion, together with a yearning for privacy, a concern for the devices and materialities of art, yet also a desire to transcend them. And these are some of the reasons—but only some—why reading and teaching literature, and writing about it, can be so much fun and also such serious business.

Opening Signals in Narrative

The end is in the beginning.
Samuel Beckett

Louis Aragon, having agreed to improvise on the subject of his own creative processes, proposed an impertinent title: *I Never Learned to Write*.[1] This title, which also provides the last sentence of the essay ("Je n'ai jamais appris à écrire"), becomes less scabrous if one remembers to quote it in full, with its coordinating particle and its final Latin word pointing to the problem of poetic or fictional beginnings: "Je n'ai jamais appris à écrire ou 'les incipit.' " For what Aragon claims never to have known in advance is the "unfolding" of his stories, the "déroulement" of his textual landscape, which he discovered, as he says, as though he were his own reader. At a paradoxical extreme, it would seem that all a text needs to be constituted and propelled forward is a first word.

The writer as reader. Aragon, as a child, discovered that hearing and lying, reading and playing, interpreting and inventing, are the same. An initial word meant the necessity of the game as well as the game of necessity. Hence the assertion: "I never wrote my novels; I read them." What is involved is the threshold of the text: not merely the generative, matricial virtue of the initial (and perhaps arbitrary) attack, but that point both in time and space where a text, separating itself from what it was and is not yet, comes into being. "On pense à partir de ce qu'on écrit": the key expression *à partir de,* referring to a supposedly dynamic point of origin, occurs again some ten pages later, as Aragon speculates on the mechanism of writing "*à partir* d'une phrase, d'une image."

The Surrealists were fond of invoking that galvanizing opening and revelatory sentence, the *phrase de réveil.* Revelatory, because the *incipit* meant the initial incantation as well as the first signal of the initiation. It is not surprising that mythical notions press themselves forward. Every opening of a novel or a poem, says Aragon, revives the image of Hercules at the crossroads. Image of destiny? It would seem that this is exactly what Aragon has in mind: "A constellation of words,

9

normally called a sentence, thus plays the role of fate." Thinking follows. The opening attack constitutes the initiation to a "mental ceremony." He remembers how as a boy he lent magic significance to any linguistic threshold.

Aragon's title echoes Raymond Roussel's autobiographical *Comment j'ai écrit certains de mes livres* ("How I wrote some of my books"), which reveals the formal aspects of his compositions, specifically the meta-grammatical mechanisms that force the hand of the writer in the invention of his story. The problem of inaugurating a text can of course be thematized, as in the work of Samuel Beckett, to whom Aragon also refers with enthusiasm. In him he salutes the literary explorer of a space that is always open and always closed, a space where nothing in fact ever begins or ends, a fictional space which indefinitely *begins without end*. With Beckett, the last words come first. And the first words point to the problematics of defining an inaugural moment. *The Unnamable* opens with the three questions that the reader expects to be answered by the ideal beginning. But here the questions have no answer: they keep the text moving: "Where now? Who now? When now?" ("Où maintenant? Quand maintenant? Qui maintenant?"). In *Molloy*, the first novel of Beckett's trilogy, compulsive writing, related to the matricial image of the first sentence ("I am in my mother's room"), is presented as an impasse. The second image is the ambivalent ambulance, leading to birth as well as to death. The aporetic process of writing thus links the end to the beginning, in fact poses it as a theme. The end of the first paragraph of *Molloy* states: "Here's my beginning"—then immediately qualifies this. "It was the beginning . . . now it's nearly the end."

These are not frivolous quips or facile pirouettes that Aragon and Beckett indulge in. Their remarks reach the heart of the constitutive elements of narrative discourse. They stress in particular the multiple linearity of any such process: that of narrated time as well as of the time of narration, the linearity of writing and of reading. But such linear modes are not necessarily perceived, or accounted for, in the same manner. Frank Kermode, in *The Sense of an Ending*, speaks of end-determined fictions, of epic and biblical models in which the end is in harmony with the beginning, of our deep need for intelligible outcomes, of man's "forward memory" linked to an "insatiable interest in the future" toward which we are oriented biologically. Modern fiction, according to Kermode, develops when authenticated accounts of beginnings cease to enjoy authority. Novels thus provide reassurance in a world that has demythologized Apocalypse.[2]

Sartre, on the other hand, views the narrative process as radically alien, and even opposed, to the time order of living. "Things happen one way and we tell them in the opposite sense," observes Roquentin in *La Nausée*. The orders of living and telling are incompatible. "One has to choose: live or tell." The reason is that in lived life the future is not there yet. Life has no fanfare beginnings and no fanfare ends. In an amusing passage which almost amounts to a parody of all storytelling, Roquentin shows that what in fact happens when one tells a story is that one begins with the end.[3] Thus the apparently innocent sentence, "As I was walking out that morning," is not at all a beginning, for obviously in life, when we walk out in the morning, we do not say to ourselves, "As I am walking out . . . ," any more than we say to ourselves, "As I am reading an essay on opening signals in narrative." The very structure of such a sentence creates suspense: the end is always there, present though invisible. The banal act of walking out of one's house is, in a narrative text, endowed with a precious quality: it announces something which is to happen. As conventional readers, we know how to attach importance to apparently unimportant details; we trust that they will turn out to be significant, and may become angry with the writer if they turn out not to be. But this, according to Sartre, is precisely the difference between art and life. Life never comes with ready-made omens.

Valid as this distinction may be, it hardly accounts for the complicated and contradictory operations of the text. For a text also has a memory—not only a projected future. Its linearity is constantly being subverted. Lessing, as well as Diderot, in distinguishing between the verbal and the plastic arts, insisted that language was made up of a succession of words in time. It would follow that literature, in particular in its narrative forms, must obey the laws of temporal sequence. Yet things are not quite so simple. The text has its own space.[4] One of the manifestations of modernity is precisely the dislocation, at times quite radical, of the temporality of language. Consequence or cause? Narrative structures tend to undermine their narrativity in favor of self-referential structures. The narrator becomes the reader.[5]

A *substitution* of this type implies that even the most eventful story, through an early interplay of grammar and rhetoric, calls for a non-diachronic reading. When the narrator, in chapter 14 of *Little Dorrit*, announces that his "history" must now be seen with Little Dorrit's eyes, he is in fact teasing us into a heightened state of consciousness concerning the early signals of the text. For Little Dorrit is present when she is still invisible, and her eyes see before she even appears. The prison-keeper's daughter, that little "angel" face touched by "divine compassion" who, in the opening chapter, watches the jailbirds being fed, prefigures the little heroine herself metamorphosed, many chapters later, into a "small bird reared in captivity." A similar telescoping blurs any distinction between early images of gloom in the Marseilles jail and later images of gloom in London's Marshalsea prison. The displacement of images seems to obey the imperatives of plot development; in reality, it serves the laws of metaphoric simultaneity.

Very often, in fact, when a novel at the outset proposes an itinerary, it also sets out to deny it. Fabrice del Dongo's destiny, in *La Chartreuse de Parme,* seems to lead him from place to place in quest of adventure. But this epic *topophilia,* contradicted by the monastic and therefore immobilizing title of the novel, implies not linearity, but metonymic transferral and ultimately an arresting metaphoric resemblance. It is the *same landscape* that accompanies Fabrice. From his prison cell in the Farnese Tower, he still sees (quite an impossibility at that distance) the chain of the Alps—that is, the unmovable setting of his childhood near Lake Como. The epic quest has been transmuted into lyric epiphany. Sometimes it is the entire first chapter that serves as a thematic spatialization. In *Moby-Dick,* which begins on the terra firma of the Isle of the Manhattoes, water is immediately substituted for rock. And this substitution of water for rock, then of the larger space of the ocean for simply water, translates the notion of departure as moral hygiene into a tragic appetite for the unreachable, the "everlasting itch for things remote." Opening signals in Melville's novel thus tell a story without telling one, by means of nonnarrative semantic displacements from plain water to "water gazers," to "ocean reveries," to "plunging," to the "magic" of meditation, to a "mystical vibration" associated with sea travel, to the adjective "holy" associated with the sea, and to the image of the "ungraspable phantom of life" linked with the story of Narcissus and his tragic drowning.

II

Louis Aragon merely hinted at a fascinating problem. His nicely illustrated little book offers semiconfessions and numerous sallies, but no sustained argument. The field of opening signals still remains fairly uncharted territory. Some probings come to mind. Claude Duchet's "Pour une socio-critique ou variations sur un incipit" is a brilliant demonstration, on the basis of the opening sentence of *Madame Bovary,* of how the language of the social group, in its *épaisseur sociale,* is from the outset inscribed into the text.[6] Raymond Jean, in a rapid survey, examined the opening sentences of a few prototypes of the Nouveau Roman (Butor, Sarraute, Robbe-Grillet, Simon, Pinget) to come to the somewhat excessive conclusion that the threshold phrases in each case summed up the entire novel.[7] Dominique Lanceraux, more modestly, focused on the expository sentence of a single novel by Claude Simon to examine in the microcosm of the initiatory verbal act the "a-chronological principles" that govern the composition of the entire work.[8] In comparison with these astute, often virtuosic, but fundamentally nonconceptual approaches, the remarks by Frank Kermode, typically made, by the way, with British grace, are more provocative. He recently returned to these questions in a somewhat more theoretical vein in an article entitled "Novels: Recognition and Deception," in which he argues, having assimilated Barthes and Derrida, that "deceptive beginnings," especially in modern texts, correspond to their polysemantic nature; that openings are the measure of the complexity of a truly satisfying coding system: that "plurality is the nature of narrativity."[9]

The most systematic, though perhaps scattered, attempts to deal with openings in fiction have, however, come from Germany. Volker Klotz, approaching the question historically, discussed the function and gradual disappearance of the muse in a most interesting essay entitled "Muse und Helios: Über epische Anfangsnöte und -weise." In this contribution to what could be termed *Eingangskritik* (the study of openings), Klotz, seemingly inspired by Curtius's chapter on muses in *Europäische Literatur und Lateinisches Mittelalter,* suggests that in epic structures, which tend to affirm themselves as a mimesis of origin, even as para-creations (epogony paralleling cosmogony), the muse traditionally functions as a numenic midwife *(Numinoser Geburtshelfer).* But the evolution from Greek to Latin and then to Renaissance epic gradually causes the muse to be relegated to a secondary role, and ultimately to disappear, until the epic beginning is itself thematized. For Byron, who sees the muse as "form'd or fabled at the minstrel's will," the beginning becomes indeed an autonomous literary problem. In the first canto of *Don Juan,* he refers ironically to the conventional epic method of plunging *in medias res,* and affirms instead that he will "begin with the beginning."[10] One could say that such thematization of beginnings is a significant feature of modern narrative. Beckett's "Where now? When now? Who now?" is paralleled by Céline's terse, self-conscious, and self-contained opening sentence in *Voyage au bout de la nuit:* "Ça a débuté comme ça" ("It began like that").

Volker Klotz's essay on the gradual disappearance of the muse is part of a collection entitled *Romananfänge,* edited by Norbert Miller, who himself contributed an interesting paper, "Die Rolle des Erzählers," which raises the vexing question of originality.[11] Mention should also be made of Harald Weinrich's fine pages on the narrative structures of myth, given in translation in the first issue of *Poétique,* which point to the importance of situational, metalinguistic, and recurrent textual signals.[12] Roland Barthes, very tuned in to the work of others, has of course greatly contributed, in *S/Z* in particular, to the popularization of the notion of signals and codes, but without granting any privileged status to beginnings. His schematic classifications of codes (hermeneutic, semic, symbolic, proaïretic, referential), his stress on linear, diachronic "reading units," tell us little about constitutive tensions, found in all narratives, between diachronic and synchronic structures.[13] At the other extreme of the spectrum, Edward Said's ebullient *Beginnings,* in spite of the array of key words all referring to the initial moment (origins, originality, initiation, inauguration, departure, radicalism), and the reference to Kierkegaard's belief that the seduction of beginnings stems from the freedom of the subject, does not focus on the precise strategies or occult intentionalities of fictional beginnings, or on the initial encounter between the reader and the text.[14]

III

On that encounter between text and reader hinges the production of meaning. "Comment s'étaient-ils rencontrés?" If the first sentence of Diderot's *Jacques le Fataliste* does not obtain an answer, it is because the question is put in the wrong terms. The author assumes that the hypothetical reader is curious about what happened before the text began. But that is an irrelevant question. Diderot's imaginary dialogue in the opening sentences ("Where were they coming from?"—"From the nearest place."—"Where were they going?"—"Does one know where one goes?") is a paradigmatic lesson in literature. What counts is not the *whence,* but the *here.* The true locus of the meeting is in the text—just as the road in question is not really the road on which the characters travel, but the narrative process itself. To be sure, Jacques and his master proceed on horseback in picaresque fashion. But the real road turns out to be the metaphoric road of storytelling, as the narrator directly tells his reader: "Vous voyez, lecteur, que je suis en beau chemin." The subject is thus not the journey referred to, but the mobility of the self-referential text. The *incipit* creates the putative reader as though to thematize from the start the fact of an essentially literary confrontation.

But beginnings are crucially important, not only in terms of road-crossings and confrontations, but because the sequential nature of the writing and reading experience comes into clash with other temporal orders. For we also read backward, and there is such a thing as the memory of the text. Literally speaking, even if in a subliminal manner, the first word of a text remains longest with the reader along the textual trajectory, and by this virtue alone acquires a privileged status. The same, a fortiori, is true of titles and epigraphs. It is this textual memory—conscious and unconscious—that structures the linear into a simultaneous order. It determines the thrust and underlies the semantic and metaphoric density of a literary work. It is not innocently that Diderot's text begins with the word *comment*. The text is inaugurated under the double sign of an interrogation—*how?*—and of the *know-how* of a literary technique.

Telescopings and projected retrospections are, however, not the only textual spatialization achieved from the outset and in dialectical tension with the opening signals. The inaugural verbal act separates the text from what it was not yet, defines and confines it. This line of demarcation, traced by any initial textual moment, explains perhaps the very real feeling of apprehension experienced by many a reader as he is about to penetrate into the verbal construct. Without indulging in metaphors of love affairs with texts (the French reader knows the additional thrill of cutting the pages!), one can indeed speak of a breaking-in (an *effraction*) or a violation which works both ways: a violation not only of the textual space, but of the reader's habits and comforts. Every threshold means resistance. "Tout début résiste," wrote Victor Hugo, who was supremely conscious of the writing-reading strategies, and symbolized the initial literary moment in the title of the first chapter of *Les Travailleurs de la mer*, a title that alludes to the name inscribed in the snow: "Un Mot écrit sur une page blanche" ("A word written on a blank page"). Thresholds may signify resistance, but they also signify passage and initiation. Hugo's statement about resistance must be completed by the sentence that follows: "Le premier pas qu'on fait est un révélateur inexorable") ("The first step taken is an inexorable revealer").[15]

The revelation, needless to say, implies a philosophical outlook. Merleau-Ponty suggested that the choice of every artistic technique ultimately corresponds to a metaphysical perspective. Indeed, all narrative structures, because of the notion of a beginning and an ending, necessarily set up a tension between linear and cyclical structures. And the specific nature of this tension in any given work also engages a conceptual, moral, or philosophical debate. Mircea Eliade's observations in *The Myth of the Eternal Return* are helpful here. According to Eliade, our biological and cultural makeup is such that we have a need to fight sheer linearity (which means submission to undoing) by invoking notions of cyclical rehabilitation. Modern man, according to this view, is in particular need of this rehabilitation, as he feels the anguish of his linear, progress-oriented notion of history, as well as of the inexorable laws of evolutionism. In Eliade's perspective, history and progress are perceived as a fall implying the loss of the "paradise of archetypes and of repetition, and a longing for the *axis mundi* that might offer resistance to concrete historic time."[16] This nostalgia for a mythical time of origins, felt with particular acuteness in the years between Leibniz and Darwin, would thus correspond to the time in history when the modern novel comes into its own.

But there exists a more endemic tension in narrative structures between figurations of freedom and of necessity. The opening page of *Jacques le Fataliste* is once again exemplary. The novel begins under the double sign of chance and destiny. The "par hasard" in the answer to the first question is countered by the words "écrit là-haut" which terminate the first paragraph. The generative element of chance is here neatly counterbalanced by the end-determined sense of necessity, setting up from the outset a paradoxical relationship between two kinds of determinants.

The overture to Proust's great novel is of course one of the most complex problematizations of the exchange economy between these apparently conflicting determinants. Serge Doubrovsky reads the first sentence of *A la recherche du temps perdu,* with its interplay between the two first persons *(référent* and *référé),* as a generator of the formal structure of the work. The very shortness of the opening statement ("Longtemps je me suis couché de bonne heure"), quite atypical of the characteristic Proustian sentence, seems to have a matricial value.[17] But it is Gérard Genette, in *Figures III,* who has most systematically examined Proust's opening strategies.[18] The difficulty and importance of any beginning appears to be projected by techniques of multiplication.

Genette counts no less than five overtures: the absolute beginning of the first sentence, with its initial temporal term "Longtemps"; the autobiographical beginning ("A Combray, tous les jours . . ."); the introduction to involuntary memory ("C'est ainsi que pendant longtemps . . ."); the specific overture to the world of Combray ("Combray de loin, à dix lieues à la ronde"); the beginning, *ab ovo*, of Swann's love. Nonetheless, the first sentence with its intriguing use of the compound tense *suis couché* retains a privileged status. The temporal signals are unmistakable. Of the traditional questions at the opening of a narrative (who? where? when?), only the third is given any relevance—and in an ambiguous fashion at that. The signal appears at the beginning of the sentence *(Longtemps)* but also at the end *(de bonne heure)*; yet the combination of the temporal adverb and the compounded past tense effaces the demarcations of a clear beginning and a clear end. What is involved is an indeterminate chunk of time.

It is thus impossible, according to Genette, not to situate the first sentence temporally; and it is equally impossible not to situate it in relation to a narrative act. A temporal analysis lays bare multiple orders: the length of the chunk of time referred to by *longtemps;* the habitual bedtime suggested by *de bonne heure;* the now of the act of remembering; the writing and reading time concretized by the shortness of the initial sentence. Temporality and narrativity are thus coupled in the initial moment. The shortness of the sentence, referring to a period of time qualified as long, dramatizes the tension between telling time and time told—between *Erzählzeit* and *Erzählte Zeit*.[19] It also sets up the tension between *discours* and *histoire,* between the narrative order and the diegetic order. This tension is heightened by anachronous implications. The sentence is analeptic in its retrospection; it is proleptic in that the first person points forward to a narration which—as we shall later learn—moves forward precisely to the discovery of a writer's vocation. Even the combination of a single statement and a multiple diegesis (one sentence referring to countless times of going to bed early) has its structural and thematic significance, calling for eventual synchronicity. The double *je* corresponds to two heroes originally split but gradually merging in the text, ultimately blending narrator and writer-hero, as writing itself becomes the subject of the writing. The mediated and the immediate voices blur any modal distinction between story and narration.

A more traditional semantic analysis of Proust's opening signals yields equally rich results. The routine regularity of habit, sickness, and ritual, conveyed by the adverbial clause *de bonne heure* in connection with the verb *couché,* is further developed in the opening paragraphs by the central image of the bed, with its varied connotations: birth, death, dreams, sex, fears, privacy, loneliness, and the adventures of the intermediary zone between consciousness and unconsciousness. The shuttle between reality and dreams, exemplified by the creation of the ideal woman from the sleeping man's autoerotic dreams, immediately subverts the notion of a mimetic narrative. The subversive nature of the opening signals is thus double: subversion of the temporal order, subversion of the notion of referentiality.

This subversion of referentiality is understood by some critics as a key aspect of modernity. For Beckett is not the only one to play out the refusal to play the game while fully aware of the supposed rules. Céline's already quoted opening sentence in *Voyage au bout de la nuit* provides a characteristic pattern. "Ça a débuté comme ça" ("It began like that"). At the semantic level, the sentence is interesting enough: the indefinite demonstrative pronoun *ça* is coupled with the pseudo-orality of an anonymous voice and a colorless auxiliary verb that undercut the dramatic initial moment stressed by the verb *débuter.* But it is in a syntactic and rhetorical perspective that the seemingly anodyne sentence is truly interesting. The subject is indeed without an object. The verb is intransitive, expressing an action strictly limited to the subject and related to nothing else. As for the comparative adverb *comme,* it points to a meaningless comparison *("comme ça"),* displaces the reader not one iota from the subject which is also *ça,* and participates in an issueless structure. The sentence, imprisoned in its very circularity, never reaches beyond itself.

It would be mistaken, however, to attribute such self-conscious strategies to a specifically "modern" movement in literary history. The subversion of the model could be said to be the law of the text. It would seem to be a constitutive element of the fiction-making process. For every such process subverts pure narrativity. Diderot and, before him, Fielding are good examples. But long before the eighteenth century, at the dawn of the European novel, the self-conscious, ironic narrative stance is already a feature of the genre. Here is how Cervantes faces the three model questions (who? where? when?) at the beginning of *Don Quixote:* "In a village of La Mancha, the name of which I do not care to recollect, there lived not long ago a knight, one of those who kept lance in rack, an ancient targe, a lank stallion and a swift greyhound." The evident playfulness of the first sentence, the intrusion of a narrative voice endowed with a capricious temper (choosing not to remember, "no quiero acordarme"), a first-person singular clearly involved in the double act of providing and denying information—all of this participates in an ironic process. But the very irony serves the realistic illusion: not only is the topographic information willfully withheld, but the temporal element of the model opening ("Once upon a time") is here transmuted into the nearby, familiar world of the "not long ago."

Much could be said about the combined awareness of, and hostility to, the literary model, the generalized image of the precursor. The anxiety of influence, the writer's Oedipal love-hate, have become commonplace notions. The undoing of the precursor, whether by denial or assimilation, is perhaps not unrelated to the novel's insistent theme of the search for a surrogate father. The authorial voice, in its double concern for origin and originality, strains to be its own beginning. Even though, as Steven G. Kellman puts it, openings of novels serve as a bridge to a supposed reality in which we are to "lose consciousness of words as words,"[20] the fact is that all openings, specifically in the realist novel, serve at the same time to create an illusion of realism and to undermine the notion of mimetic representation. Philippe Hamon quite rightly stresses the importance of the *incipit* in any realistic discourse as an *indicator* of the genre; but it must equally be stressed that such realistic effects are usually charged with ironic self-negating potential. In this respect, the great nineteenth-century texts in the so-called realist canon are in greatest need of a rereading.

Balzac's *Le Père Goriot* may serve as a useful illustration of how a beginning—in this case a first paragraph—conveys an intentionality in conflict with its more explicit intentions. But first the title. The name Goriot, distinctly plebeian and even vulgar (*goret* means young pig); the word *père* referring to age and perhaps decrepitude, but also to patronizing familiarity when thus used as a colloquial epithet; the implicit refusal to propose in the title a name indicative of conventional heroic dimensions—all this points to a mimesis of very ordinary life, associated with realistic intentions. The deliberate degradation by means of the word *père* is underlined by the outraged comment of M. de Restaud when Rastignac refers to the latter's father-in-law as *le père Goriot:* "Vous auriez pu dire Monsieur Goriot!" ("You might have said Monsieur Goriot!") But of course the word *father* also has a proleptic function: the theme of paternity is inscribed in the title. And indeed Goriot, a latter-day Lear, acquires grandeur as the profaned Father, the

"Christ of paternity"—just as Rastignac's education is in large part a father-search under the sign of Telemachus, whose mythic adventures are illustrated in a cheap, degraded, yet symbolic manner on the varnished wallpaper decorating the gloomy sitting room of the pension Vauquer.

The entire first paragraph is structured around contradictory signals of surface realism and of simultaneous subversions of the realistic discourse. The first words ("Madame Vauquer") echo the title, proposing a name that is also plebeian and animalistic (the syllable *vau*). As for the added information "née de Conflans," it has the official ring of vital statistics. The aristocratic Conflans is, moreover, an indicator of social mobility (from Conflans to Vauquer implying a loss in social status), just as the references to street and quarter (the rue Neuve–Sainte Geneviève, the Quartier Latin, the Faubourg Saint-Marceau) are not mere topographic bits of information, but metonymic signals of social stratification later illustrated by the difference between the Chaussée d'Antin and the Faubourg Saint Germain. All this directly points to a sociological texture, suggests a historically grounded representation of a referential reality, and functions as a disclaimer that this could possibly be a fiction.

But the most potent de-fictionalizing signal is the deliberate use made of the present indicative, suggesting that all we read truly exists, that this is faithful reportage of facts anyone can verify. Madame Vauquer *is* an old woman who . . . Her boarding house *is* open to a mixed clientele. Even the verb *commencer*, thematizing the beginning, undermines the convention of the beginning-in-time by placing it at a nonnarrative proximity in the present: "époque à laquelle ce drame commence." The temporal signal of the present indicative abolishes the distance between subject and object; or rather, it serves to create the illusion of unmediated contact with a reality that is nonliterary.

In this respect, the recurrent word *drame* deserves a special gloss. The formula *époque à laquelle ce drame commence* serves indeed to deny the literariness of the text—and it does so at several levels. First as a generic disclaimer, denying precisely what the book is, namely a novel, and invoking what it is not, a dramatic work. But the word *drama* is of course misused—not only by Balzac, but by his period. Hence the reference to the discredit of the word *drama,* which has been overworked, strained, and twisted ("la manière abusive et tortionnaire dont il a été prodigué"). It has been applied not only to what is not strictly dramatic, but to what is not, strictly speaking, literary. This, of course, is a matter of common usage. One speaks of a human drama—and quite specifically of one that occurs in ordinary life, not in the theater. In that sense, instead of the stage representing the real world, that *real world* becomes the stage. The opening section of *Le Père Goriot* refers indeed to Paris as a "scène pleine d'observations," a stage that hardly distinguishes between spectacle and spectator. What has happened in the initial paragraph is that the repeated use of the word *drama* suggests the transparency of a text that interposes no mediation whatsoever between the reader and the reality to which he is referred.

The referential fallacy is flagrant.[21] For it is precisely around the word and the concept of the real *(souffrances réelles)* that the text is articulated. For these so-called real sufferings are seen as filling the huge metaphoric valley extending between the heights of Montmartre and Montrouge, a valley of crumbling stucco, where metaphoricity *(vallée de plâtras)* conjures up the biblical valley of tears and of the shadow of death. The rhetoric points not only to symbols but to allegory (the valley is an agglomeration of vices and virtues), as well as to myth (the chariot of Juggernaut relentlessly crushing hearts and bones). The principle of literary mediation is furthermore proposed toward the end of the paragraph through a direct reference to the reader's delicate white hand holding the novel that pretends not to be one.

But there is better still—and it comes at the end of the first paragraph. The narrator affirms that what the reader has in front of him is neither fiction nor a novel *(ni une fiction, ni un roman)*. And he concludes in English and in italics: *"All is true."* These italicized words in the provocative code of a foreign language are the ultimate signal of absolute referentiality. Yet it is at this precise point that all is inverted and converted. For the English words *All is true* are also a reference to Shakespeare. An important article by Philarète Chasles indeed informed the readers of the *Revue de Paris* (10 August 1831) that Shakespeare's *Henry VIII*, at the time it was first produced, had been announced under the title *All Is True*.[22] In the first edition, the English words, appearing as an epigraph, were in fact explicitly attributed to Shakespeare. The extreme signal of realism *(all is true)* thus places the elaborate opening disclaimer of literarity under the sign of literature. The allusion to Shakespeare, symbol of literary genius for Balzac's generation, moreover strengthens the thematic links between Balzac's profaned and dispossessed father and the tragic figure of King Lear.

IV

Such an analysis clearly suggests that opening signals in fiction can alert us to the duplicities of the narration. In the particular case of Balzac, the analysis lends support to the hypothesis that so-called "realistic" texts call for an ironic reading of the message of realism. Much of nineteenth-century fiction may thus be an open field for fresh investigation. Larger questions are obviously involved. If subversion of narrativity is constitutive of the novel as a genre, what then are the modalities that govern the relation between history and storytelling, and between storytelling and poetic constructs or *poesis?* The problem becomes particularly acute in a fictional mode for which the nineteenth century displays a special fondness: the historical novel. How does the principle of self-referentiality affect texts that pretend to be not only sociohistorically situated, but ideologically committed? The works of Balzac and Victor Hugo might be fruitful testing grounds.

Natalie, or Balzac's Hidden Reader

The basic tensions of *Le Lys dans la vallée* are introduced in the novel's opening letter. Writing to Natalie de Manerville, Félix agrees to "offer" his past, while making an appointment for that same evening, and from the outset reveals the major time schemes of the book. The story of his childhood and of his idealized love for Mme de Mortsauf is played against the present, on which the past continues to weigh. Death nourishes life. It is one of the ironies of the novel that the past cannot be turned into an objective reality, cannot be exorcised. Despite appearances, the story is open-ended: one has to go on living. The tensions between past and present are further heightened by a range of psychological times. Moments of the past are relived in their fragmentary immediacy, but also perceived as a total experience. Yet the narrative necessarily proceeds in a proleptic fashion, since the retrospective view is inseparable from knowledge of subsequent events, inseparable from a retrospective wisdom that provides a strong sense of fate. This interplay of time schemes is sharply illustrated by the use of the present indicative in the first description of the lyrical setting: "If this woman . . . *lives* anywhere in the world, it is here!" What we are given is a kind of interior monologue accompanying the initial epiphany at the sight of the "voluptuous" river Indre. But in the same paragraph, we read: "ever since that day, *I rest* every time *I return*"—a reference to the walnut tree beneath which he stopped that first day, but also many times later, and even *now* that Mme de Mortsauf is no longer alive (29).[1]

The letter to Natalie provides early reading signals. The temporal ones, concerned with opening and closure (the buried memories are offered to the one he will see "tonight"), imply a fictional reader in the text who is engaged in the reading process much as is the actual reader of the novel. They suggest moreover a multiple experience of women, a progressive sentimental education. The confessional mode, with its tensions between speech and silence, and the underlying fear of imparted secrets (there is talk of wounding, of violating) is closely linked to the strategies of love (submission to the demanding woman) and the ambivalent psychology of the hero. While Félix makes himself appear interesting, hinting at the contradictions in his character, at the repressed feelings and memories hidden deep in his soul, he also betrays his weakness with the opening words of the novel: "Je cède" ("I submit").

From the very beginning the texture of Le Lys dans la vallée is remarkably dense. For beyond these tensions a basic antithesis of water and desert imagery ("productions marines"—"grève") emerges, which announces not only the floral exuberance on the arid, pebbly lande, but also a thirst that cannot be quenched, a death-in-life. This principle of death is not one that appears after the event; it is seen as constitutive of the act of living. The repression or negation of the vital principle is no doubt compensated here by the act of confession—the "labor" necessary to "express." This labor, or "travail," is at the same time a failure (Félix with Natalie) and a success (Balzac at the level of the "work" of literature). As early as the prefatory letter to Natalie, the novel thus questions the relation between the experience of living and the act of telling, thereby affirming the specificity of the writing process.

The letter is of major importance in the strategy of the novel. Yet the idea of an epistolary confession came to Balzac rather late, at a time when it would seem that the novel was already largely written; the name Natalie first appears in the corrected proofs. Félix's letter presenting the story of a former love to the woman he is presently courting is visibly an addition. As for Natalie's answer—her rejection of the man who continues to live with a ghost—it was clearly added by Balzac in extremis.[2] That the prefatory text was an afterthought does not, however, diminish its significance. The device might well have been conceived as an ironic protection, for this novel of a confession is also a confession in the form of a novel. What is more important is that the frame corresponds to a reaction of the author as reader, that it suggests a creative process determined by the already written text, or rather by a text in the process of being written. Correcting proofs was for Balzac a creative stimulant. The added beginning thus provides more than a frame; it participates in the fictional elaboration. That Balzac was an attentive reader of his own text is of course confirmed by Natalie's letter at the end of the novel. This seems to be the true function of the opening and closing epistles: the author embodies the reader that he is, as well as the reader that *we* will be, in the person of Natalie, a character present throughout yet visible nowhere.

The "you" that refers to Natalie is in fact addressed to us, a complex *us* required by the novel and which is part of it. "In order to describe this moment to you . . ." The evocation of the idyllic hour engages our own experience of happiness. The syntax itself functions as a signal. Henriette touches the water "as though to cool a secret ardor" (203). The "as though to" is an invitation to decipherment.[3] Acknowledging his female readership, his "censors in petticoats," Balzac invokes an abstract reader through the mediating presence of Natalie—a compassionate observer of the human heart, one of the many who understand and forgive because they too have suffered. Hence the strategic appeals at the end of Part I and Part II to a *you* that is not at all Natalie: to all the "unknown holy Clarissa Harlowes," all the "dear martyrs," all "you who are in love" (96, 223). Hence also the many maxims and epigrammatic references to the wisdom and maternal comprehension of a sentimental elite. On the syntactic level, recurrent demonstrative adjectives—"*cette* science de l'existence" (231), "*cet* amour qui . . ." (232)—presuppose a common fund of knowledge.

But to the extent that the substance and the tone of the confession are bound to displease Natalie, the *vous-nous* that she embodies also implies a transfer, a psychological identification of the reader with the "judge" she turns out to be. She is a jealous judge, no doubt, but above all irritated by the weakness, complacency, egoism, duplicity, and bad faith of the man who is courting her. The response in the form of a letter which comes at the end of the novel thus reflects a *different* reading of the text which, in apposition to sentimental empathy, maintains a much less indulgent viewpoint.

To be sure, Balzac uses other devices to determine or displace the reader's perspective: the doctor's "observing glance," for instance, or the "eyes" of the worldly Abbé de Dominis (208, 215). But the *you* represented by Natalie remains the privileged mediator, especially since her invisibility in the body of the story makes it possible at the same time to control the perspectives and to provide a sense of closure. And this apparent closure of the text is important because of the ironies it involves. It is a story that is not over; it is a confession that leads to a failure in the present; it points to a wide open (empty?) future, particularly painful to one who has "no faith in tomorrow" (39). Balzac enjoys playing with structures. The "two childhoods" of Part I are, in fact, "the same childhood" (84). The two women in the title of Part III are two different women (Mme de Mortsauf, Lady Dudley), but they are also the two faces of the same woman. Mme de Mortsauf indeed reveals herself as being "two women," Henriette and Blanche (214). Yet behind these two versions of Mme de Mortsauf we discover a third, unknown until the very end, the one who reveals her thirst for sensuality too late, who has been undermined by a life of repressed desires. The structural arithmetic remains flexible: behind the couple Henriette-Arabelle, behind the double and even triple Mme de Mortsauf, there stands a third woman, Félix's mother, who is present at the outset and who, through her coldness and her demands, determines her son's emotional life. And even these figures fail to account completely for the structural complexities of the novel. In addition to the feminine triad (mother, beloved, mistress) there are two other feminine presences, both important for their judgmental role and their act of rejection: Natalie and Madeleine. Five women, not two, are thus at the core of this book.

These arithmetic complications confirm the importance of structural elements in Balzac's work. The preliminary and concluding letters, while functioning as a frame, highlight thematically the drama of language and communication. Not only does Félix's letter "obey" the woman who requests a confession (while her letter, at the end, ironically reproaches him for having obeyed her "unwise request"), but within the opening letter there are already contradictory signals of oscillations, affirmative and negative movements, conflicting desires to tell and not to tell. The verb *céder* in the first line is soon opposed by the expression "the rules of common sense"; the idea of *wanting* someone else's past is countered by "invisible resistances." And so it continues throughout the paragraph. The coquettish anger of the demanding woman is contrasted with the notion of silence, the "secrets" in question with the idea of *knowing* everything, "every word" with "buried memories." The dangers of language, its potential cruelty and destructive power, are all foreshadowed. Félix is surely right, and more than he knows, when he refers to verbal communication as capable of inflicting wounds.

The relation of language to catastrophe is taken up early in the story. This would seem to be one of the functions of Félix's mother, who is not merely an autobiographical presence in Balzac's novel. She comes to Paris to bring her son home just as he is about to be sexually initiated. (Is she not a castrating mother?) Balzac stresses repression of tenderness no less than "repressed desires." But this tension between longings and repression is entirely played out at the level of language. At each relay on their return home, Félix is determined to speak up; but every time, his mother's cold unresponsiveness paralyzes him. Discouraging and provocative at the same time (is she tempting him?), she ends up by reproaching him for his silence. But the flow of words with which he opens his heart to her is quickly met with a stinging rebuke. His mother accuses him of playing a comedy of emotion. This brief episode in which silence alternates with fervent words ends symbolically with the mother's most unjust accusation and the son's impulse to kill himself.

The novel is filled with situations that bring the exigencies of speech into conflict with the imperatives of silence. The pact—Félix calls it "le contrat"—which supposedly governs his relations with Mme de Mortsauf links the need for confidences to the sense of a prohibition. In Félix, Mme de Mortsauf seeks a friend who will "listen" to her, a trustworthy and sensitive person to whom she can confide her sorrows. But if she retains the right to "cry out" her suffering in his presence, she does not want him to speak out his love for her. She wants to have "nothing to fear" and refuses to be exposed to the "heat" of his words. "Keep silent" is her typical admonition (92–94, 146). She desires the impossible, a one-way linguistic communication. In reality, the verbal contract is disturbing from the outset. Explanations and clarifications tend to be postponed or repressed. "Depuis quelques jours une explication flottait entre nous . . ." (80). The sentence reads like a vague threat. Fear of words transcends ordinary reticence. Their brutality is dreaded, almost like the contact with another's body. Verbal exchange is in fact perceived as a disguised sexual contact. Hence the bizarre choreography of orders and counter-orders which at times takes on a stylized quality: " 'Keep quiet,' she told me." " 'Well,' said she, 'speak up!' " And on the same page: " 'Let's not talk any more about these things,' said she." " 'No, let's talk about them!' said I" (82–83).

Communication—not to say communion—can be achieved only beyond, or outside of, ordinary language. The river excursion allows for an exceptional moment of plenitude, when the "mysterious grace" of words seems fully operative (203). Most often there is withdrawal to the region of inner language. Mme de Mortsauf hears a "soft voice" speaking to her "without words" (179). Similarly, Félix converses with a star. Such solipsistic communications encourage all manner of illusions and misunderstandings. The language of bliss has little to do with the "precise language" (163) that characterizes the harsh realities of social relations. Children prattle for the pleasure of prattling. Lovers like to invent a private language which is less innocent. Félix thus requests and obtains the permission to call Mme de Mortsauf by "a name belonging to no one": Henriette (93).

Nothing in the novel illustrates this inadequacy of language better than the distinction made between the voice and the word. It is the voice that stirs the emotions. Félix explains to Henriette how unimportant words—even her own words—seem to him compared with the "sound" of her voice (144). When they first meet, he hears only her cry of surprise and the simple word "Monsieur." Yet he later has no trouble recognizing this voice which "penetrated" his soul and filled it "as a ray of sunlight fills and gilds the prisoner's cell" (37). This internal *son-lumière* suggests at the linguistic level an experience analogous to that of insight through blindness: "like a blind person, she was able to recognize the agitation of the soul through imperceptible speech intonations" (37). Balzac carries the bold comparison to its logical conclusion with the striking formula "spoken light" ("lumière parlée"). What counts is the song of the syllables, the caress of the consonants, the rhythmic unfolding of the sentence. Semantics are transcended. What remains is the harmony of that which cannot be spoken. "She was thus able . . . to extend the meaning of words" (40).

This extension also occurs in the less harmonious register of the cry. The mother's inner cry of anguish for her child, the silent cry of the unhappy woman which can be read in her eyes—these silent outcries are an ultimate manifestation of the priority of the voice over speech. Félix does not dare to break certain moments of silence, preferring the communicative "inebriation" of the exchanged glance (99). And if Henriette knows how to be "affectionately silent," it is not only because a "woman's silence" is full of meaning but also because harmony cannot be achieved through words. Balzac's novel suggests throughout a poetry of silence, a poetry of repressed language which lends itself to "mysterious meanings," while serving the demands of modesty and the duplicities of hidden desire (123). "When words were lacking, silence faithfully served our souls" (113). This dream of a language without words corresponds at another level to the incompatibilities between living and the act of telling. The word that says or describes is destined for the realms of absence and emptiness. "It would seem that I can speak to you about yourself only from afar" (144).

Literary structures thrive on such tensions or gaps. But for the protagonists this means being condemned to an impossible mediation. Language reveals itself to be forever inadequate, out of tune with every emotion. At best, it functions as a sublimation, a derivative, an alibi;

most often it deceives and wounds. It is at the same time inept and dangerous. More or less unconsciously, the characters try out other forms of mediations, but soon discover their tragic limits. Even the language of the eyes is shown to be brutal and lustful, an ironic negation of the motto of Clochegourde castle: "Voyez tous, nul ne touche!" Everything in the novel tends toward the sublimation of desire; yet everything exacerbates and distorts it. If Balzac chooses never to reveal directly what goes on in Henriette's psyche, this is not merely for aesthetic or technical reasons, to avoid a simplistic conflict between sensuality and virtue. Symbolic transfer is properly the subject of the novel.

The symbolism, which is announced by the title, continues throughout to be of central concern. The landscape is from the outset conceived as a guarantee of peace and harmony. The river Indre, the woods, the birds, the cicadas are all part of a general "melody" (30). This song of nature resembles the voice of the "eternal Song of Songs." The biblical image, reflecting the title of the novel, is that of nature inviting its creatures to a feast of love. But very soon this peaceful and paradisiac setting undergoes an erotization which profoundly negates peace and innocence. The valley is a "cup of emeralds," the river flows with "serpentine movements" (29). Elsewhere the valley is compared to a "bed" (72). The image of the snake is later developed—"rivière serpentine" (77); "sinuosités vaporeuses" (180)—and explicitly loaded with sexual connotations. Referring to the "undulations" of his reverie while facing the river, Félix explains to Natalie what she must surely have understood: "le désir serpenta dans mes veines" (113).

This stylized landscape which mirrors and camouflages unacknowledged yearnings is far from reassuring. It turns out to be not a symbol of harmonious plenitude but a setting that hides the truth. "Nature was the mantle that cloaked her thoughts" (180). But nature refuses to be thus used or tamed. It takes its revenge. This is Henriette's lesson as she lives out her destiny of repressed desire. Her beloved valley becomes a source of suffering. And nothing is more distressing as she reaches the end of her terminal illness—symbol of a more generalized wasting away—than the haunting complaint of the woman whose need for love and caresses has been so cruelly frustrated by her own doing, and who in her awareness of approaching death suffers more than ever from a "burning thirst" which is only exacerbated by the sight of the river. The most painful experience is the realization of a fundamental lie, of a thoroughly false relation with nature. "Everything has been deception in my life" (301).

The available forms of mediation are perilously seductive, precisely because they seem to promise both contact and innocence. The language of flowers evoked by the title suggests a "délicieuse correspondance" (119). It is in fact a transposed language. Floral arrangements are repeatedly presented as rivaling other forms of artistic communication. Through the bouquets he offers, Félix attempts to "describe" a feeling. He himself reacts emotionally to the "musical phrases" with which he produces these "floral symphonies" (115, 119). But the main intent of the bouquets is to serve as substitutes for words, or for the art of language. They are translations of translations. Balzac raises simultaneously the question of bad faith and of artistic communication. The flower arrangements constitute a "poetic work," a "discourse," a "poem." As a form of *écriture*, they are in fact seen as superior to the insipid flowers of rhetoric, "les fleurs de l'écritoire" (116, 117, 122). Harmonizing with one another, the different flowers seem to encourage harmony between human beings. It is with the help of Henriette's children, Jacques and Madeleine, that Félix tries out his first floral discourse. But can such an alliance remain innocent? He would like to believe it: "all three of us delighted in planning a surprise for the one we loved" ("notre chérie"—115). In reality, Félix makes use of what he takes to be innocuous intermediaries to create a language of complicity ("cette langue à notre usage"—123), a language that the beloved alone will know how to decode. The text is explicit: "Love has its heraldic emblem; the countess deciphered it in secret"(115–116).

How, then, can one pretend that these floral poems are "neutral pleasures"? Nothing is in fact less neutral than this secretive language of seduction and provocation. Do the floral declarations not work like a "contagion"? Do they not unambiguously speak of the inebriation of fertility, the "ivresse de la fécondation" (119)? The flower imagery gives expression to Félix's sexual longings; he glimpses shapes and forms that suggest to him feminine languor and yielding. But that same imagery is also highly provocative. The terminology is far from neutral: "échevelé," "déchiré," "déchiqueté," "tourmentées," "désirs entortillés"— these images of dishevelment, of twistings and tearings, hardly suggest serene senses. As for the "magnificent red poppy with its seeds about to burst open," it is only one of the many images that contrast violent colors and fertility with the solitude and whiteness of the lily. The aphrodisiac intent is more or less explicit. "Place this floral discourse in a sunlit window frame . . . and she will soon be ready to surrender" (122). The "discourse" will indeed have its intended effect, as is evidenced by Henriette's ecstatic fever ("fièvre expirante") when, in her final moments, she surrounds herself with flowers. "Flowers had thus caused her delirium."

Mediation is shown to be malefic. It invites forbidden love, and functions as deceit. One can easily imagine the irritation Natalie feels as she reads the following sentence: "Never since then have I prepared a bouquet for anyone." And it is impossible not to anticipate her stern indictment of the following statement: "When we had created this private language, we felt a satisfaction akin to that of a slave who deceives his master" (123). A doubly nefarious deceit is involved here, for it is surely they themselves who are deceived by the protective and heady symbolism they utilize to compensate for their abstinence. The "neutral" pleasures ultimately cheat nature itself. But nature does not allow itself to be deflected or repressed with impunity.

There can be no innocent mediation. Nothing proves this better than the role of the children, and the symbolic motif of childhood. This family symbolism, more complex even than the flower symbolism, links up with the flower imagery at critical points in the novel. At the beginning, it is with Henriette's children that Félix composes his bouquets. At the end of the book, surrounded by flowers which proclaim her disordered imagination and her impending death, Henriette herself becomes a child again ("like a child who wants a toy"), forcing Félix into a reversal of roles, making him act toward her "as a mother with her child" (300–301). The image of the child in this context takes on an extraordinarily mutable shape. The real and imaginary network of family ties inside the novel is woven of substitutions, dreams, and ambiguous fictions. Félix and Henriette discover that they have had "the same childhood"; they consider themselves, as it were, brother and sister (there is talk later of her smiling like a "sly sister"—275). But Félix also embodies the son and the spouse, insofar as he plays brother and father to Henriette's children. Yet none of this prevents him, as we have seen, from becoming a father to her, not only at the end of the book (when, in her illness, she regresses to something like a second childhood) but already at the time of the first flower arrangements: "I had to calm her, to promise never to cause her any pain, to love her at the age of twenty as an old man loves his youngest child" (115).

These transfers and displacements in human relations surely point to the realities of deprivation. Thus, Mme de Mortsauf's loving aunt, who was herself a substitute for an indifferent mother, is in turn replaced by Félix now that she is no longer alive. In the logic of the novel, there is nothing surprising if, within the same paragraph, Henriette refers to

Félix's protective and reassuring role ("you who replace her") while describing him as her "adopted child" (156). For she wants him as her child precisely because he means something else to her. ("Enfant, vous serez aimé"—190) Félix-the-aunt and Félix-the-son are evidently screens. The mutability and instability of such mediating figures have their origin in an initial self-deception illustrated by an expression such as "homme-enfant," which Henriette uses in her letter (156). The image of the child merely serves as an alibi. The truth lies rather in the cry of surprise and the simple "Monsieur" with which she reacts, in the early ballroom scene, to the aggressive male he really is. On the other hand, her own multiple and elusive image (sister, mother, woman, child) corresponds to the incestuous nature of the desired adultery ("too well-loved sister," "secretly loved mother"—189), that is, to the attraction and fear of a fundamental prohibition.

As for the real children in the novel, their mediating function is equally complex. They bring the protagonists together, divide them, serve as pretexts, and finally become their judges. Henriette takes bitter pride in her maternal duties. In reality, these duties prove useful to her, for they protect her against herself ("perhaps children are a mother's virtue!"—253). This idea is foreshadowed on the page dealing with floral aphrodisiacs: "it will take an angel or her child's voice to keep her from the edge of the precipice" (122). But this rather ambiguous virtue is not truly effective. By placing her own daughter between herself and Félix, Henriette admits that she needs to set up barriers to protect herself. But they are useless: "barrières impuissantes" (319). In this realm of equivocation, Balzac maneuvers with brilliant and delicate touches. It is, for instance, precisely while remarking to Félix that children are "a mother's virtue" that Henriette caresses her daughter's hair. But are these caresses meant for Madeleine? Is it not an indirect caress, destined to be so understood by her interlocutor? Another scene provides a telling analogue: "all the while caressing the head of her dear child . . . , she described to me the nights she spent at his bedside during his illness" (175).

What we have here is an indirect language that needs to be deciphered. Yet there can be no doubt that Natalie, the hidden "reader," understands perfectly that when Henriette calls her son "Dear heart!" and kisses him with passion, it is not so much maternal tenderness as amorous passion that is revealed by her gesture and words of endearment. She communicates not with her son but with Félix. This oblique discourse is made more meaningful by the fact that Henriette has just been "affectionately silent" (152–153). These communicative indirections imply a double irony: through the mediating presence of the children, the woman expresses herself in a veiled and incomplete fashion. But the mother ends up by resenting her children precisely because she has made use of them too well. In the long run, subterfuges and bad faith undermine her motherly virtues far more than a candid adultery might have done. "I have sacrificed a great deal to you," she says one day to Madeleine and Jacques, pushing them away from her bed (293). Small wonder if Henriette, like Natalie, rejects Félix at the end of the novel. Félix's hypothesis is nonetheless pertinent. He believes that Madeleine's resentment is directed not so much against the one who might have been responsible for her mother's death, as against a world of feelings and emotions intuited too late, a disturbing and even threatening world from which she feels excluded ("Madeleine hated me . . . ; she would perhaps have hated us both, her mother and me, had we found happiness"—325). Once again, nature takes its revenge. The end begins to come into view. Madeleine's rejection of Félix merely anticipates Natalie's.

The first page of Le Lys dans la vallée announces a story about "poor oppressed hearts." Up to a point, the novel can be read as a drama of repression. Certain key verbs come up insistently: constrain, confine, compress, contain, arrest, choke, constrict, prohibit—a full lexicon of repressive terms. It is not order but perversion that is served by these references to a stifling control over nature. Lady Dudley, Félix's English mistress, provides a telling illustration. Seen as a product of a country where the tyranny of law, rules, and "form" encourages hypocrisy, Arabelle, who is "encaged" by those iron "fortifications" with which society surrounds women, rebels by cultivating a taste for the unusual. In all her activities, especially in her emotional or amorous life, she requires powerful sensations. The lies of society are paid for by depravity.

Yet such an observation represents only a partial reading of the novel. If it is true that even small defects turn out to be devastating "if they have long been repressed" (198), there nonetheless exists a beauty to rules and controls. Félix refers to lovers' delights in obstacles. He is sensitive to the poetry of constraints, which is confirmed by the invocation at the end of Part II: "You who are in love! do impose beautiful obligations on yourselves; do take on rules to obey" (223). Even the rules of social life can appear in a positive light. Félix speaks with respect of the social code, the "second education" which is that of worldly

33

experience (47). As for Henriette's letter, which is to serve as a vade mecum, it preaches acceptance, submission, reserve, a "middle line," and the social virtues of *silence*. But Henriette does not fool herself; she knows that worldliness (the "fatale science du monde"—163) is ultimately destructive. She deludes herself only when it comes to the world of her own sentiments, for she thinks that there, too, order can rule, that "tranquillité" is compatible with love. She conjures up a reassuring image of love, almost devoid of passion: "I imagined it like an immense and bottomless lake, where storms may be violent, but rare and contained within boundaries that cannot be transgressed" (266). Such a notion of contained tempests is of course a delusion, as is the satisfaction of having paid tribute to the laws of society. Henriette will learn this, but too late. There is great bitterness in a sentence of her last letter referring to the social laws: "we have complied with human laws" (316).

Only in the realm of intellectual labor, and more specifically in the realm of art, do rules prove unambiguously beneficent—even though success in that case is achieved at the cost of some kind of death. When Félix was an adolescent, his repressed desires "constrained" him to devote himself heart and soul to his studies. He understood then that labors of the intellect could become a passion. He also saw that all hope for order, form, and expression was to be found there. He himself will not follow that road—at least not in the narrated time. But then, does this time of narration not correspond to that which, in the opening letter, he calls the "travail" of expression? The centrality of the question of art is confirmed by the first two sentences of the actual narrative: "What great talent inspired by tears will one day give us the most moving elegy . . . ? What poet will tell us about the sufferings of the child . . . ?" This interrogative invocation clearly places the story of so-called real events under the aegis of literary creation.

The intrusion of artistic images into the body of the story is moreover so intense that one could properly speak of a thematic priority of art within the novel. Whether in matters of landscape or feminine beauty, "nature" seems to imitate artistic models. Mme de Mortsauf's forehead is that of the Joconda, her "Greek" nose seems to be designed by Phidias, her hand is as though modeled on those of ancient statues (41–42). As for the Indre valley, not only does Félix love it "as an artist loves art," but flowers make the riverbanks resemble "tapestries," while the landscape represents a "scene" framed by trees, and the church is the kind that "painters seek for their paintings."

Nothing is more difficult to define than Balzac's attitude toward nature, or the relationship in his work between "reality" and "art." One might talk of an economy of exchange, of mutual nourishment, of symbiosis. The ambiguities of this relationship are reflected in the double aspect of Félix—a character in a novel, but at the same time a persona of the writer. Evoking his childhood, he conceives of himself as destined to become a "seer."

> I often attributed these sublime visions to angels entrusted with preparing my soul for a supernatural destiny. These visions endowed my eyes with the power to see the intimate life of things; they prepared my heart for all those magic experiences which make the poet suffer when he has the fateful ability to compare what he feels with what he is, his immense desires with the little he has achieved. They inscribed in my head a text where I could read what I had to express. (12–13)

Much is to be found in a passage such as this, including an allusion to the prophetic mode. As creator of the text, Balzac constantly mirrors himself in it. Or rather, it is the larger world of *La Comédie humaine* that is reflected in the reduced model of the novel. Hence the allusions to Balzacian figures (Mme de Beauséant, the Marquis d'Adjuda, Mme d'Aiglemont, the Marquis d'Espard) who do not appear in the story proper.

Life and art are, however, ultimately conceived of as incompatible orders. If they do communicate, it is by means of a transsubstantiation which establishes the priority of the lived over the act of living—that is, the priority of the purified message, of the posthumous language of distance and absence. Perhaps this is the true significance of the combined floral and astral images. The lily is perishable, but the star shines across time. "You left her when she was a flower . . . ; you will find her consumed, purified in the fire of suffering, pure as a diamond" (294). These edifying words spoken by the priest evoke no doubt the astral transfer achieved in the mind of the unloved child (his dialogues with the stars), but also the artist's transfigurative "work" that can express and organize through a special language these "ancient emotions" which, suddenly reawakened, can do so much harm to the living.

Le Lys dans la vallée is an exemplary novel in many ways. Between reality and verbal expression a shadow falls. One must choose. But even the option of literary language does not provide intellectual comfort. No code and no communication can be devoid of equivocation. This fact is perfectly illustrated by the invisible yet pervasively present figure of Natalie. For Natalie, the hidden reader (and are we not hidden also?), exists on two levels, both of them indispensable to the dialectics of freedom and necessity. A sympathetic complicity with the characters in the face of their suffering is held in check by a severe and even hostile judgment implying a moral stance. But there is more. Natalie, hidden and present, while suggesting a current that flows through the reader, reminds us also that every author is first and foremost a reader of himself.

La Peau de chagrin:
The Novel as Threshold

At the beginning of *La Peau de chagrin* the infernal gambling den, with its impassioned addicts, initiates us into a frightening Parisian "mystery." This somewhat purple passage, an immediate and startling descent into a modern Hades, is an excellent introduction to the narrative world of Balzac. In 1831, Balzac took the literary scene of Paris by storm with this unusual novel. Its immediate success was largely due, no doubt, to the sensational nature of the work. The thirty-two-year-old author had been determined to show off his virtuosity. And indeed, the first impression the book gives is one of extraordinary vitality. But Balzac's quasi-Rabelaisian verve, his ability to exploit without self-consciousness his own dreams and nightmares, are permanent features of his art. A certain flamboyance, a desire to see things big, concern for details and at the same time an indomitable urge to amplify—all these are traits that continue to delight readers who do not feel that good literature must necessarily be lifeless.

La Peau de chagrin is an exciting introduction to the fictional world of *La Comédie humaine*. Bravura passages succeed each other at a quick pace. The gambling establishment where the hero Raphaël, having lost all he possesses, confronts suicide; the uncanny antique shop where, in unutterable chaos, the anachronistic debris of a few dozen civilizations seems to come to life again and all the shapes that have ever haunted man's imagination appear to dance as in an apocalypse or a witches' Sabbath; the description of the magus-like, Mephistophelian antique dealer who offers the hero the magic talisman, the ass's skin, that gives the book its title, thus bestowing upon him supernatural powers for which, like Faust, he will have to pay with his death—all bear witness to Balzac's taste for the spectacular. But such tours de force are not limited to passages dealing with the supernatural. Later in the story, the Taillefer orgy, for instance, is not only an extraordinary orgy of food and words in which Balzac piles up mad crescendi, from whispers to demonic tutti, suggesting the growing clamor of drunkenness; it also challenges him to outdo Roman decadence as depicted in Petronius's *Satyricon:* same universal hiccup, same insolent wealth, same garish coupling of the macabre and the obscene.

It is not at all insignificant that *La Peau de chagrin* appeared in 1831. Balzac's first major creative outburst, with its stylistic and thematic fireworks, coincides with a period of unusual ferment. Around 1830 the first wave of Romanticism reached its full height in France. Lamartine, Hugo, and Vigny in poetry; Stendhal in the novel; Berlioz in music; and Delacroix in painting are some of the names that come to mind. Not many periods can rival these years in the profusion—and often confusion—of ideas and systems. A civilization aware of its own sickness seemed to be calling forth its own prophets: the utopian social ideas of Saint-Simon and Fourier; the positivistic philosophy of Auguste Comte; Lammenais's vision of a democratic and even revolutionary Christianity; the authoritarian dogmas of de Maistre and Bonald; the fashionable eclecticism of Victor Cousin, and the historical and philosophical panoramas of Michelet and Jouffroy. All these, with the emergence of a large daily press—and vociferous public opinion—created a cacophony of ideas. In this stimulating climate there is only one common element: a pervasive sense of Change, Time, and History from which the idea of Revolution is never totally absent.

Obvious historical reasons account in part for this generation's awareness that it could not live on inherited values. Balzac's own life in this respect was not atypical. Born in 1799, at the end of the Directory, he grew up during the Consulate and the Empire, became an adolescent with the Restoration, and reached manhood with the July Monarchy. Having witnessed an impressive acceleration of history, his generation was haunted by the very ideas of instability, erosion, and transformation. The moral climate—a certain religious and metaphysical anxiey, ancestor to our own—was largely due to the newly acquired sense of historical *fatum* (fatality). Other factors contributed to the intellectual tension: the clash between eighteenth-century rationalism and religious aspirations; the political ferment at work as an emerging proletariat developed class consciousness and the middle class a bad conscience; the ambiguous attitudes of an intelligentsia rebelling against a social order while enjoying its comforts. Writers like Hugo, Vigny, and Lamartine, whose preoccupations at first had been almost exclusively aesthetic, turned with increasing concern to the social, political, and moral problems of the day.

Historical circumstances do not, however, account for the private tensions underlying Balzac's novel. The peculiar turbulence of *La Peau de chagrin* echoes something of that in Balzac's own life, specifically some of his early Parisian experiences still fresh enough to be unsettling. Torn between asceticism and an urge to taste life to the fullest, dreaming simultaneously of producing a profound masterpiece written in austerity and of enjoying quick success and dissipation, Balzac, like Raphaël his hero, had known all the frustrations of a moneyless, secluded existence in a garret. He too had developed the art of making debts, and must have often longed for supernatural powers that would enable him to conquer Paris. From age twenty to thirty he had been a hack writer and had had contacts with unscrupulous literary impresarios, with the cynical world of Parisian journalism. He knew at first hand the power of money. Driven by a compulsion to become rich fast, he had thrown himself into utterly unrealistic business speculations which literally made him slave to life-long insolvency.

But it is Balzac's "student days" in a Parisian attic, his "sépulcre aérien" as he called it,[1] that *La Peau de chagrin* most movingly evokes: his enforced chastity, the claustral discipline he adopted, his monastic dedication to books in the little cell overlooking the roofs of the city, so close to but so far from the life of the huge metropolis. In no other work has Balzac written more lyrically of the joy of studies, of the pleasure of intellectual work, while at the same time describing the temptations of luxury, success, and sensuality that assail a young hermit. Behind these conflicting demands of his temperament is one all-consuming dream: to write a masterpiece. And with it goes Balzac's stubborn belief in his own destiny as a genius.

II

In 1831, Balzac did not yet know that he was to write *La Comédie humaine,* an astonishing fictional universe with its more than two thousand characters who appear, mingle with each other, disappear, and then show up again. *La Peau de chagrin* is only one small segment of this fresco. Many a theme, many a character in *La Peau de chagrin* was to reappear. Years later, in his famous introduction to *La Comédie humaine,* Balzac summed up his grandiose ambition as novelist. It was an ambition that had developed, so to speak, organically, in the very act of creation. Only gradually, after many of his novels had been written, did Balzac understand the direction his work was taking. As the volumes accumulated, he began to understand that his persistent dream had been to construct a fictional edifice that would also be a "total history" of his time, a work in which the novelist, competing with the statesman and the philosopher, would account for the very causes of the historical process. The task was almost impossible: to grasp, to analyze, and to describe the whole historical and social life of a nation. The very title, *La Comédie humaine,* reminiscent of Dante's summa, suggests a scheme nothing short of total vision and total insight.

La Peau de chagrin provides the reader with a fair sampling of the characteristics of *La Comédie humaine.* To begin with, its major defects: lengthy digressions, a verbal exuberance that easily becomes sheer verbosity, a tendency to overstate and overcolor, a mania for name dropping and allusions, an incurable attraction to the sentimental and to the melodramatic. Showing the effects of years of hack writing, the finest novels of Balzac tend to be too bulky, overdrawn and sensational, and even trite. These would be serious defects in a lesser writer: Balzac can afford the luxury of defects. For *La Peau de chagrin* typically contains many admirable traits: a love of words that is truly sensuous, technical prowess in the massive build-ups, exciting crescendi after a slow, ominous preparation. No novelist, either before Balzac or after, has so successfully revealed the dramatic interplay of great forces behind the trivial acts of daily life. Here, the grimace of the miser, the smile of the dandy, the furniture in an apartment are not merely picturesque. They point to abstractions, indeed are often determined by an abstraction. With Balzac the *roman de moeurs* (novel of manners) is not merely an exploration of the quaint, a search for romantic "local color" in the here and now. The courtesans who appear in *La Peau de chagrin* (they are among Balzac's favorite characters) are not there just to titillate our imagination: they incarnate the principle of excess, combining in their way of life dramatic antitheses: luxury and poverty, beauty and disease, life and death. They are the very embodiment of abstract or even occult forces larger than any individual. Even Balzac's taste for detailed descriptions, for inventories, this *bric-à-bracomanie,* as Félicien Marceau called it, is only another manifestation of his visionary tendencies. What *La Peau de chagrin* reveals above all is Balzac's attraction to the irrational, to all forms of mystery, his deep social pessimism, all so typical of a writer who combined a sanguine temperament and deep mystical yearnings.

La Peau de chagrin reflects the most basic and paradoxical Balzacian characteristic: a vision both realistic and supernatural. This ambivalence has perhaps never been more acutely diagnosed than by his young contemporary Baudelaire. In one breath he called Balzac a "great historian," obsessed with the minutest detail, and a pursuer of dreams in search of the absolute. Baudelaire's preference was of course for the "passionate visionary," but he knew that Balzac's vision depended on his ability to observe and to describe. The demonic for Balzac must always assume a palpable shape. It is no coincidence that some of the most "scientific" passages in *La Peau de chagrin* (Raphaël's visit to three professors and the shattering of the huge press used in an attempt to distend the diabolical skin) are also most charged with supernatural overtones. The name Pascal, evoked when the professor of physics recalls that it was Pascal who invented the hydraulic press, further suggests the paradox of a highly rational mind bent on exploring the world of the irrational.

La Peau de chagrin thus contains in profusion some of the basic traits of *La Comédie humaine*. And every one of its themes was to give birth to further novels. Raphaël's loss of innocence and ideals is more amply treated in *Illusions perdues* (published in three parts: 1837, 1839, 1843); the destructive power of thought, the tragedy of intellect, the psychophysical relation of mind and body are the subject of *Louis Lambert* (1833) and of the other *Etudes philosophiques;* the modern epic of money and business speculation is at the heart of *César Birotteau* (1837); the satanic elements are embodied in the character of Vautrin, who first appears in *Le Père Goriot* (1835); the fascination with the supernatural and the occult inspires *Séraphita* (1835); and the cold-blooded war of the sexes, in which the dandy sets out to conquer society using his elegance as a weapon, is a recurring motif in at least half a dozen novels. And in many novels the reader is again thrust into Paris. That immense and ever-moving, that frightening and alluring city, with its shipwrecked souls and "hidden" districts, its weird light, the mystery of its fog, its contrasts of wealth and poverty, suffering and joys, was for Balzac the symbol of the social force against which the individual, if he is to affirm himself, must wage a desperate and heroic struggle.

And throughout *La Comédie humaine* the dynamics of society and the dynamics of the individual continue to clash. Raphaël is brother to the lean, young provincials who rush to the capital, hungry for fame. They share the same fever of *arrivisme* which racked a whole generation of moneyless young men born too late to distinguish themselves on Napoleon's battlefields or in his administration. They know the same temptations of quick money and easy success, the same trap of conformity. Society will always be the sworn enemy, too, of Balzac's superior men. Many of Balzac's future young heroes will accept like Raphaël the challenge of this uneven battle, echoing Rastignac's famous words: "A nous deux maintenant!"[2] Many too, Raphaël among them, as they survey the Parisian jungle, could say with Lucien de Rubempré that there was his kingdom, there the world he must subdue. More important still is the struggle in which the individual, a slave to self-inflicted obsessions, lacerates himself and drives himself to self-destruction. For many a Balzacian hero—whether in pursuit of some worldly desire or in mad quest for the absolute—his enormous willpower seems, ironically, to bring about his undoing. Thus genius becomes a disease, and intellectual greatness a form of suicide. This is the basic theme of *La Peau de chagrin*.

In Balzac, death itself, and destruction through steady decay, are permanent motifs. The shrinking skin in *La Peau de chagrin* symbolizes the relentless erosion of life by life. All great novelists, no doubt, deal implicitly with disillusionment, the awareness of evanescence. With Balzac, however, these become major themes. They reveal the anguish of a writer haunted by his own dark thoughts and by the dance of life and death.

III

The first pages of *La Peau de chagrin* are an eloquent warning to myopic readers who think of Balzac's art in terms of petty realism. Realism there is, to be sure. The world of surfaces and palpable objects holds an endless fascination for Balzac. He never tires of situating his human dramas in a social and political context. Quite often the social and political context is far more than a setting. It provides the dramatic tension, and is ultimately translated into a dramatic force. Long before Taine and Zola, Balzac insisted on the threefold importance of historical moment, environment, and heredity. The opening section of *La Peau de chagrin* serves to remind us, however, that Balzac deals in much more than surface realism; it offers a lesson in "how to read" Balzac.

All the details in the description of the gambling den—and they are there in profusion—point to symbols and abstractions. No account could be further removed from sheer representation. The little old man in the coat room of the gambling house is more than a shabby old attendant who takes the client's hat: he illustrates the evils of gambling. In just over two pages of seeming digression, Balzac turns this individual into a universal type, embodying moral degradation, bearing the weight of all suffering and despair. His face, we are told, reveals the miseries of an entire hospital, the ruin of families, the calamities of suicide, exile, and damnation. Moreover, he is presented as a pale shadow, crouching *(accroupi)* behind his barricade as though lying in wait for victims. The image of this insensitive doorman placed at the gates of a gloomy den conjures up memories of the mythological underworld. To strengthen this impression Balzac transmutes the old man into a living "warning" placed there by Providence, and depicts him as the Cerberus-like watchdog of the nether regions.

Balzac develops this impression further by transforming Raphaël's act of handing over his hat into a ceremonial, ritualistic gesture. His trivial act becomes a kind of "parable," and suggests some infernal contract by which, symbolically, the traveler to the Parisian Hades surrenders, together with his hat (intelligence? self-possession?), any rights he may have over himself. It is an act of submission, an act of abdication. Balzac draws similar effects from his description of the other gamblers who are the spectators in this scene. Victims of their own obsessions, they are the true inhabitants of this hell. Glimpsed in the livid light of the "cursed hour," they appear to Raphaël, in their ter-rifying calm, like "human demons" expert in tortures.[3] Finally, the gam-bling house itself looms as a place of damnation, a place of death, a prison whose forced laborers greet the new prisoner with tragic respect.

No matter how picturesque, there is hardly a detail which does not imply a mythical dimension. The metaphoric tissue of Balzac's prose transfigures reality; it gives a permanent, underlying unity to seemingly unrelated experiences. The images of death, prison, and hell; the analogy of the gamblers and perverse demons; the hat ritual; the allegories of disease and debauchery; the hero's first appearance as a "prince" of suffering, as a fallen angel deprived of the halo of his innocence—these themes, which will be developed throughout the book, illustrate Balzac's metaphoric inventiveness.

Metaphors transfigure. They also enlarge. The opening section of *La Peau de chagrin* clearly points up the relation between a writer's love of metaphor and his taste for amplification. Although Balzac provides us with local color that is definitely Parisian, the perspective is foreign; the here and now are explored so as to provide simultaneously an excursion into time and space. Raphaël's specific degradation and suf-fering in a specific locale assume epic proportions. They sum up *all* degradation and *all* suffering. Temporal and spatial "tourism" in turn produce unexpected parallels. The gambling house is compared to the "place de Grève," the Parisian square where crowds used to gather to await the lurid spectacle of public executions. Then again, Balzac turns it into an arena where, at set hours, a tragic ritual of death is enacted. Rome had its gladiators; Spain its bullfights. Paris, with the Palais-Royal of 1830, provides a no less dramatic ritual of death.[4] This descriptive method obviously implies that details are subservient to meaning. This is the very opposite of surface realism. In fact, with all his slow build-ups and patient inventories Balzac, as Erich Auerbach has demonstrated in *Mimesis*,[5] is a master at bestowing demonic significance on the most trivial detail.

Because of this systematic fusion of the physical setting and the mysterious influences that pervade it, Raphaël's fate, like that of most of Balzac's characters, is predetermined. The dramatic and conceptual synthesis presiding over the novel comes first, and it is upon this foundation that Balzac then *constructs* his characters. His point of departure is an idea. "The mores of all the nations of the world, as well as their wisdom, were summed up in his frigid face," writes Balzac of the strange antique dealer in *La Peau de chagrin*.[6] He sees him as held captive by universal forces. The man is not free to work out his individual destiny.

Every technique and every perspective implies selection. Balzac concerns himself with the interplay of massive occult forces. What may appear as digression is often the very substance of his book. The strange inconsistency of gamblers who yearn for money and luxury, but sit endlessly in a dingy gambling room, is only a pretext for Balzac's more general speculations on the nature of antithesis—the lover who loves on a sordid bunk; the power seeker who grovels in the mud; the merchant who amasses millions in a dank shop—antitheses which in turn provide the pretext for a still broader meditation on human nature and human duplicity.

The first six or seven pages of *La Peau de chagrin* thus point to the ambitious nature of Balzac's fictional work. His novels are not mere case histories or concerned with the tragicomedy of manners. All his novels reveal his visionary temperament and his proud awareness that it is he, the poet, who creates a universe into which he has a privileged insight.

Finally, the very "details" of the opening paragraphs function, in retrospect, as preparatory symbols. The contrast between the young man who gambles away his last coin and the old attendant who takes his hat is a prefiguration of the central contrast between youth and age which Balzac elaborates in Raphaël's subsequent encounter with the antiquarian. Ultimately the conflict between youth and age will take place in the mind and body of Raphaël, and will culminate in a struggle between the forces of life and death. Gambling, too, is only another symbol for the act of living in which passion becomes a principle of destruction. And this, of course, is related to the diabolical skin, the "peau de chagrin," that power-giving but steadily shrinking talisman in which Balzac symbolizes the eternal dialectic of desire and death.

IV

Balzac's ambitions are philosophical in nature. When Blondet, one of the characters in *Illusions perdues,* defines the novel as "the most immense modern creation," it is precisely because the novel as he—and Balzac—see it must have an intellectual substructure and reflect a metaphysical vision. Such above all is the view of D'Arthez, who wants to be a "profound philosopher," just as Balzac himself knew, long before he had fully charted his course as the author of *La Comédie humaine,* that he wanted to compose works of philosophical import and establish himself unequivocally as one of the luminaries of his generation.[7] Early in his life—no doubt influenced by the Saint-Simonians—he thought of the writer as a high priest of humanity, as a spiritual legislator, a prophet, a seer. In a significant essay, "Des Artistes," written barely a year before *La Peau de chagrin,* he glorified the artist as a thinker, and in turn exalted the thinker as a "sovereign" ruling over his century and molding the future. "We have reached the era of intelligence," he proudly confided to Madame Hanska. His own ambitions in this new "era" were almost Napoleonic: "I want to govern the intellectual life of Europe."[8]

Though the statement is somewhat pompous, Balzac was aiming high. It is revealing that as early as 1831, *La Peau de chagrin* is part of a series entitled *Etudes philosophiques.* And it is characteristic that at the heart of this particular "philosophical study" he placed a symbol which he himself translated repeatedly into philosophical terms. For what is the devilish talisman, the skin that shrinks with every desire, if not the symbol of self-consuming life? The ass's skin represents two of the most dynamic but also most destructive of principles: *Vouloir* and *Pouvoir,* volition and power. *Vouloir* consumes and *Pouvoir* annihilates. But it is clear from the beginning that the talisman is the symbol of human destiny which condemns men to the terror of witnessing their own gradual self-destruction. Desire and Death are inescapably bound to each other; that is the essential truth symbolized by the ever-shrinking ass's skin.

Around it minor symbols or symbolic episodes cluster, all related to one another as well as to the main theme, so that in spite of lengthy digressions and the episodic nature of the novel a strong sense of unity emerges. The gambling scene symbolizes suicidal thirst for possession and power. The antique shop, with its inventory of civilizations and its variations on the theme of "ruins," points to the death wish of the hero Raphaël, while communicating the fever of experience and individual incarnation. Here again, there is the mystical marriage of vitality and annihilation. With Raphaël's visit to the antique shop the central philosophical issues of the novel are broached: the pathology of thought, the incompatibility of possession and contemplation, the systematic discrediting of Civilization. The episode of the Taillefer orgy strengthens the idea of the fatal bond linking possession and destruction. The gardener who brings back the ass's skin which Raphaël, in a desperate gesture, has thrown into the garden well, clearly symbolizes the impossibility of eluding one's destiny. As for the fate of the gigantic press, shattered in an attempt to distend the now fast-shrinking skin, it is clearly symbolic of the failure of all science in the face of the deeper mystery of life.

The characters Balzac created also seem to embody parallel principles: the antique dealer and Foedora, equally afraid of life, are equally stingy with their emotions, and their life thus becomes a premature death. In contrast, the gambler and the courtesans defiantly spend themselves in the passion of the moment, and destroy themselves in the act of living. Terrified by life or flirting with death, Balzac's human beings appear unable to avoid excess and ruin. The entire novel seems to have been conceived under the sign of the big Orgy.

The larger issues with which *La Peau de chagrin* is concerned stand in bold relief. The characteristic social pessimism underlying the whole novel is not countered by any optimism concerning the destiny of the individual, who can only choose between two types of death: "to kill emotions in order to live to old age, or to die young by accepting the martyrdom of passions."[9] It could be argued, of course, that Raphaël's destiny is bound up with failure, that he is a *raté:* he himself comes to understand that power raises the stature of those only who are already tall. But although the theme of the *raté* is never totally absent from Balzac's work, *La Peau de chagrin* is far more concerned with the exemplary nature of Raphaël's destiny, and with the human allegory it sets forth.

46

In Balzac's allegory is enacted the perpetual clash of thought and action, the *agon*—as the Greeks called it—which has haunted man's mind ever since he became capable of seeing himself simultaneously as subject and as object. It was Goethe who said that thought and action, *Denken und Tun,* were the sum of all wisdom, like the rhythm of question and answer. Yet this rhythm has been the source of much anguish. And perhaps no period has been more tragically aware of the beauty, but also of the irreconcilable nature, of this dialogue than the one in which Balzac began to write. If Romanticism bequeathed us one theme which modern literature and modern philosophy have not yet exhausted, it is the irremediable clash between life and the knowledge of life.

Balzac's own temperament made him especially vulnerable to this antinomy. His conflicting desires for cerebral creation and for worldly glory brought him face to face with an insoluble dilemma: the deepest joys of the mind required an almost inhuman deprivation, while possession meant the dissipation of genius. The hesitation between silence and tumult once more appears as a choice between two forms of death. In the last analysis, *La Peau de chagrin* appears as a fictional meditation on opposing modes of suicide.

"What young man has not meditated on suicide?" Viewed in the light of this question, *La Peau de chagrin* is more than a meditation; it is the story of a slow suicide. Raphaël, it is true, gives up the idea of killing himself, as he leaves the antique shop and meets his friends. But as the old man puts it so well when he explains the deadly pact: "After all, you wanted to die? Well, your suicide is only postponed."[10] Raphaël finds out that no matter where he turns, he will stare into the mask of death. He can *use up* his existence in pleasure, become a *galérien du plaisir,* and consume himself in the act of living. Or he can abdicate life in order to outlive himself: a form of castration. No matter what he chooses, he is trapped. In fact, prison is one of the recurring images in *La Peau de chagrin:* there is penal servitude in the wild gamble of life as well as in the willful withdrawal from it. And it is this nightmarish view of human destiny as a form of imprisonment and disintegration that this novel, and so much of Balzac's work, movingly dramatize.

Hugo's *William Shakespeare:*
The Promontory and the Infinite

Ce sera le manifeste littéraire du 19e siècle.

During his exile on the English Channel island of Guernsey, in between two visionary dialogues with the sea, Victor Hugo noticed, atop a promontory, a column commemorating a general by the name of Doyle. But who was this Doyle? The promontory and the column struck him as symbolic. England honored an obscure man of war, instead of its national poet. Hugo was scandalized. Where indeed was the column for Shakespeare?

General Doyle's column looms in Hugo's most celebratory text, *William Shakespeare*. He had agreed to write a preface for his son's translation of the complete works of the poet. But the "preface" grew so exceedingly in size and scope, it became such a dithyramb in honor of genius (his own included), that Hugo published it separately, in 1864, the year of the three hundredth anniversary of Shakespeare's birth.

The text reaches indeed far beyond its original purpose, far beyond a discussion of Shakespeare's art. Shakespeare became a pretext for dealing with what Hugo himself defined as the "mission of art" (153).[1] This is not to deny that these heady pages provide striking observations on Shakespeare's fantasy, thematic coherence, power of vision. Hugo beautifully evokes the dreamlike haze, the complicity of sobs and laughter, the carnivalesque effects of Shakespeare's theater, the plumbing of the imagination, the baffling joy—"gaîté inintelligible" (236)—of a poetic world where virgins coexist with monsters, where man subconsciously fears what he most desires and desires what he most fears. Shakespeare exuberantly challenges all repressive laws, including those of rhetoric. "Il enjambe les convenances, il culbute Aristote—" (240). Mighty contrasts and parallels are established between the works of Shakespeare and Aeschylus, between the figures of Hamlet and Prometheus. Hugo is an "intertextual" critic *avant la lettre*.

But the chief concern of *William Shakespeare* is not a single literary achievement or even a single genre. Hugo's broader ambition in having the "poet of France" (his own words!)[2] face the "poet of England" was to provide the definitive manifesto of nineteenth-century literature—an overwhelming assessment of the responsibility of the writer, as well as of the nature and function of genius. The oceanic exile, as he approached his mid-sixties, meant to confront the *hommes océans*, the unfathomable, inexhaustible creative spirits of all time. The confrontation was of course also to be an exercise in self-assessment.

The image of the promontory sets up the opposition of warrior and poet. That Hugo's own father had been a general only invests column and promontory with added significance. *William Shakespeare* proclaims the demise of the warrior-hero, the entrance of the real giants on the scene of action, the victory of the pen over the sword—in a sense the victory of the son over the father. In the final section, the men of violence, whose names fill history books, are seen in eclipse: the human butchers, the "sublimes égorgeurs d'hommes" (312) who have for so long usurped the rightful place of the thinkers, are fated to vanish in the general twilight of the traditional hero. But this hoped-for twilight of the "hommes de force," this liberation from hero-worship, have their own sad grandeur. Not only is there nostalgia for the glorious old exploits, but irreverent rejoicing would be out of order. The hero deserves a worthy funeral. "N'insultons pas ce qui a été grand. Les huées seraient malséantes devant l'ensevelissement des héros" (323). Yes, jeers would be unseemly. Nonetheless, the death warrant of the warrior has been signed.

The fading away of the traditional epic virtues is seen, however, not as an end but as a beginning. It signals the emergence of a new symbolic epic. In his self-chosen political exile, Hugo develops a revolutionary ideology all his own. The saga and aspirations of the French Revolution are read into the lines of a new providential text that sings the adventure of the human spirit and the prowess of the creative mind. Not only does genius take precedence over the hero, but the inkstand *(l'écritoire)* is destined to become the emblem of the era of ideology. "The supreme epic is being enacted" (323), announces Hugo as he glorifies *l'écritoire* and specifically relates the civilizing mission of the nineteenth century to the institution of literature. "Thought is power" (285), he declares in a spirit quite unlike that of Foucault, who, a century later, equated *savoir* and *pouvoir* in order to denounce traditional humanism. The power of Hugo's new "conquerors," of the poet-prophets who will crush the heroes, serves spiritual values. But these values, contrary to first assumptions, are not easily compatible with a historical notion of progress.

A curious anachronism, affecting Hugo's utopian vision, sets up indeed a basic contradiction. For the dynasty of men of genius, whose recognized superiority means the advent of a new era, remains totally unaffected by the notion of progress. Shakespeare is not inferior or superior to Aeschylus; Dante is not inferior or superior to Homer. The dynasty is made up of minds responsible, as it were, for their own origin and originality. "Supreme art" integrates the artist in the "region of Equals." There is no primacy among masterpieces, no hierarchy to be established between genius and genius. Each superior artist takes his place in a timeless collegium, participates in what Hugo calls the "famille dans l'infini" (242). Needless to say, this glorification of a communion in the absolute of art is altogether different from Baudelaire's or Flaubert's idealization of the freemasonry of artists which Sartre diagnosed as an escape into the realm of the posthumous. But there is no doubt that Hugo also stresses, though in a far more complex manner, the artist's ontological presence-in-death, hinting at the implicit desire to see himself, while still alive, as posthumously communing with an atemporal elite. "To be dead is to be all-powerful," he writes in the chapter entitled "Après la mort." This cryptic statement is clarified a few paragraphs later: "The poets being dead, their thought reigns. Having been, they are" (295). The living man of genius is thus a statue about to enter into the future that is already the past (350). But this statue comes to new life. There can be no greater glorification of the institution of literature than this apotheosis in death. "The poets are dead; their thought is sovereign" (295).

When Hugo asserts that art is more lasting than any given religion (202), this is not to undercut the religious impulse, but to affirm more strongly the sacerdotal function of the artist. The poet, according to Hugo's definition, is *sacerdos magnus*. The poem "Les Mages" had already established the vatic poet as the true spiritual leader. *William Shakespeare* echoes this poem emphatically: "There is a high priest in this world; it is genius" (170). Sharing the Symbolists' visionary and esoteric concerns, Hugo sees the Book as a spiritual instrument, and poetry as a second Creation. Interestingly, the Symbolists rarely attacked Hugo; Mallarmé in fact reprimanded Claudel for speaking ill of him.[3] What distinguishes Hugo from the Symbolists' as well as from Flaubert's glorification of literature as an absolute—what separates him from the Chevalerie du Néant as defined by Sartre—is that Hugo's notion of "création seconde" never leads to the cult of negativity. God remains present to the mystery of art. "Dieu crée l'art par l'homme" (170). The artist collaborates, substitutes, competes—he is never alone. To suggest this association, Hugo invokes honored symbols and metaphors: Socrates' demon, the bush of Moses, Numa's nymph, the spirit of Plotinus, Mahomet's dove—above all, the image of the summit *(la cime),* point of encounter between God and genius (172). Equality reigns not only between the Equals. Hugo speaks of the poet's apparent "égalité avec Dieu" (243).

The theory of Equals leads Hugo into interesting difficulties. In an oxymoronic juxtaposition of images, the "immovable" giants of the human mind are defined as a "dynasty" (189). This word, referring to a succession of rulers, implies a sense of temporal continuity. But art, Hugo insists, is precisely not successive or cumulative. The originality of masterpieces rests in their own origin: they are always *other.* Poetry is "immanent," he explains, stressing thereby the immediate and irreplaceable plenitude achieved by genuine masterpieces.[4] For art is not perfectible, not susceptible to improvement. It is governed by the absolute, exists in an eternal time, and constitutes the one exception to the law of displacement and replacement. The ideal does not budge; it knows no shifting horizons. The master poets do not outshine one another, do not climb on one another, do not use one another as stepping stones. Each masterpiece is its own world: the result of a control that leaves no room to chance. "There is no chance in the creation of the *Oresteia* or of *Paradise Lost.*" Each creation is the offspring of will. "Un chef-d'oeuvre est voulu" (198).

But how compatible is this notion of atemporal plenitude with the belief in historical process and progress to which Hugo is so strongly committed? Hugo comes out rather categorically. "Art is by its nature not subject to progress" (197)—a statement which leads him to make an important distinction between art and science. If one looks for progress, he maintains, one must turn to scientific achievements. Gutenberg's invention of the printing press, for instance, holds out promise of perpetual movement and uninterruptible progress. It can happen, of course, that the distinction between science and art is illustrated by one and the same figure. "Pascal the scientist is superseded; Pascal the writer is not" (201). For in the realm of science, contrary to that of art, all is relative and subject to the principle of replacement. There all is subject to linear time and chance; discoveries are the result of endless gropings and productive errors. Each successive scientist casts previous achievements into relative oblivion. Science goes on ceaselessly erasing itself, but these are fruitful erasures—"ratures fécondes" (198).

The contrast between the linear time of science and progress, and the timeless space of art, led to another major difficulty that nettled Hugo during his exile years, as he tried to reconcile his beliefs in the autonomy of art with a deepening interest in the cause of Revolution. Having assumed, after 1851, a prophetic political role, Hugo felt increasingly the need to neutralize the charge that he had been one of the earliest proponents of art for art's sake. Of course, Hugo continued to believe in the primacy of form. As late as 1864, in a piece called "Les Traducteurs," he asserted that each and every stylistic detail has metaphysical implications (375). But that section of *William Shakespeare* entitled "Beauty, Servant of the Truth" is clearly designed to dispel the persistent image of its author as an advocate of the self-serving function of art.

The coining of the expression *l'art pour l'art* was indeed often attributed to Hugo. After all, he could not deny that, some thirty-five years earlier, in the first preface to *Les Orientales,* he had proclaimed that there are neither good nor bad subjects, that the poet is free and has no accounts to give, that a so-called "useless" book of "pure poetry" needed no justifying. But much as he liked to have been the first in anything, he hated to be trapped by his own formulas. And so, in *William Shakespeare,* the formula *l'art pour le progrès* is proposed as a loftier one. The mission of men of genius, we are told, is the forward march of humanity.

An even more paradoxical development on the usefulness of the Beautiful was finally not included in *William Shakespeare.* In pages entitled "Utilité du Beau," Hugo tried to adapt the aesthetic views he held in the 1830s to his more recent political and metaphysical concerns—a somewhat acrobatic task. By means of curiously modern-sounding remarks on the hidden intentionality of the text, as well as Victor Cousin–inspired ideas concerning the identity of the Beautiful and the Ideal, Hugo boldly sketched a theory about the utility of the useless,[5] which foreshadows the rich developments, to be found in *Les Travailleurs de la mer,* on the mysterious ways God makes himself manifest in the apparently destructive toiling of the sea.

Hugo in fact goes far beyond establishing a relation between aesthetic pleasure and virtue. He places all of nineteenth-century art squarely in the service of Revolution. Hence, the baffling association of genius with progress. First we were asked to see men of genius in a timeless scheme (though Hugo cautiously uses the expression "intrinsic progress"). We are now told that God continues to add to the great roster of exceptional poets "when the needs of progress require it," that the function of genius quite specifically is to espouse and promote Revolution. The benefit is supposedly mutual. The cause of Revolution in turn serves the cause of art—and, beyond art, the spiritual needs of man. "Never have the faculties of the human soul deepened and enriched by the meaningful ploughing of revolutions, been profounder and loftier" (194). The nineteenth century, which in this optimistic view marks the coming of age of humanity, also confers a new role on the writer. The political apocalypse signifies a new beginning, imposes new obligations, provides new opportunities. What Hugo is really saying is that political commitment defines the modern writer's originality.

The association of modern genius and Revolution is thus spelled out in apparent contradiction to art's supposed freedom from the laws of historical progress. In a preliminary note, Hugo went so far as to write: "Poets, above all, are devoured by the idea of progress" (345). The nineteenth century, according to Hugo, is without precedent. It is the offspring of an idea. And that idea—Revolution—is the grand climacteric of humanity, the turning point in a providential plan in which good can take the form of the hydra, and every thinker carries in him something of the *monstre sublime*. Hence Hugo's fascination with the figure of Marat. But the monstrosity of Revolutionary violence (for that is what above all obsesses Hugo) also explains the dream of transcending Revolution, of seeking higher harmony through an exit from history, through the negation of the destructive principle associated with any linear historical scheme. This dream of an exit from sequential and violence-ridden history is of course Enjolras's message, or rather sermon, from atop the barricade at the end of *Les Misérables*, as it will be the subject of Gauvain's visionary meditation at the end of the historical novel *Quatrevingt-Treize*.

What then is this notion of genius—at once committed to change and permanence, free from the laws of temporality, yet serving God's mysterious will-in-history? Hugo appears to reject any system. His theory of literature pretends to be thoroughly untheoretical. ("Shakespeare is a genius, not a system"—268.) Yet the underlying pattern is clear. It is that of self-canceling contradiction. Great art brings into fruitful and self-effacing clash will and predestination; it is based on what Hugo called "double reflection," the faculty of seeing the two sides of things simultaneously. Shakespeare is *totus in antithesi*, mirroring the ubiquity of opposites (236–237). The connivance between genius and the supernatural is the corollary of this insight into the "universal antithesis." The suggestion is that genius is more than human: a universal spirit, an "âme cosmique" (226).

Recurrent sea images convey the sense of power and of mystery, the sea changes that are part of the games of infinity, the fecund interplay of anger and of peace. The *hommes océans*, the creative and revelatory poets who hear and understand what the mouth of darkness has to say—they know the "intoxication of the high sea." Reflecting the divine principle, they are "All in One" in their "inexhaustibly varied monotony" (159). The sea metaphor projects a double axis: the horizontal expanse (analogue of the desert image associated with the voice of the prophet and a transfiguring fall); the depth to be plumbed, inversion of the image of an elating ascent. Each genius, according to Hugo, is an abyss as well as a summit. Hence, the symbol of the promontory, specifically associated with the apocalyptic vision of Patmos—the frightening "promontory of thought" from which the visionary artist perceives the shadow (224). Revealingly, Hugo's list of the world's fourteen great men (the fifteenth remains modestly unnamed) includes at least five prophets or biblical figures: Job, who achieved greatness at the bottom of his spiritual pit; Isaiah, the "mouthpiece of the desert"; Ezekiel, the fierce "demagogue" of the Bible; Saint John, the man of Patmos, who faced revelatory violence with the tongue of fire and the "profound smile of madness"; Saint Paul, who, on the road to Damascus, fell into truth (173–183). And it is telling that the last two words of *William Shakespeare* should be the name Jesus Christ.[6]

Three elements remain constant in Hugo's portrayal of genius: symbolic power, religious awe, and *démesure* or excess. The potential for symbolization appears boundless. It is as though all of human experience could be contained in a single brain. Elsewhere, Hugo wrote that a poet is a "world" locked up in a human skull. "Un poète est un monde enfermé dans un homme." Some of the chief tenets of Symbolism are affirmed in *William Shakespeare:* the poet's intuition of the occult sense of existence, the heroic quality of poetic vision, the gospel of correspondences, the belief that the world is a text that speaks to us but needs to be deciphered, semiotic links between the realms of the visible and the invisible binding infinite manifestations to a single principle. The Symbolist poets, though often made uneasy by his overpowering voice, were perfectly aware of Hugo's contribution. Baudelaire had earlier praised Hugo's ability to decipher the great dictionary of nature, and to dig into the inexhaustible treasure of the *universal analogy.*[7]

The relation between this pervasive symbolization and a yearning for the *sacred* is obvious. Hugo stresses the poet's sense of religious terror. "He shudders at his own depth" (242). The *vates,* or prophetic voice, surrenders to an all-consuming "religious meditation." Even in the great poets' lighter moments, one can detect the pressures of the unknown, the all-powerful *horreur sacrée* of art. Their vision hurts our minds' eye, much as Bishop Myriel's goodness in *Les Misérables* hurts and saves Valjean's conscience.[8] The breath of genius, the "souffle du génie," is defined as the "respiration of God through man" (302). Appropriately, the section that concludes with the metaphor of the promontory ("Un génie est un promontoire dans l'infini") evokes the elation of gazing at a beclouded headland jutting out into the sea, eerily inviting one to perambulate among the winds.

This image of the promontory takes on a special meaning if one recalls that one of Hugo's grandest animistic metaphors is that of "Le pâtre promontoire au chapeau de nuées," that the prophet's revelatory activity is repeatedly modeled on Moses' ascent of the mountain, and that shepherd and promontory are indeed featured in the important poem "Magnitudo parvi."[9] But more significant still is the title of Hugo's striking text on the relation of genius to dreams, *Promontorium somnii.* This symbolic promontory of dreams—the name evokes a lunar summit Hugo glimpsed through Arago's telescope at the Observatoire—proposes itself as a mental topography of visionary extravagance ("allez au-delà, extravaguez"), of *fureur sacrée,* of poetic madness. In *Promontorium somnii,* Hugo in fact inverts the old adage: *"Quos vult AUGERE Juppiter dementat"*—God makes mad those he wants to elevate (464).

These themes of extravagance and madness bring us closer to Hugo's definition of the nature of genius. For the most important characteristic of genius, from an aesthetic point of view, is what Hugo calls *démesure*—mad excess, overabundance, boundless prodigality. Shakespeare recognizes no limits; Aeschylus makes of sea and mountains the colossal protagonists of his drama. Genius simply cannot be measured by the restrictive norms of that "good taste" against which Hugo had inveighed ever since the preface to *Cromwell* and the polemical pages of *Notre-Dame de Paris.* Impossible exhaustion is the corollary of impossible sobriety. Great art is orgiastic; it has profound affinities with the carnival, the Mardi Gras (216). Sacerdotal obscenity is at the heart of Aristophanes. The mysterious ferocious laughter of art testifies to an excess of sap.[10]

The sexual connotations of *démesure* are aggressively obvious—especially when related to the sterility of criticism. Genius offends the academician as the stallion offends the mule (214). Chastity is the eunuch's pride; the seraglio displeases the impotent visitor. For genius is a condition of "orgiastic omnipotence" (241), a steady intercourse between "lewdness and thought," a movable orgy with the "bacchant" called inspiration (215, 239).

In rhetorical terms, the praise of *démesure* calls for a defense of hyperbole, declamation, amplification. Hugo challenges the castrating prescriptions of rhetoric. Aeschylus's metaphors, Hugo claims, are outsized; his tragic effects are like blows struck at the spectators (215). What value then is there in textbook wisdom, what value in classifications and prescriptions, when deeper wisdom lies in such extravagance? Ever since his early pages on Mirabeau's eloquence, Hugo has been aware of the protean metamorphoses of his own images.[11] But this theory and praxis of metaphoric profusion serve a deeper fusion.

The praise of excess has indeed political implications. *Bon goût* is denounced not merely as a form of gastritis (241), but as submissiveness to Law and Order. Dethroned "good taste" is treated as a *ci-devant* form of divine right. Hugo equates the question of Taste with the question of Power. Ironizing on sobriety as nothing but a servant's qualification, Hugo sees a certain type of criticism as a literary police force faithfully serving the establishment, the "grand parti de l'Ordre" (260). But there are philosophical implications as well. Hugo's stance could, by anticipation, be called antistructuralist. Hostile to all reductive schemes, he proclaims the irreducible uniqueness of genius. Just as divinity for Hugo is the "I of infinity," so genius is "absolute personality." Hugo's cult of the singular voice means that, even though entire periods can be summed up by one figure (320), the true identity of a great work is with itself. There can be only one Homer. Hence, the inappropriateness of all poetics. How applicable, Hugo asks, are the poetics of the *Odyssey* to Milton's *Paradise Lost*? Awe is the beginning of all sound criticism. It is as though poetics had to be reinvented to account for each great text. No matter what the laws of a given genre may be, a superior work of art is always a transgression, and this transgression instills in the author himself the horror of "his own depth" (242).

This fear of transgression is the obverse of the *pro domo* defense of orgiastic creativity. The prohibition against haunting the "tavern of the sublime" (238) is very much perceived in terms of a self-glorification, which ends up by converting God himself into Supreme Poet. The motto *totus in antithesi*—the characteristic of Hugo's own art—applies first of all to divine creation (236–237). It is the perpetual yes *and* no which allows the man of genius not only to fill and fulfill an entire century, but to participate in the tragic delight ("volupté tragique") of all nature. Hugo's own apotheosis is inscribed in the tribute to Shakespeare, as he sees him(-self) bending and weeping over human suffering, and achieving his transfiguration as he stands up, tender and terrible, above the *misérables* of this world (271).

Genius is ultimately associated with sacred lasciviousness, the "rut universel" of perpetual becoming (215). And this exuberance of all creation, this terrifying hilarity which is the tragic laughter of art as well as the ominous laughter from below ("Le mot pour rire sort de l'abîme"—216), perhaps provides the deepest link between genius and the prophecies of history. For Hugo, the hour of laughter is indeed the hour of Revolution. And Revolution is that reading of the text of history which most clearly establishes God as preexistent, coexistent, and immanent author-genius mirrored or postulated (mimesis and poesis) in the literary text.

The Edifice of the Book

Quel édifice égale une pensée?

Hugo, *William Shakespeare*

The chapter entitled "Le Massacre de Saint-Barthélemy" in Victor Hugo's *Quatrevingt-Treize*, depicting the martyrdom of a rare book about a martyr, is a humorous episode dealing with an act of vandalism committed by three little children. Their act of violence against a beautifully bound and illustrated *in-quarto* in the library of the Tourgue castle merely concerns the destruction of a book. What are such mischievous games compared with revolutionary violence and the horrors of civil war? Yet these are more than childish games. "The appetite for destruction exists," comments Hugo. The very title of the book in question evokes the infamous massacre of Protestants that began on August 23, 1572, Saint Bartholomew's Day. One may therefore wonder why Hugo treats the extermination of the "majestic book" in such a lighthearted manner. The impish exterminators, all pink and giggly, are called "angels of prey," and the annihilation of the precious volume ends with a poetic image of "swarms" of bits of paper floating into the sky to a little girl's delighted cry of "Butterflies!" (XV, 440–442).[1] What is the meaning of all this playfulness in the context of historical atrocities and of the violence against the book?

It is worth recalling that for Hugo the destruction of even a single book was tantamount to sacrilege. Only a few years before writing *Quatrevingt-Treize*, in *L'Année terrible*, he had denounced the "outrageous crime" of setting fire to that collective spiritual treasure called a library. Violence committed against books was nothing short of rabid impiety (XV, 161–162). The poem "A qui la faute?" is much more than an expression of infinite sadness in the face of brutality and ignorance (the imaginary arsonist is illiterate); it refers obliquely to the violence of history, as well as to all forms of political oppression. Burning books is the crime of Omar against which Hugo inveighs at length in *William Shakespeare*, evoking the horror of libraries going up in flames. It is said that on Omar's orders, the books of the Alexandria library served to heat the public baths. The real scandal, however, is not orgy or debauchery. Burning books is an act of fanaticism equivalent to burning human beings.

According to his wife, Hugo witnessed scenes of book vandalism in February 1831 when the Parisian rabble looted and destroyed the library of the archbishop's palace. It would seem that the memory of the event was quite personal and traumatic. One of the books thrown into the Seine happened to be the only copy of a book Hugo had recently consulted to write *Notre-Dame de Paris*. The violation of the printed word does, however, glorify the book in a tragic and ironic manner. What the mob throws into the river, what Omar throws into the fire, is precisely that which makes war on violence. A library is an "act of faith" (Hugo puns on the Inquisitional expression *auto-da-fé*); it is a curative agent (a "médecin"), a guide, a guardian—above all, in a pseudo-mystical context, it is a spiritual abyss, a "gouffre des bibles" (XV, 161).

This glorification of the book takes on the most diverse forms throughout Hugo's life. The dream of having the pen replace the sword, of having the poet overcome the warrior, assumes a very special symbolic value, if one remembers that Hugo's father had been a general in Napoleon's army. It is true that Marius in *Les Misérables,* like Hugo himself, admires the "Homeric stanzas written on the battlefield." But *Les Misérables* nonetheless proclaims the death of the sword wielders, the advent of the true heroes: the poets and the thinkers (XI, 472, 287). It is precisely the mission of genius to compete victoriously with the *gloria militar*. A book is a *force,* as it can be a weapon. Woe to the tyrant—even the group can be tyrannical—who does not love and respect this force. Napoleon's great error, according to Hugo, was to have failed to see that books are a dawn of ideas, and to have held the future in contempt (XI, 283, 288).

Hugo's cult of democratic virtues, always associated with the image of the printed page, may amuse his reader. "Instruction Gratuite et Obligatoire. Mangez le livre." Or with equal grandiloquence: "Annoncez les bonnes nouvelles, prodiguez les alphabets" (XII, 277; XI, 443). This kind of utopian rhetoric repeatedly proclaims the book's power to destroy the scaffold, liberate men and women, protect the child, point the way to progress, give renewed life to dead souls.

Let us not smile too quickly. For Hugo the glory of the book is not a simple matter of public utility. What is involved is an agonistic relation with death. Survival is at stake. All the scriptural signals tend to be testamentary. Marius carries on his person, like an amulet, a brief note which is his father's spiritual last will. Valjean brings a dowry of 600,000 francs—his worldly legacy—wrapped in a package that looks like an "octavo volume" (XI, 926). In *L'Homme qui rit,* Dr. Genardus Geestemunde's ultimate scriptural message—the confession of a crime—is entrusted to the ocean in a sealed bottle. All these signals point to the afterlife of the text. But images of survival are also images of dissemination. The spirit of destruction has no hold on the book. The book's substance is always elsewhere. Gutenberg is great because his invention made the book invulnerable. Once printed, the book is freed from time and space: it is at the same time here and everywhere.

The ambiguities of writing, inscribed under the dual signal of destruction and dissemination, of the equally "sacred" future and past, also have much to do with their insertion in a historical, and more particularly a revolutionary, becoming. The expression "This will kill that" ("Ceci tuera cela"), which serves as the title of a key chapter in *Notre-Dame de Paris,* refers specifically to the power of the printed book in confronting the hieratic and archaic architectural constructs of former periods. There was a time, according to Hugo, when architecture was the writing—the *écriture*—of humanity. But thanks to the invention of the printing press, the written text becomes the new architecture— an architecture both more powerful and more durable. The reign of marble alphabets and granite pages is over. The cathedral is an ultimate and supremely beautiful illustration of such texts of stone. The façade of Notre-Dame de Paris is described as "one of the most beautiful architectural pages"; each of its stones is viewed as a "page" in the history of our civilization (IV, 92, 95). Much like the pages of any text, they have to be "read," that is, deciphered. Frollo is fascinated by the symbolic portal which he decodes like hermetic scripture—a "page de grimoire" (IV, 125). The metaphor of the hieroglyph is a recurrent figure suggesting lapidary inscription and initiatory decipherment.

The archdeacon and the narrator, though they both consider the invention of the printing press a turning point in history, do not, however, interpret the relationship between writing and architecture in the same manner. For Frollo, the printing press signals the subversion of priestly power and the erosion of dogma. It is anticlerical in its very essence. For the narrator, on the other hand, the monuments of the past—the obelisks and columns of Karnak, the pagoda of Eklinga, the temple of Solomon—were the magnificent structural expressions of total ideologies. But their "visible majesty" (Hugo significantly refers to architecture as the "art-roi") is ultimately destined to be dethroned. The political motif is clear. Architecture, this stupendous handwriting in stone, has been a collective enterprise and a collective achievement. But it neither represented the people nor spoke to them. Its nature has remained hostile to the democratic spirit. It addressed a hierarchical and hieratic elite. Its rigid forms seem to resist all change, to oppose the very notion of progress. When dogma is engraved in stone, it is doubly petrified.[2]

Gutenberg's invention is a major spiritual event to the extent that it both signifies and provokes the transition from theocracy to democracy. What Frollo fears as the end of the world is in reality the beginning of a new one. In *William Shakespeare,* Hugo was to call Gutenberg a "redeemer" (XII, 219): freeing thought from materiality, he made it possible for literature to become thought-in-action. The press is the mother of revolutions—"la révolution mère" (IV, 141). But this matricial nature is also the source of a paradox. For the book, like Revolution itself, can only be conceived on the basis of the cumulative experiences of a cultural past. This double interdependence of the printed text and of revolutionary action casts a telling light on the significance of the book-destroying children in the library about to go up in flames. The book prepares the Revolution. But it is ironically in the very library where the young aristocrat Gauvain was inspired by books to become a revolutionary that the Vendéen children, adopted by the revolutionary battalion, tear up the beautiful *in-quarto* that recounts the life of Saint Bartholomew. The library is a sacred repository, it is the "civilized side" of the Tourgue; but it is also a transformational locus that teaches how to question what has been transmitted. The library preserves, but also challenges and demolishes. The destruction-survival of the book is thus related to a fundamental question. If the spirit of Revolution is fed by the experience and culture of the past, how then can the revolutionary future radically deny that which brought it into being? On the other hand, the book—much like the revolutionary process itself—is a relentless march forward, an action destined to permanent incompletion. Hence the disturbing image of the thousand-storey edifice, an ever-growing building already reaching to the moon, which in the final sentence of this key chapter is symbolically described as mankind's second Tower of Babel (IV, 144).

The image of the unfinished tower has a specific relevance to Hugo's notion of creative work. The unfinished nature of the book represents its mode of being and its transformational force. The omnipresent image of Babel in his own writings signals the obsession with language and *work in progress*. Throughout his texts, one can trace the central metaphor of the edifice in transition, and of architectural hybridity which brings to mind the *Zwitterarten*—those hybrid artistic forms—which accord-ing to Hegel characterize the modern novel.[3] The incompleteness of the book's edifice is for Hugo the very condition of its dynamic power. His is a synoptic vision of mankind's labors. Each word, each text, much like the living stones brought to a symbolic building site, implies not only addition but transmutation. Revealingly, the inscriptions on the cathedral's walls merge with and even efface one another. Like all acts of language, like all collective effort, they participate in a ceaseless becoming. As early as "La Pente de la rêverie," the multilanguage tower occupied a central and enigmatic position. It was, at the same time, an exalting and disquieting image. "Pendent opera interrupta" (IV, 95). It is significant that in order to describe the cathedral, Hugo alludes to Virgil's literary "monument."

The paradox is obvious. Hugo's explicit ambition is to "totalize" himself in a book. The prescriptive sentence in *Feuilles paginées* could not be clearer: "Se totaliser dans un livre complet" (III, 1195). Yet Hugo's vast literary enterprise, much like his proposed image of creation itself, postulates at the same time fundamental unity and endless process. His entire work, as Jean Gaudon has shown, brings into conflict the demands of the poem with those of poetry, embraces "totalitarian" and "unrealizable" projects, and strains toward a poetics of perpetual move-ment, a textuality without boundaries.[4]

Such a poetics of process and becoming cannot be simply explained by the refusal to be immobilized in the display cases of anthologies. Effacements and disappearances are central themes. The material dis-persion of the torn pages in *Quatrevingt-Treize,* their flight into the sky ("évanouissement dans l'azur") have an emblematic value. All through Hugo's writings, one can trace the motif of scriptural effacement sym-bolizing transfiguration: the effacement of the word *ananké* engraved on the stone wall of the cathedral (the verb *effacer* appears three times in the short preface to *Notre-Dame de Paris*); the effacement of the anonymous verses penciled on Valjean's tombstone at the end of *Les Misérables;* the effacement of Gilliatt's name written on the "blank page" of the snow in the opening scene of *Les Travailleurs de la mer.* The book itself, like the waves of the ocean, is constantly seen in a process of "decomposition" and "recomposition." A striking image in *Les Tra-vailleurs de la mer,* which calls for an intertextual reading, casts light on the principle of destruction-fecundation-birth: the deck of the ship-wrecked boat, whose "belly" has been torn open during the salvage operation, is compared to a book that has been pried open ("comme un livre qui s'ouvre"). The carcass of the Durande is exposed to the air ("offerte"). The word "démembrement" is followed in turn by a series of surgical images ("incision," "opérée," "coupure," "fracture"), leading to specifically obstetrical images suggested by terms such as "délivrer" and "enfantant" (XII, 711, 733–734).

Such imagery strongly problematizes the text. For if indeed writing is destined to be effaced, and the book destined to be dismantled, what then is the relationship between the text and that which it claims to represent? What can be the link—poetic or mimetic—between a system of vanishing traces and a reality (nature?) itself conceived as a process of disintegration, a vast laboratory of death? Some of the most complex passages in Hugo's novels deal with this problem. But the complexity also hides an affirmation. For if "reality" itself is an endless project (all realizations are merely sketches), if it is subject to the same law of dissolution, then this double negativity, this double effacement of the book as text and of the world as text, turns out to validate the mimetic function of poetic language. What Hugo has succeeded in doing is to create for his own use a contextual system comprising all his writings (even those still to be written), as well as the imaginary *hypertext* of the supreme author, to whom he would relate both as spokesman and rival.[5]

Hugo clearly comes close here to a cabalistic tradition which also seems to have influenced modern philosophers and critics who tend to view the world as a "space of inscription."[6] Many of Hugo's writings bear witness to this notion of the world as a book and of creation as a text. In this perspective, God's work is the supreme example of the indestructible text ("this book, in which the zodiac is a sentence"—XII, 67). Even the Donkey in Hugo's Faustian extravaganza speaks of the "pagination of infinity" which must forever elude our understanding.[7] Such a text is both indestructible and indecipherable. In fact, it is a palimpsest, for the act of inscription is never completed, and proceeds layer by layer. In *Philosophie: Commencement d'un livre,* referring to prehistoric sea-formations, to strata of rocks, to stupendous geological constructs, Hugo speaks of the "pages of a palimpsest"—and this precisely while dealing with the thematic relationship between "putrifactions" and "transformations," and exalting the *birth* of forms.

Not only nature but history is conceived as a relentless act of writing, a tragic composition. God, in *Quatrevingt-Treize,* is seen as the "enormous and sinister" writer of the somber pages of the Revolution (XV, 380). An important passage in *Les Misérables* sets up a vast hermeneutic system of translation and interpretation of historical events. The event, "geste de Dieu," is a mysterious script, forming part of the "scénario divin" (XI, 862–863); it can be understood (badly at that) through a writing/reading effort, a mysterious but productive mutual exchange opening the way to comprehension, but also to misunderstanding. "God makes visible to men his will in events, an obscure text written in a mysterious language. Men make translations of it forthwith; hasty translations, incorrect, full of mistakes, gaps, and misreadings" (XI, 605–606).

Granted this notion of *liber mundi,* only a short distance remains to that of God-the-literary artist (and, by implication, to that of the literary artist-as-God). Throughout Hugo's work, the poet is seen as the celebratory participant in divine creation. "God creates art through man," Hugo writes in *William Shakespeare.* This type of assertion must be read against other passages stating that works of genius are man's "superhuman" creation. Such affirmations of equivalences between the writer and God are even more striking when they occur with the word "device" *(procédé):* "one can see God coming . . . one can almost make out his device. A little more, and it seems that one could also create." In *Les Travailleurs de la mer,* where this passage appears, God is in fact presented as a master rhetorician: figures of speech, antitheses, analogies, synonyms—these are his *devices.* Even his repetitions, or redundancies, are humorously expressed in terms of writing: "omnipotence copying itself." The book of God, a palimpsest where all traces are erased as they repeat themselves, allows for no discontinuities. "Tout est coefficient" (XII, 810–811). All contradictions merge and amalgamate. All nature is linked to an original project, though its "mask" suggests the reign of contingency.[8]

The disturbing link between the artistic and the divine projects is humorously illustrated when Gilliatt, after his rescue exploit, is described as both author and demiurge. Hugo plays on a word which is obviously dear to his heart: "Here is the author." This auctorial image comes up again when Gilliatt's name, much like the name of a successful playwright, is "on the tip of everyone's tongue" (XII, 774, 790). The evocation of Gilliatt's creative inebriation while at work on his reef is surely ironic. "His work went to his head" (XII, 704). It is, moreover, a creative exaltation that Hugo associates with the names of Prometheus, Aeschylus, and Shakespeare. Such humor and self-directed irony only stress the equivocal nature of the God/artist analogue. Gilliatt the de-miurge, in his superhuman struggle against the elements, is himself associated with the forces of darkness. Local superstition refers to his "nocturnal" work. His nickname is "le Malin."

The disquieting cosubstantiality with "infinite selfhood" (*le moi de l'infini* is the definition of God given in *Les Misérables*—XI, 82) implies complicity and rivalry between author and *auctor*, between two different creative principles. The act of writing is intimately associated with me-taphysical anguish. It is on the same page where the printing press is called "la révolution mère" that the renewal of human thought is com-pared to the change of skin of the "symbolic snake" which, ever since Adam, has represented intelligence. Frollo, in his intellectual quest, is struck by the age-old symbol of the "snake that bites its tail" (IV, 141, 124). This double reference to the snake in *Notre-Dame de Paris* suggests a convergence between the narrator's point of view and Frollo's. "Ceci tuera cela" is a key chapter insofar as the true subject of this poetic fiction about the dead and the living stones of Paris is the disturbing relationship between the letter and the spirit.

This malaise associated with writing does not prevent Hugo from imposing his "Babelic" signature on his own mental landscape. Archi-tecture remains the privileged metaphor. This is particularly true in *Les Travailleurs de la mer*, where the action takes place far from man-made structures. Piranesean sea constructs suggest both ruin and incomple-tion. Weird entablatures, pediments, and colonnades stand side by side with truncated columns, broken bridges, barred entrances, and leaning towers. Other "dizzying constructs" introduce the utmost architectural heterogeneity: pagodas, pyramids, dungeons, alhambras, and sepulchres stand next to sunken cathedrals and massive citadels, introducing every-where a conflict of designs ("un combat de lignes"). Underwater urban images—fragmented walls, segments of streets—can be glimpsed next to Babel-like constructions. And on the immense pedestal of the reef besieged by the ocean, an outsized rock formation in the shape of a huge capital H stands as though to glorify the master architect. It is his granite signature.

But this signature endorsing Babel is the same signature that endorses the disturbing edifice of the book. The link between chaos and writing in Hugo's work suggests a not-so-secret collusion with the monstrosity of all creation. Writing is ominous, even in the parodic perspective of *L'Ane:* it represents not only a rattling and a clashing of words, a carnivalesque orgy of language, a deluge of ink, but the great whisper of the Unknown.[9] More serious than this ambiguously comical complaint of the Donkey is Hugo's own conviction, so often expressed, that true genius is necessarily a *noir génie*. The complicity of the artist with the forces of darkness to which he gives form and expression ("ce monde obscur qui se mouvait en moi"—VIII, 889) is explicitly illustrated by the exemplary figure of the sculptor German Pilon, to whom Hugo attributes the creation of the grotesque "mascarons" in the poem *La Révolution*. It is revealing that Hugo felt compelled to transfer this connivance with darkness from one art to another. But Germain Pilon clearly embodies Hugo's notion of the artist in a generic manner. He becomes the model of the "funèbre artiste," of the dark genius forever drawn to the darkest side of the great mystery (X, 232, 228).

The tragic rehabilitation of the monster—Hugo's poetic message—must be understood in terms of what for him is the monstrous nature of any poetic message. The sealed bottle entrusted to the sea by the fearful leader of the *comprachicos* is a traditional symbol of the survival of the literary text. At the supreme moment of the shipwreck, the disappearing arm holds up the flask as though to "show it to infinity" (XIV, 108). But here, the posthumous message—the confessional manuscript—is clearly associated with evil. The surviving text is literally the story of a crime. Doctor Gernardus Geestemunde, the criminal seer surrounded by the chaos of the ocean, composes his text *in extremis* on the verso of the old parchment. Self-parody could not be more evident. Hugo had only recently written a long poem entitled "Le Verso de la page." But the author of the second verso, the one who dies leaving behind him the seaborne bottle containing the confession of his guilt, is explicitly a baleful genius, a sinister visionary of the abyss.

Geestemunde's iconic gesture, holding the flask up to heaven as he is about to be swallowed by the ocean, implies a double verticality. This upward and downward movement illustrated by a drowning human figure transformed into "the speaking statue of darkness" must be read against the inverted Tower of Babel which haunts Hugo's imagination (XIV, 107). Such a nightmare tower is repeatedly associated in his work with the anguish of writing and with a threat that is far more disturbing than that of the book's destruction by mischievous children, illiterate vandals, or all the Omars of this world.

V.H.: The Effaced Author
or the "I" of Infinity

The literary destiny signaled by the two initials V.H. begins with an execution. It has been said that Victor Hugo's second birth to literature, the one that granted him access to visionary poetry, required a double caesura in his life: the death of his daughter Léopoldine and his own exile. Hugo's monumental sense of selfhood, the *Ego Hugo,* "rises up on an island, at death's very core."[1] In fact, the preface to *Les Contemplations* invites us to read this collection of poems "as one would read the book of a dead person." If Cocteau's quip—"Victor Hugo is a madman who took himself for Victor Hugo"—has any pertinence or even some depth, it is because the mythmaker-artificer, appearing as an absence in his text, becomes a text himself. Long before Léopoldine's drowning in 1843, or his political exile in 1851, Hugo had already transformed his voice into writing. *Le Dernier Jour d'un condamné* (1829), this record ("procès-verbal") of agonizing thought, this haunted monologue provoked and terminated by the blade of the guillotine, can be seen as the threshold. Hugo, at twenty-seven, while still far removed from the mourning and exile that were to mark his second birth, already imagined a death that opens onto literature.

To be sure, there are many other motifs and concerns in *Le Dernier Jour d'un condamné:* the symbolic and controversial figure of the executioner, the questioning of social and moral assumptions, an impassioned argument against capital punishment. Long before Sartre, Hugo chose to give his reader—and society—an uncomfortable conscience. The hallucinatory confrontation with the *idée fixe* of the severed head, the intellectual autopsy of the Condemned Man, the imprisonment in the present indicative—all these not only feed the black humor of the novel, but allow us to read between the lines a more subversive story of suggested parricide and memories of regicide. Metonymic substitutions put the king in the place of the Condemned Man, and Charles

X in that of Louis XVI, thus hinting at a revolution that remains to be completed or started anew. As for the strident chain gang, this truly demonic carnival of vociferating and grimacing convicts, it initiates us into the Kingdom of Slang, a horrendous and grotesque language, the "verbe forçat" of the world of criminals and of *les misérables*.

In depth, however, the novel tells another story. It is not by chance that Dostoevsky, in a letter written to his brother Mikhail only a few hours after his ordeal of the mock execution, quotes the cry of Hugo's Condemned Man. This cry—"ça voit le soleil"—expresses Dostoevsky's somber relief at being condemned merely to forced labor in Siberia. For Dostoevsky as well, but in this case as a lived experience, the condemned man's status symbolizes a break. It is interesting enough that the lived experience is textualized through the imaginary fabric of a text. Even more telling is the rest of Dostoevsky's letter, which, in association with Hugo's fiction, reveals the break between the former aesthete and the writer to come. Dostoevsky, who knew *Le Dernier Jour d'un condamné* by heart, it would seem, probably understood that the problem of the Condemned Man was his own in more ways than one.

It has indeed been insufficiently noted that the nameless hero of *Le Dernier Jour d'un condamné,* in contrast to Claude Gueux and Jean Valjean, both of whom are illiterate at the start, is a cultivated person, and even something of an intellectual. He is "refined by education," knows Latin, tends to have a bookish view of the world, seems to have read Pascal, asks for paper and ink, is nostalgic for his study, and even collects and annotates a song in slang.

But there is more. It is precisely in the prison, conceived as a *space* of writing (with its graffiti, mutilated inscriptions on the walls, its pages of stone), that the Condemned Man, now that the spoken word no longer communicates, now that there is no one to talk to and nothing to say, begins to write, aware that *everything* is to be written. The walls covered with tracings—chalk, coal, carvings, black letters, forgotten names, dismembered sentences seemingly branded with fire—objectify his own voice that has become silence, a voice that his own little daughter no longer recognizes. It is striking that many years before *Les Contemplations* everything seems already to be articulated on *before* and *now* ("autrefois" and "aujourd'hui"), around a gap filled by the silent biography of a man who no longer counts. The posthumous glance, the perspective of death on life, was indeed to be that of *Les Contemplations,* whose dedicatory epilogue "A celle qui est restée en France" binds the exiled poet not so much to his country as to the place where his daughter now abides—the tomb. It would seem that, beginning with *Le Dernier Jour d'un condamné*, Hugo places himself at the frontier of infinity, at the transgressive borderline where speech is replaced by the text, and the human being by the writer.

The paradox of Hugo's boundless ambition is the disappearance of the self into writing. The preface to *Les Contemplations* (Hugo's prefaces must never be taken lightly) maintains that the volume should be read as one would read "le livre d'un mort," but seemingly denies any otherness with regard to the reader: "O fool who believes that I am not you!" A strategy of effacement animates Hugo's entire work. Pierre Albouy has most convincingly spoken of the dispersion of the *Je* in certain lyrical texts. This dispersion of the first person singular, a signal of a totalizing ambition, manifests itself through a voice that articulates the individual on the collective, a "sonorous echo" which depersonalizes, and through recurrent grammatical shifts from *je* to *tu* to *il*, to the dispossession of *on*.[2] But one must be careful to add that this dissemination of the "I" always serves the apotheosis of genius. If the visionary artists and thinkers, the *mages,* are described as "splendid histrions" invested with collective humanity and wearing the changeable mask of the entire human comedy, it is because they are ultimately dispossessed of their personality. They are the supreme actors in a cosmic drama.

The strategy of effacement is nonetheless very real. Actors, mimes, histrions, buffoons, high priests of laughter, the *mages* appear and disappear on the great stage of the world, and participate in the mysterious vanishing act of undoing and becoming. Very significant is the recurrence in Hugo's lexicon of the verbal substantive *le passant* (the passerby). The narrator in *Les Misérables* is a "passant" in the historical landscape of Waterloo; Cambronne is a "passant de la dernière heure" as he reaches tragic grandeur in flinging the most obscene of words in the face of destiny; Jean Valjean first appears as the "passant" in the town of Digne, before he becomes a "passant" in Cosette's life, only to end up as a passing figure in a nameless tomb. Even the four anonymous lines of poetry penciled on the tombstone, which end with an image of disappearing daylight, are eventually washed away by the rain and erased by time. The effacement of the personality and the effacement of the text are both part of a process of transmutation.

The system of effacement evidently functions at the thematic level of writing. In *Notre-Dame de Paris,* where the text of history is itself subject to the principles of hybridity, transition, and incompleteness, architecture is replaced by writing, and the hieroglyphic sign by the book. But the book itself remains uncompleted. It is a writing-edifice in progress, a disturbing Tower of Babel, both ruin and construct. Hugo's novel about the cathedral begins, in fact, under the sign of effacement. The untitled preface explains that the whole book grew out of a single word—*anankē*—engraved in the stone, and that this word has since been whitewashed or erased. The verb *effacer* appears no less than three times in the same paragraph of this very short preface. An effaced author, an effaced word, a great cathedral that may also one day be "effacée" . . . What remains is the book.

This system of effacement is even more clearly scriptural in the opening scene of *Les Travailleurs de la mer*. The image of the name traced in snow corresponds to the title of the first chapter: "A Word Written on a Blank Page." As for the book itself, it seems destined to perform an intertextual vanishing act. Its recomposed substance always feeds the text to come. We have seen that in *Quatrevingt-Treize,* the dismantling of the book at the hands of the children, its physical dissemination as the torn pages are carried away by the wind, are poetically described as "un évanouissement dans l'azur."

The "desirous quest of writing"—Alfred Glauser's expression[3]—is nowhere better illustrated than in another snowy landscape, early in *L'Homme qui rit,* when the abandoned child meets with the decomposed body of the hanged man. The dead figure and death itself are metaphorically linked to the dynamics of writing in the context of an immense white page.

Ever since his earliest writings, certainly since the period of "La Pente de la rêverie," Hugo's scriptural thematics seem to have been subject to an implicit law of erasure, attrition, evaporation, disappearance. For the persona of the poet, all visible forms seem to pale, crumble, vanish. The barely perceptible but dangerous slope of reverie, about which the poem warns the reader from the outset, becomes the "dizzying spiral" of the self.[4] Moving from a didactic to a prophetic tone, the poem first addresses a group of familiar figures ("amis") in the name of a gently hortatory first-person singular, but soon proceeds from this still limited *je* to a broadened self (his "spirit" presented as an awestruck third person), while the temporal movement of the poem carries us from the cozy present indicative to the still familiar imperfect, and from there to the dramatic preterit, to conclude with a transcendental pluperfect which totalizes and universalizes the awesome experience. A gradually enlarged and depersonalized self seems to be engaged in a quest for the absolute.

This essentially solitary experience does not, however, glorify the otherness of the personality. Rather, it strives toward an enlargement of the self that allows the two notions of *solitaire* and *solidaire*—both of them terms dear to Hugo—to merge and become synonymous.[5]

Effacement, in this context, is obviously conceived as a limitless amplification. It proclaims a self so large indeed that it blends with totality. Nothing could be further removed from a poetics of negativity. In an important passage of *Promontorium somnii*, Hugo derides those he calls "the visionaries of negation," and he does so in the immediate vicinity of the verb *s'effacer:* "to disappear, to erase, to dissolve, to dissipate oneself, to become smoke, ashes, shadow, zero, never to have been, what happiness! What encouragement to be! It is so sweet to hope Nothing" (XII, 480). Hugo's irony is heavy. But he feels strongly about affirming the work's immanence, and even more strongly about the immanence of the creative act. His is at the same time a poetics of effacement and an affirmation of plenitude.

This double tendency is confirmed by the wide range of poems projecting the figural presence of the poet. No one, even at a time of high claims for poetry, believed with more fervor than Hugo in the special function and mission of poetic genius. Mazeppa, violently carried beyond the bounds of reality, crosses the "domains of the possible," acquiring total vision. The contemplative explorer of "La Pente de la rêverie," adrift between the "ineffable" and the "invisible" (tropes of negativity) discovers eternity at the bottom of the abyss. The magus-king of the poem "Sagesse" tests all nature in the crucible of his soul. Olympio, blending his spirit with the "grand harmonies" of the world becomes himself an abyss. Palestrina, in "Que la musique date du XVIème siècle," is not only the "dark examiner" ("scrutateur ténébreux"), the knowing interpreter of a secret language, the initiated listener discovering the muted parable of the world; his mind, symbolically amplified to the point of infinity, becomes itself a "profound universe." As for the poem entitled "Au statuaire David," it further develops the image of the mental universe containing the ominous architecture of the "age-old Babel."

But it is in certain poems of *Les Contemplations* that Hugo proposes an enlargement of such dimensions that the figure of the poet ultimately seems dispossessed of his personality, dispossessed and evacuated, as it were, of his biographical self. The poetic drive in "Ibo" assumes Promethean dimensions. And "Les Mages" properly defines the visionary poets and thinkers in terms of the image of the skull-as-container-of-infinity. But these "dark witnesses of space" do more than assail the heavens. They uncover and dislodge the supreme being.

> Ils tirent de la créature
> Dieu par l'esprit et le scalpel;
> Le grand caché de la nature
> Vient hors de l'antre à leur appel. (IX, 362)

Assaulting the sky, they are committed to an even more extravagant enterprise. The high priests of infinity, inebriated by space and time, dream of the ultimate vanishing of all lines of demarcation. They yearn for the disappearance of heaven itself: l'évanouissement des cieux!" Such metaphysical extravagance is—if at all conceivable—pushed even further in "Le Satyre," where the orphic faun sings of chaos as a lascivious spouse of infinity. In the poem's final section, the Satyr, who is about to humiliate Jupiter and all of Olympus, appears as an increasingly frightening figure, a dark shape containing all of space and still continuing to grow—the figure of excess itself. The effacement of the poet's figura is thus conceived as the very opposite of a disappearance. It signals his fusion with the cosmos.

> Place à Tout! Je suis Pan; Jupiter! à genoux. (X, 601)

Such a defiant merger with universals lends added meaning to some remarks Hugo planned to use in a preface to a volume he thought of entitling *Les Contemplations d'Olympio.* These remarks clearly situate his mythopoetics at the very confines of depersonalization. "There comes a certain moment in life when, the horizon having broadened ceaselessly, a man feels too small to continue speaking in his own name. Poet, philosopher, or thinker, he then personifies and embodies himself in an imaginary figure. It is still a human being, but it is no longer the self."[6]

This abstract, figural presence can easily become the point of departure for an allegory of the poetic process—a process which Suzanne Nash has studied with great care in her book on *Les Contemplations.*[7] In this allegorization of the poetic activity, certain symbolic figures are identified or suggested: Lucifer, Adam, Prometheus, and of course Orpheus, whose bitter and tender voice, according to Hugo, can stir the dark folds of shrouds and move stones. As a constitutive textual consciousness, the figure of the poet no doubt tells us more about the constitution of the text than about the individual who holds the pen. *Autrefois* and *aujourd'hui* cease to be the slopes of a lived life's divide; they become the two testaments of the same great BOOK that proclaims the transcendental signified ("Car le mot, c'est le Verbe, et le Verbe, c'est Dieu"—IX, 81) and affirms—or seems to affirm—Being as an ontological presence anterior, exterior, and superior to the limited text.

But to read the author's figural presence either as an affirmation of the constitutive self-consciousness of the text or as an act of faith in transcendence—that is, astride self-referentiality and the will to sing the world—might imply an overly simple choice. Hugo's poetics of authorial presence also need to be read against the parodic, therefore ironic and subversive, authorial incarnations that characterize his works of fiction.

It is indeed remarkable that, while Hugo's poetic work is rich in figures glorifying the artist, the poet, and the genius—at times taking as a point of departure a historical figure (Dürer, Virgil, Palestrina, Dante)—the novels instead seem to offer, at best, caricatures of the writer: hybrid, incomplete, or bizarre beings. Pierre Gringoire, the charming though ineffective poet-playwright in *Notre-Dame de Paris,* is called an "esprit essentiellement mixte" (IV, 67). He is an insecure dreamer, a wise fool, a philosophizing dramaturge, who is also something of a mountebank and a clown. Yet this comic and pathetic creature is also the perfect *flâneur,* a yearner and seeker after the intangible, an explorer-contemplator who leads us into the labyrinth of the Parisian streets, who guides us downward into the somber and picturesque poetic world of the *truands'* Cour des Miracles. Mediator between surface reality and the underground world of dreams, he moves as though he were himself led by some Ariadne's thread. At the frontier of his reverie, Pierre Gringoire becomes a metanarrative and metatheatrical consciousness, a seer of visible and invisible spheres, a decipherer of inscriptions in search of living stones. He seems to have access to "imaginary spaces."

Gringoire seems to prefigure an even more extravagantly self-parodic figure Hugo was to create many years later. Ursus, the ventriloquist mountebank in *L'Homme qui rit,* whose polyglot soliloquies are overwhelming "verbal excrescences,"[8] provides an obvious caricature of the rhetoric of excess ("démesure"), and of the metaphoric inebriation which Hugo, in an earlier account of Mirabeau's almost supernatural eloquence and protean style, had considered typical of his own writing.[9]

Proteus indeed. "What Proteus did for the eyes, Ursus did for the ears." In a scene that seems to compete with Diderot's *Le Neveu de Rameau,* Ursus produces all by himself an entire orchestra of human and animal sounds. Metamorphosing himself into a crowd, he becomes All and Everyone. Mime of the multitude, capable of the widest range of imitative virtuosity, Ursus appears as the living emblem of the theater (XIV, 291–292). And his own allegorical and illusionist fairy play, performed in the fairground atmosphere near a tavern, recalls inevitably the carnivalesque performances of the Elizabethan theater as Hugo evoked them in *William Shakespeare.*

Yet his parody of the writer remains positive and reassuring on the whole. The case of Doctor Gernardus Geestemunde, that strange and somber philosopher-bandit in *L'Homme qui rit,* is another matter. Although this sinister spiritual leader of a criminal gang disappears in a shipwreck early in the novel, his disquieting presence continues to cast its shadow on the rest of the book. The image of the manuscript in a sealed bottle (Hugo surely recalled Vigny's "La Bouteille à la mer") is a common symbol of the posthumous message. But the message here is the record of a mutilation. Guilt seems to accompany self-parody. A haunted and haunting figure endowed with inner vision, the learned Gernardus Geestemunde scrutinizes the forces of darkness, enters into a dialogue with the abyss, and descends into his thoughts "like a miner into his shaft." An avatar of Hugo's visionary embarked on the dangerous slope of reverie, he hears the "monstrous voice" and witnesses the mysterious processes of nature (XIV, 77, 85, 87).

The textual elements are at the same time parodic and unavowable. A perpetrator of the most heinous crime against a child (thus against God), Geestemunde is a disciple of chaos and of the occult. His is an oracular voice, the voice of a "magister" and of an "augur." Hugo jokingly calls him a "pedant of the abyss" (XIV, 80)—a reflexively ironic appellation, if one recalls the frequency of the word "abyss" in Hugo's vocabulary. Yet Gernardus obviously transcends humor, and even any particularization as a specific character. He is much more than a Dutch outlaw. The narrator explains that he is one of those figures in whom nationality itself is "effaced" (once again the motif of effacement!— XIV, 76). He is nothing less than the visionary poet, the tragic dreamer assuming a sacerdotal stance—"posture pontificale." As he goes down to the bottom of the sea, he becomes "the speaking statue of darkness" (XIV, 107). But this visionary poet remains an accomplice of evil, seems in fact to carry evil in his being. Or rather, it is this complicity with evil that seems to endow him with supernatural vision. From the very start, the portrait is disturbing. His baldness, which is compared to the tonsure of a priest (Frollo's sinister profile unavoidably comes to mind), the swollen veins on his forehead, his unhealthy complexion—all point to inner tensions and contradictions, to spiritual chaos, to yearnings for transcendence that are potentially perverted and converted into a fascination with the fall. Hugo has created no figure who suggests the mythopoetic link between poetic vision and attraction to evil more powerfully than does Geestemunde.

What hidden confession, what underlying anxiety and even sense of guilt about the creative act might be implicit in the description of this "pedant of the abyss"? It is clear that once again the figure of the poet-seer is that of the evil genius, the *noir génie*. This goes further than merely to state somewhat vaguely, as did Hugo in *William Shakespeare*, that every genius is an "abyss," or to play with the inverted corollary proposed in *Les Travailleurs de la mer*: "What an artist is the abyss!" Discussing the uncanny laughter of art, and specifically the darker side of laughter, Hugo hit on the following formula: "Le mot pour rire sort de l'abîme" (XII, 203, 693, 216).

To grasp how meaningfully the banalized image of the abyss is wedded in Hugo's mind to the hell of poetic creation, one need but read the poem "O strophe du poète" in Book V of *Les Contemplations*. This short poem is articulated not only on a split identity, but also on a fundamental temporal rift between *before* and *now:* in the past, the poet's facility gave itself free rein; his poetry, separated from his true self, frolicked in the country amid the wildflowers, at the surface of reality. But "now" things are different. The deep self, the HE of the poem—the dark inhabitant of the pallid cave—has done violence to his muse, has taken her and ravished her, brought her down to his underworld, and imposed on her an infernal marriage with the ghost-hunting king of darkness.

Toute en pleurs, il t'a prise à l'idylle joyeuse;
Il t'a ravie aux champs, à la source, à l'yeuse,
Aux amours dans les bois près des nids palpitants;
Et maintenant, captive et reine en même temps,
Prisonnière au plus noir de son âme profonde,
Parmi les visions qui flottent comme l'onde,
Sous son crâne à la fois céleste et souterrain,
Assise, et t'accoudant sur un trône d'airain,
Voyant dans ta mémoire, ainsi qu'une ombre vaine,

Fuir l'éblouissement du jour et de la plaine,
Par le maître gardée, et calme, et sans espoir,
Tandis que, près de toi, les drames, groupe noir,
Des sombres passions feuillettent le registre,
Tu rêves dans sa nuit, Proserpine sinistre.

And Prosperina, who has been carried away by Pluto, became queen of the nether regions.

Hugo seems to have understood very keenly that what we might designate in today's critical language as the "auctorial voice" is neither the voice of the author, nor the voice of the person, but a combination of signs which in a textual corpus constitutes an identifiable authority responsible for the writing. In this perspective, it is not the psychological identity that matters, but the relation of the self to its own voice. And that is precisely what Hugo suggests in "O strophe du poète," when he dramatizes the tragic intimacy between a self already become fiction (an "I" that has become "He") and his own poetry.

Seen in terms of such an authorial selfhood become otherness, Hugo's texts remain subject to a basic tension. They affirm at the outset rupture and discontinuity, the point of view of death, a system of effacement, a voice which, having become silence, absents itself from the subject into the immanence of writing, an intertextual vanishing in the service of poetry rather than of the poem, and therefore immersed in a scriptural *becoming*. But on the other hand, the system of effacement implies an enlarged self, the affirmation of a plenitude, a theater of the consciousness so enormous that it can embrace infinity. "Poeta omnis est." Yet this outsized consciousness, whether in the parodic, lyrical, or visionary register, asserts a complicity with darkness, and even with evil. This *poète noir* is ultimately the auctorial presence-in-the-text. It is true that Hugo, speaking about himself, has said: "I am the one who pays attention to his nocturnal life"; and again, in the same notes, that he was a "night bird," that he inhabited "l'azur noir" (X, 1175, 1189). Such remarks refer, however, less to the man and to his habitat than to the space of writing. In *Les Misérables,* more precisely in the important pages on the lower depths where the embryonic future germinates, Hugo evokes the splendid blackness of the scriptorium—the "noirceur sublime de l'écritoire" (XI, 533).

Through a significant displacement, the most dramatic and most symbolic embodiment of *noir génie* is worked out, as we have seen, not in the figure of a writer but in that of a sculptor. In the poem "La Révolution," Hugo attributes to the "powerful" Germain Pilon the creation of the grotesque stone figures of the Pont Neuf, the grimacing and threatening *mascarons* that were already evoked in the carnivalesque election of the Pope of Fools in *Notre-Dame de Paris*. In "La Révolution," that "horrible populace of statues," those petrified specters of a "sinister Mardi Gras," represent proleptically the tyrannized popular masses—*le peuple*—sneering with anticipation, for Revolution will be the hour of laughter and vengeance. Germain Pilon, the artist, is thus seen as a "shaper" of dark forms, a prophetic hewer of images announcing "le carnaval de l'infini," whose form-giving vision is capable of creating the revolutionary force that has not yet come into being. "Tu fis le peuple, toi!" (X, 226, 228).

Yet there can be no doubt: this visionary shaper of the people and of Revolution, this prophet of a new apocalypse, is not only a "nocturnal" genius but an intimate of the darker forces, always drawn to the heart of mourning. In the concluding lines devoted to Germain Pilon, attraction to the mystery of evil seems to accompany the apotheosis of genius:

> Qui sait si tu n'as point contemplé l'affreux deuil
> De la nature immense, et si, funèbre artiste,
> Tu n'avais pas en toi le souffle le plus triste
> Dont puisse frissonner un esprit sous les cieux,
> La désolation du Mal mystérieux,
> Quand, regardant ces flots, tu penchas, noir génie,
> L'éternel grincement sur la plainte infinie?

But there is more. For this complicity of the somber genius with evil ultimately blends into a complicity with God, whose collaborator he is shown to be. This collaboration, however, remains equivocal. Who collaborates with whom? Hugo writes:

> Dieu! collaborateur ténébreux et serein!
> Qui sait si le génie, effrayant souverain
> A qui les astres font dans l'ombre un diadème,
> A l'intuition totale de lui-même? (X, 231)

The syntax is more than doubtful. The grammatical uncertainty causes the text to say something *else,* or rather several things at the same time. For is it genius that collaborates? Is it not rather God, referred to as "shadowy" and serene—"ténébreux et serein"? And in this case, is it not God, the supreme author, who is drawn to the darkest side, the "côté le plus noir du mystère" (X, 228)?

It is a revealing ambiguity, but one which hardly surprises Hugo's reader. For the author of the work and the author of the world do meet in a common theology of darkness. We have already seen that Hugo, referring to revolutionary violence in *Quatrevingt-Treize*, speaks of God as the "sinister" author of the Text of History ("rédacteur énorme et sinistre"—XV, 380). Once again, the syntax is telling: the adjective "sinister" refers not so much to the text as to its author. God as baleful *scriptor:* the stress is on the relationship between authority, textuality, and malefic forces.

The association and even identification Hugo suggests between the author as God and God as author is, to be sure, quite different from Baudelaire's affirmation that the artist is accountable only to himself, that he perpetuates only himself, that he is his own kin, his own priest, his own God.[10] It is quite different also from Flaubert's image of a God-author present everywhere in his work, but visible nowhere. It is true that in the Preface to *Cromwell*, Hugo wrote: "Like God, the true poet is present everywhere at once in his work" (III, 72). One might even wonder whether the statement did not linger in Flaubert's memory. But for Hugo, the metaphor was almost an act of faith. In *Philosophie: Commencement d'un livre*, which is something of a spiritual testament originally meant to serve as a preface to *Les Misérables*, Hugo writes: "authority implies the author (XII, 61).[11] Without knowing Dante's *Convivio*, might Hugo have been similarly led to speculate on the etymology of the word *autor?* According to Dante, that word—not to be confused with *auctor*—was derived from the Latin verb *avieo*, meaning "to bind." The author, a binder of letters and of vowels, is thus seen as entrusted with the spiritual secret of language, the mystery of the *logos*. The "letter," in this perspective, is quite precisely the "scriptural transposal" of the world's *sacrality*.[12]

Hugo was to push to its logical extreme this confrontational equation between the authority of the text and the authority of the Word. The two authorities were to become indistinguishable in his mind. One can follow this rivaling and equalizing process in *William Shakespeare*, where Hugo, after defining the work of genius as a "second creation," a "divine action accomplished by man," proclaims the *equality* of genius and of God. This equality seemingly turns into identity. Aware of the enormity of the affirmation, Hugo comments: "It is an equality whose mystery is understood when one reflects that God is internal to man" (XII, 243).

To clarify the interplay between divine interiority and exteriority, it may be useful to recall Hugo's favorite image of the poet's skull containing infinity. "Un poète est un monde enfermé dans un homme," he writes in *La Légende des siècles* (IX, 654). In an article on Hugo's metaphysical poetry, Michael Riffaterre refers to the recurrent metaphor of the *vault* of an inner world which translates the "logically inconceivable antithesis" of infinity contained by the poet.[13] The skull-dungeon is indeed a typically Hugolian trope. Charles Baudouin, in his psychoanalytical study of Hugo, sees this image primarily as the emblem of a psychological imprisonment in an original trauma of guilt. The figure of a skull-dungeon has in fact more extensive meanings in Hugo's work. It symbolizes the eternal adventure of the dreamer who, in his transgressive quest, confronts the wall, yet loves the very obstacle that incites him to go beyond. The prison metaphor signals, at the same time, a desire to occupy the space of writing and the need for a salvational transcendence.[14] This articulation of an inner reality on an outer reality aims essentially at abolishing all distance and effacing every line of demarcation in the traditional binary opposition between man and the cosmos, between the author of the text and the text of God. The two authors end up by amalgamating (a word dear to Hugo), to the extent that the infinitely expanded inner world is ultimately assimilated into the universe. According to Albert Béguin's suggestive formulation, "a formidable appetite of the self has swallowed everything."[15] Perhaps the most awe-inspiring manifestation of this cosmic ingestion is provided by the spectacular enlargement of the Satyr growing into the measureless figure of Pan. "L'espace immense entra dans cette forme noire" (X, 600). The dark form is evidently the consciousness of the poet—the *poète noir,* at once finite and infinite.

ONCE again the notion of *effacement* refers to a boundary. But what about the effacement of the author? At the outset, if one thinks of the inscription/decapitation motif in *Le Dernier Jour d'un condamné,* the point of view of death signifies rupture, discontinuity, dispersion of the self. This evacuation of the living self implies an auctorial self dilated to such an extent that it merges with infinity. "L'infini fait irruption en moi," Hugo writes in *Philosophie: Commencement d'un livre* (XII, 36). But this particular image of a breakthrough creates a poetic space at the same time restricted and boundless. Hugo's rhetoric inflects the thematics of effacement. It reconstitutes what Anne Ubersfeld calls the "atomized self" ("le *je* pulvérisé").[16] This ultimate denial of effacement implies a mythopoetic self, the figura of the creator whose figural presence in the work is enigmatized by an implicit assimilation of the author of the work with the author of the *hypertext*. And this assimilation is further complicated because it establishes the very principle of the author—that is, of a constitutive authority, as the accomplice of dark and sinister forces. The author of the literary text turns out to be not merely a privileged interlocutor of God.[17] Given the state of complicity between God and the author, evil and creation are inseparable. The very notion of utopian progress and political eschatology is thus called into question, since Hugo sees God as the "enormous and sinister" author of the text of history.

The exchange system between the self and the infinite moreover presupposes a concurrence as well as a rivalry between the two authorial principles. Hence the importance of the Tower of Babel, an image endowed with both positive and negative potential. Skyscraper, or rather sky-aggressor, having language as its foundation but also threatened by language, the forever uncompleted tower is the emblem of the ominous dynamics of creation. Hence also the image of the "promontory into infinity"—the definition given of genius in *William Shakespeare* (XII, 250). For the promontory is associated not only with Saint John at Patmos unveiling the apocalypse, but with Moses encountering God on Mount Sinai, and finally with the notion of poetic transgression. The "promontory of dreams" becomes the mental topography whence it is possible to conceive the poetics of transcendence, the escape from confinement, the breaking out into the beyond—or, to use Hugo's powerful image, "the scaling of the steep slopes of the impossible" (XII, 480). Ultimately, the "I" facing infinity becomes the "I of infinity." Identification turns into maximal identity.

The question of identity haunted Hugo, who never tired of spreading his name or his initials in large letters, like living and threatening figures, across his graphic work. In his writings as well, there are repeated onomastic self-references: Hougomont at Waterloo, the old cell built by Bishop Hugo of Besançon in *Notre-Dame de Paris,* the bandit Hogu-Homère in *Les Misérables*.[18] At times, he imposes his signature by a single letter, such as the huge metaphorical capital H of the two towers of Notre-Dame, or the two rocks of the reef in *Les Travailleurs de la mer*. Identity, for Hugo, means Being. This by itself might explain why, in *William Shakespeare,* he insists on the superiority of "named" over anonymous works (XII, 190). It also explains the vehemence with which he rejected the idea of reincarnation,[19] for death, in his view, far from signifying the dispersion or transformation of being, was to guarantee real identity, the integrity of the self.

Hugo's aphoristic statements about genius are revealing: "To be dead is to be all-powerful"—"Having been, they are" (XII, 294–295). The posthumous literary perspective leads to what has been aptly called a "theology of the self."[20] The visionary poet, the *vates,* thus illustrates absolute personality, the infinitely expanded self, the *moi de l'infini.*[21] But this definition of the persistent selfhood of the author is also exactly the same as that of the "living infinite," the "latent self" of God. The "I of infinity" corresponds quite precisely to the definition of the supreme author given by the Conventionnel in *Les Misérables* a few moments before his illuminating death: "Ce moi de l'infini, c'est Dieu" (XI, 82). And this same God is defined by Ursus in *L'Homme qui rit,* amusingly no doubt, but also with deep meaning, as a "maker of beautiful poems," as the "first among the men of letters" (XIV, 204).

Hugo thus leads us to think of his poetics in terms of an authorial theology. It is a theology that is disturbing in more ways than one. For what is involved is far more than the point of encounter between *mimesis* and *poesis,* between song and creation; far more in fact than the exorbitant ambition to be his own procreator, his own origin, to give birth in and through himself to the divine. Some may wish to dismiss this venture as an arrogant illusion. Yet the divine laughter, the "vaste rire divin" (XII, 233), which Hugo attributes to genius is nonetheless profoundly disquieting. Whether it be called collaboration, rivalry, or identity, what seems to be involved is a fear of complicity with the underside of creation. The *moi de l'infini* appears to be associated with Evil. Among Hugo's work notes for *William Shakespeare* can be found a sentence he deliberately kept out of the final text. It is a strikingly ambiguous sentence, precisely in that it tries to answer Job's age-old question about the mystery of evil: "Evil, in nature as well as in destiny, is a dark beginning of God continuing beyond us into the invisible" (XII, 356). It is a troubled and troubling sentence. One recalls Hugo's comments about the *noir génie,* the "sob" of creation, nature's deep "mourning," the attraction to the darkest side of mystery. It is a sentence which all by itself casts doubt on any naïvely optimistic, utopian, or redemptive reading of Hugo's work.

Sartre, Hugo, a Grandfather

Spanking literary figures was one of Sartre's favorite occupations. "I have spanked Maurice Barrès," Roquentin records, on Mardi Gras day, in *La Nausée*. True, it was only a dream. The outrageously chauvinistic Barrès, in that dream, tells a soldier with a hole in the middle of his face that he should put a bouquet of violets in that hole. Roquentin and his two fellow soldiers, after indulging in an obscenity, proceed to take Barrès's pants off, spank him until he bleeds, then draw the face of Déroulède on his buttocks.

This dream-wish has many extensions in Sartre's work; Barrès is not the only victim. Metaphorical spankings occur in almost every text dealing with literature. The more famous victims are called Baudelaire, Flaubert, the brothers Goncourt, Leconte de Lisle. The list is in fact much longer; it includes all those major and minor writers who in one way or another have promoted and embodied the institution of Literature as it came to flourish in the nineteenth century.

Why then, one might ask, such relatively gentle strictures against Victor Hugo? Why does Sartre grant what amounts almost to immunity to the figure who perhaps more than anyone else in his time symbolized the *cléricature* of letters, who in fact presented himself to his contemporaries and to posterity as nothing less than its high priest, or as the Word incarnate?[1] Why is such privileged treatment granted to the one writer whom Sartre, only half-ironically, calls the supreme lord of his epoch, the "incontestable souverain du siècle"?[2] One would, on the contrary, imagine Sartre to have had little sympathy or tolerance for a man of letters capable of proclaiming that France is a supreme spiritual power because of its "literary priesthood" ("clergé littéraire") and its great writers who are the modern Popes![3]

The answer lies in part in the specific diagnosis of the nineteenth-century writer, and of his situation, as it appears in Sartre's study of

Baudelaire, in *Qu'est-ce que la littérature?* and in that summa, *L'Idiot de la famille*. The main points are worth recalling. According to Sartre, when the aristocracy collapsed at the time of the Revolution, the French writers, who until then had been the parasites of a parasitic class, showed themselves unable and unwilling to express solidarity with what was, on the whole, their own class, the bourgeoisie. This mythical rupture with their own origin, this tearing themselves away from their own class, was necessarily accompanied by bad faith, alienation, and a permanent sense of betrayal. The need to reconstitute a fake aristocracy in a vacuum led to a mystical integration into a self-created aristocratic order (the institution of Literature), as it also led to a literature of negativity founded on doubt, denial, and contestation—a literature of revolt, though not of revolution. The nineteenth-century writer, filled with duplicity, wants to consider universal man; but in his desire to be above it all, he becomes a stranger to the here and the now. He is attracted to the newly glorified notion of the *Peuple,* as a potentially great subject; but, filled with contempt and fear, he avoids real contact and remains incomprehensible to the proletariat. He enjoys the metaphysics of curse and damnation (leading to the notion of the *poète maudit*), yet he refuses to confront the reality of suffering and evil. Perhaps even worse: in spite of his willed separation from his own bourgeois class, he secretly espouses its repressive ideology insofar as it allows him to justify his aesthetics of opposition and resentment.

In discussing Baudelaire and Flaubert, Sartre defined the vocation of the nineteenth-century French writer in terms of a spiritual freemasonry, an atemporal communion of saints, an at-homeness in the vast cemetery of culture, a viewing of oneself as already posthumous while still alive. The rights of genius replaced the divine rights of monarchy, just as the sacralization of the collegium of artists instituted an extrahistorical order in which each writer took his place side by side with the great figures already dead, or still to be born, in the cultural necropolis. Flaubert's particular obsession with the posthumous stance (the word "necropolis" occurs repeatedly in his writings) explains in part why Sartre singled him out as foremost among the Knights of Nothingness.

Surely Sartre could have used Hugo to illustrate the desire for a communion with an atemporal elite, as well as the postulation of a presence-in-death which gives a privileged status to the point of view of posterity. In *William Shakespeare,* which Sartre knew well enough to quote from in *L'Idiot de la famille,* Hugo indeed extols in a self-

83

serving manner the dynasty of men of genius who, coexisting in a nonsequential time, belong to the "region of Equals," and who, their work accomplished, join what is described as the "famille dans l'infini."[4] The same text—but about that, too, there is no comment from Sartre— proclaims the coming reign of the poet-prophet and glorifies communion in the absolute of art. More strikingly even than Baudelaire or Flaubert, Hugo affirms the genius's ontological presence-in-death. "Etre mort, c'est être tout-puissant." Again, even more tellingly: "Ayant été, ils sont."[5] And could Sartre have forgotten that Hugo, in a well-known preface, specifically asked that *Les Contemplations* be read as "le livre d'un mort" ("the book of a dead man"), that he never tired of presenting himself as vatic poet and *sacerdos magnus?*

Sartre could certainly have made use of Hugo for polemical purposes. Yet he chose not to do so. The superficial reason may well be that, no matter what his sins, Hugo did not fit into Sartre's theoretical schemes of alienation and negativity. In discussing the metaphysics of failure in *L'Idiot de la famille,* Sartre suggests that Hugo's vitality and success must necessarily have made the Knights of Nothingness ill at ease. Feeling cursed neither by destiny nor by his mother, Hugo appears to them as triumphant, at ease in his fame, prestigious in his political exile—in fact, a political party all by himself: "il possède je ne sais quelle puissance surhumaine" ("he possesses an unfathomable superhuman power").[6] It is hard to tell whether this sentence is free indirect discourse (expressing the awe of the confraternity of writers), or whether Sartre speaks in his own name, and once again only half-ironically. Might it not be that it is Sartre himself who is made ill at ease by Hugo?

Interestingly enough, if one is to trust *Les Mots,* Sartre's awareness of Hugo goes back to his earliest childhood memories. Just as his interest in Flaubert's problem with words has its origin in his own childhood experience of "idiocy" when he first encountered *Madame Bovary* and the opaqueness of language, so a private family mythology had early crystallized around the figure of the Guernsey patriarch. Except that Hugo precedes Flaubert by a good twenty-seven pages in the Gallimard edition. This anteriority, or priority, of Hugo is, however, not a simple matter of textual strategy. Hugo is clearly associated with even earlier childhood memories than Flaubert—is associated specifically, in fact, with the figure of Sartre's grandfather, a substitute for the absent-dead father. The grandfather himself takes the grandfatherly figure of Victor Hugo as a model to imitate in thought and gesture. Charles Schweitzer not only had a cult of Hugo (for him, all of literature led straight from

Hesiod to the author of *La Légende des siècles*), he lived in a state of symbiosis with him. Photogenic like Hugo, he enjoyed being photographed and he assumed Hugo-like poses in front of his family—to the point where it is hard to tell whether it is to his beard or to Hugo's that Sartre refers as he evokes the childhood impressions of Poulou (the little Jean-Paul). Both Schweitzer and Hugo had perfected the art of being a grandfather; both were inebriated by their own theatricality. Schweitzer's inebriation (producing poses, attitudes, a sense of petrification, "moments of eternity" when he becomes, as it were, his own statue) corresponds to Hugo's inebriation with himself. Playing on Cocteau's famous quip, Sartre states that his grandfather was a nineteenth-century man who, like many others, like Hugo himself, took himself for Victor Hugo.[7]

"Un homme du XIXe siècle" ("a nineteenth-century man"): the formula is clearly meant to suggest a significant anachronism which, in the case of Poulou the boy and Jean-Paul the adolescent, is first lived out at the family level. The heavy presence of the substitute father, who has replaced the dead/eclipsed begetter, corresponds to the intrusion of, and return to, the past. The child comes under the spell of a figure belonging to another century, who imposes on him—and this fifteen years after the death of Mallarmé!—ideas that were currency under Louis-Philippe.[8] One may well wonder whether Sartre did not recall the dramatic relationship, in *Les Misérables,* between Marius and his grandfather, Monsieur Gillenormand (defined as a man of the eighteenth century!), who also replaced and displaced the eclipsed father (first banished, then dead), and imposed on the childhood of Hugo's young hero (himself a fictional account of Hugo's own childhood) the conservative views of another century.

The problematic bond between family structure and ideology obviously complicates Sartre's judgments as well as his silences concerning Hugo. Blended and confused with the image of the grandfather, Hugo remains an oppressive, paradigmatic, and very intimate presence. Mention of his name sends contradictory signals. On the negative side, he strikes Sartre as the embodiment of idealistic humanism and spiritual arrogance. God's self-appointed interlocutor, the "favorite interviewer of God"[9] appears to him hardly as an intellectual subversive, a questioner of the order of things. His repeated claims to be the teacher of the invisible world all seem to derive from a self-publicized, unmediated contact with the voice of darkness. Sartre might have been amused— if he did not already know—that Hugo himself inscribed under one of the countless photographs taken by his son Charles (in this one, he was perhaps just dozing): "Victor Hugo écoutant Dieu" ("Victor Hugo listening to God"). In any case, the "superhuman power" and undeniable "sovereignty" to which Sartre alludes clearly indicate misgivings about the *vates* posing as spokesman for transcendence.

What he must have known, however, though he chose not to dwell on it, is that Hugo had expressed himself against a certain notion of militant art *(l'art enrôlé)* and that history, when it was not strictly speaking raw material (very raw) to be changed by and into art, remained for him, in spite of his lifelong fascination with it, an ominous and evil force. If Enjolras, the revolutionary student-leader in *Les Misérables,* dreams of an exit from the forest of events, it is no doubt because Hugo came to question not only the historical perspective, but the historical process itself. In "La Pitié suprême," he denounced "inexorable history" ("l'histoire où le sang reparaît"—"history where blood reappears") as the accomplice of crime. History is darkness and violence. The "grand sanglot tragique de l'histoire" ("great tragic sob of history") bewails the reenactment, in various forms, of the eternal crime of Cain.[10]

Equally disturbing to Sartre must have been Hugo's continued fear of the masses. For in spite of his abstract glorification of the *Peuple* (a concept to be given concrete form by none other than the artist), in spite of his courageous defense of the repressed Communards, Hugo felt hostile to the *peuple* as a social, physical, and historical reality, and regularly allowed his pen to glide from the word "people" to the French equivalents of crowd, mob, plebs, rabble, scum. Sartre must have been in some sympathy with Proudhon, Marx, and Lukács, all of whom criticized Hugo for espousing a liberal utopian view which was essentially a justification of the bourgeois order, and for not understanding, or not wishing to understand, the class struggle and underlying socioeconomic problems of the industrial age.

The gentleness of Sartre's treatment of Hugo remains noteworthy, colored as it is by an only partly concealed admiration. "Cet homme étonnant" ("this surprising man"), he calls him in *L'Idiot de la famille* (III, 383). Once more, Sartre's recorded childhood memories are telling. Hugo was ubiquitous; he was on all the bookshelves, manifest in all the genres. "Victor Hugo le multiple nichait sur tous les rayons à la fois" ("The multiple Victor Hugo was on all the shelves at once"). And Poulou had cried over the destinies of Jean Valjean and Eviradnus.[11] The admiration in depth is, however, closely linked to Sartre's own destiny or vocation as writer, insofar as *Les Mots* is centered on the relation between *lire* and *écrire*. The most remarkable feature of the phenomenon called Hugo is indeed, as Sartre seems to suggest, his readership: he may not have been the only one to intuit the existence of a new potential reading public, namely the proletariat; but this bard of the disinherited and the underprivileged (Sartre surely knew "Les Pauvres gens" as a schoolboy) was and still is the only one to be read by the working classes.

In this context, Sartre almost forgets about Hugo's camouflaged complicities with the dominant ideology; he remembers only that Hugo turned against art for art's sake, that he became the "chantre des pauvres," and that this astonishing individual, this sacerdotal anarchist who had and still has a popular readership, expressed as his last wish the desire at once "childish, theatrical, and sublime," to be brought to rest in the "corbillard des pauvres," to be given a pauper's funeral.[12]

It is thus a kind of *engagement* after all that Sartre values in Hugo, a commitment and sense of mandate confirmed, it would seem, by a proletarian reading public. Sartre's own notions of the writer's responsibilities are, as is well known, explicitly set forth in *Qu'est-ce que la littérature?* and in the short manifesto introducing the first issue of *Les Temps Modernes:* the writer must not miss out on his time; he must espouse his period; he must avoid indifference, and understand that silence can be a scandal. Flaubert's decision not to protest made him an accomplice of the repression which followed the Commune. More fundamentally still—and more permanently—the writer must give society an uneasy conscience *(conscience malheureuse),* and thereby necessarily clash with all conservative forces. Ultimately, *engagement* is of course philosophical: the acute awareness that evil is not a simple product or by-product; that it cannot be avoided, reduced, or assimilated by the rhetoric of idealistic humanism; that evil remains absolute, and that literature therefore has an obligation to deal with "extreme situations."[13]

By Hugo's definition, too, there can be no innocent bystander. "Qui assiste au crime, assiste le crime" ("Whoever is the witness to a crime abets it"). Any bystander is necessarily an accomplice. Hugo's aphorism has, by anticipation, a Sartrean ring. There is in fact much in Hugo— and Sartre well knew it—that is a praxis of involvement. *Le Dernier Jour d'un condamné,* partly the oneiric projection of a psychodrama, is a polemically charged, militant plea against capital punishment and the inequities of the Law. It is a novel clearly designed, as the Molièresque dialogue-preface suggests, to create maximal unease (Hugo's equivalent of the *conscience malheureuse*) in the reader. It is a book which, moreover, projects its powerful and creative shadow over all of Hugo's subsequent writings. Hugo's capacity for social and political indignation was alive indeed. We hardly need speculate about whether he would have remained silent or not on the subject of concentration camps and genocide. Certainly it would not have taken him several decades to discover that there had been such things as the Stalinist purges, the Holocaust, and the Gulag archipelago. Sartre knew very well that, even though Hugo had inveighed against *l'art enrôlé*, [14] he had denounced the autonomy of art, precisely in the name of progress. Sartre even quotes from *William Shakespeare* about "l'art pour le progrès."[15] And he knew that for Hugo, too, evil was not just a metaphysical shadow, an idea to be dissolved or dismissed in and by an abstraction, but an immanent reality which galvanized the salvational mission of the writer.

The soteriological impulse of the writer, the assumption that he has a mandate to save the world, was of course not Hugo's monopoly. For Sartre, it was a very personal subject—almost too personal for comfort. If society needs to be given a *conscience malheureuse*, it is no doubt because the unease is first and foremost the writer's own deeply painful experience insofar as his mandate—about which he feels both doubt and guilt—seems to imply, on his part, a condescending solicitude which he judges with severity. In his "Présentation" of the first issue of *Les Temps Modernes,* Sartre stresses the importance, for the writer, of binding himself to a social class, of not allowing himself to look down *(se pencher)* from a privileged, lofty position. *Se pencher* over problems and human beings means, figuratively, to take interest and to show concern; but it unavoidably suggests the more concrete image of bending down, of condescending. Where, after all, *was* the writer? "In the air?"[16] And is that not the preferred position of Victor Hugo, the vatic poet, writing in his glass-encased "lookout" all the way on top of Hauteville House on the island of Guernsey?

But what about Sartre himself? Does he not also, like the false prophet Clamence, in Camus's *La Chute,* feel irresistibly drawn to heights and supreme summits? In *Les Mots,* he in fact admits to his delight at living and writing at a great height; he refers to his childhood obsession with reading and writing as an early desire to live in the rarefied air of the upper spheres, "parmi les simulacres aériens des Choses."[17] Even the desire to *come down* is perceived ironically as the obverse of the vocation of verticality and altitude.

But the feeling of guilt accompanies not only the climb to the *cîmes,* it sticks more stubbornly still to the writer's yearning for private salvation—and in particular to the opportunistic desire to be saved by politics. In *L'Idiot de la famille* (III, 91), Sartre makes a revealing comment about how Hugo, "lost" to poetry in 1848, was "saved" by the coup d'état of Louis-Bonaparte in 1851. The implicit accusation is one of political parasitism. Obliquely, the accusation is self-directed. Sartre knows that his relation to History is problematic; that no matter what his proclaimed intentions, he too remains dedicated to the institution of Literature. He cannot forget (or quite forgive himself) that many years earlier, exactly at the time he confused the beard of his grandfather with that of Hugo, he "gave himself to Literature," and by so doing "took holy orders" ("j'entrais dans les ordres"), banking on a "posthumous beatitude."[18] Even as he reminisces and writes his autobiography by a tenth-floor window symbolically overlooking a cemetery, he confesses to feeling something akin to terror at the thought of the eventual cooling of the sun, a catastrophe which would deprive him of the millions of survivors whom he would like to continue to haunt and to save. The end of the world would deprive him of his posthumous stance!

With little indulgence for Poulou, Sartre recalls how he never doubted for a moment that a place was reserved for him in the Pantheon.[19] Next to Hugo, perhaps? He does not say. It is clear, however, that if the image of Hugo continues to serve Sartre's self-incriminating bent, it also mirrors a permanent longing. Sartre denounced in others, and in himself, the big lie of any literary *cléricature*. Yet he was never to give up the ambition he describes, as he nostalgically evokes his friendship with his fellow Normalien, Paul Nizan: the hope of bringing about salvation, "notre salut et, avec un peu de chance, celui des autres" ("our salvation, and with a little luck, that of others"). The hope, and the shame that went with it, were intimately related to the use of *words,* quite specifically—though both he and Nizan were atheists—to a religious vocabulary: "Nous gardâmes longtemps, lui et moi, le vocabulaire chrétien" ("For a long time, he and I retained the Christian vocabulary"). But words were also to be terrorist weapons: "ces bombes, mes paroles" ("these bombs, my words")[20] Revealingly and ironically, Sartre titled his autobiography *Les Mots,* a title that becomes even more ironic if one remembers that it was Hugo—and this precisely in a poem that stands next to the famous assertion concerning the explosive, revolutionary impact of his own literary language—who proclaimed the transcendence of the *Word:* "Car le mot, c'est le Verbe, et le Verbe, c'est Dieu."[21]

The Will to Ecstasy:
Baudelaire's "La Chevelure"

L'ivresse est un nombre.

Two surprising lines, at the heart of "La Chevelure," alert us to the inadequacy of reading the poem literally, as a glorification of sensuous love.

Je plongerai ma tête amoureuse d'ivresse
Dans ce noir océan où l'autre est enfermé . . .   (lines 21–22)

These lines are no doubt suggestive of a physical experience, of what appears to be the central motif of the text. The verb *plonger* signals full immersion in the erotic-exotic imagery that can be traced back to the first stanza; the double enclosure ("dans," "enfermé") fuses the evocation of the lovers' alcove with the magic workings of synesthesia; the adjective *noir* qualifies the woman's hair, but also the bounded intimacy, and the descent into the secrets of the body which, by association, becomes the precious repository of memory. Yet things are not quite so simple. Two striking features of line 21 cannot be quickly dismissed. The first is the tense of the verb—"Je plongerai": a noteworthy use of the future in an evocative context stressing the past ("souvenirs dormant," "presque défunt"). The other, even more remarkable, is the metaphoric inversion "amoureuse d'ivresse" (not intoxicated with love, but in love with intoxication), which reverses the expected order of priorities, making not love but intoxication the ultimate end. The adjectival form "amoureuse" in fact relegates love to a desiderative attribute.

It is the head ("ma tête") that counts, yet not the head of hair but that of the poet's persona: the head that accomplishes the erotic movement, but also the seat of reverie and skilled perception. The expression "mon esprit subtil," two lines later, clearly supports such a reading. As for the metaphoric complexity of line 21, it serves to remind us that the true inebriation, announced by the exclamation "Extase!" in line 3, refers to the poetic sensibility, or more precisely to the poetic function itself.

That "La Chevelure" is in part about the poet should not come as a startling discovery. The pervasive use of the first-person singular; the topos of the ecstasy-providing yet anonymous mistress; the imagery of quasi-death, resurrection, and timelessness ("souvenirs dormant," "presque défunt"; "retrouver," "rendez"; "éternelle," "embaumé," "toujours") all give credence to such an interpretation. Moreover, the specific inebriation is linked to a figurative notion of drinking: it is the *soul* that wants to drink (line 16)—a notion that is delicately summed up in the concluding line, when the verb *humer,* applied not to a banal libation but to the very essence of memory, serves as an intermediary between the image of drinking and the more abstract one of breathing in. Any reader who recalls that, in discussing the deep joys of wine, Baudelaire focuses immediately on the man who *drinks genius* ("l'homme qui boit du génie")[1] will of necessity make a further link between intoxication and the experience (or activity) of art.

The question is enriched by the ambivalent aesthetics of intoxication. The reference to Hoffmann's *Kreisleriana,* at the beginning of *Les Paradis artificiels,* may seem trifling: Baudelaire recalls the advice given to the conscientious composer to drink champagne to compose a comic opera, Rhine wine for religious music, and Burgundy for heroic strains. This light-hearted reference in the opening section does serve a purpose: it provides a framework within which the notion of inebriation is explicitly placed in the service of art. The "qualités musicales des vins," illustrative of the system of synesthesia and foreshadowing the decadent "orgue à bouche" of Huysmans's hero Des Esseintes, are further related to temporal and spatial expansion, to the dynamics of escape. (The prose poem "Enivrez-vous" specifically recommends drunkenness as a way to avoid the martyrdom of Time!) Conversely, it is not surprising that music is directly evocative of the tormenting and delicious elation of artificial paradises: Wagner's *Tannhäuser* provides Baudelaire with the "vertiginous concepts of opium" (1214).

The relationship *art-ivresse* is further complicated by the dialectics of will and passivity: although the intoxications by drugs and art clearly imply a liberation, a "trip" (in the sense of a transport, or the literal meaning of *ecstasy*), it is not at all clear whether this signifies a weakening or, on the contrary, a concentration of the volitional powers. The dilemma is, of course, crucial to the poetic activity as understood by Baudelaire. On the one hand, any form of intoxication represents excess:

it involves (the metaphor once again points to the aesthetic experience) "le développement poétique excessif de l'homme." The cost is always an extraordinary expenditure, a self-destructive "dépense de fluide nerveux." It marks a falling-off, a loss of the most precious substance: will. On the other hand, not only do some intoxicants (wine, for instance) "exalt willpower," but poetry specifically requires the "assiduous exercise of will and the permanent nobility of intention" (341, 342, 384, 387).

A great deal has been said about Baudelaire's interest in drugs. It might be worthwhile, for a change, to look not at what the poet says about inebriation, but at how he relates inebriation to the problems of poetry. What justifies such a perspective is a threefold dialectical tension in *Les Paradis artificiels* paralleling, at the level of the discussion about wine and hashish, the fundamental opposites of the creative method: egocentricity and depersonalization, passivity and control, intoxication as self-possession and artistic self-possession as inebriation.

FIRST, depersonalization. The subtitle of "Du Vin et du hachish" refers to intoxicants as "moyens de multiplication de l'individualité": multiplication, but also dispersal, evanescence. A few pages later, Baudelaire asseverates that certain drinks possess the virtue of increasing ("augmenter") the personality enormously; they create, so to speak, "a third person" (333). After a while, the personality disappears altogether (twice Baudelaire uses the formula "la personnalité disparaît"—339, 365), and this vanishing act is brought into revealing juxtaposition with the poetic act, namely that of the "poètes panthéistes" (365). Ultimately it is the generic "enthusiasm" of all poets and creators which is metaphorically illustrated by the painful delights of intoxication (369). The lyric mode exists for Baudelaire in terms of a structured depersonalization: the poem functions as a specular system allowing the subject to disappear in the object. In section VII of "Du Vin et du hachish," the "great poets" are indeed seen as exercising their will to achieve a state in which they are simultaneously "cause et effet, sujet et objet."

"Multiplication" is a key word. Baudelaire likes crowds because they provide him with the dizzying "jouissance de la multiplication du nombre." Inversely, concerning the multiplication within the individual: "L'ivresse est un nombre" ("Inebriation is a number"). But this form of numerical, demultiplying, centrifugal intoxication seems contradicted by an intoxicating effect (or metaphoric use of intoxication) that stresses the self as the center of the universe. *Les Paradis artificiels* insists on this opposing centripetal, and even solipsistic, trend. Hashish "develops excessively the human personality"; drugs in general encourage "solitary pleasures," they "exaggerate" the individual, they wed him tragically to himself. Eventually, this movement carries the individual to believe in his own godhead. He becomes the monomaniacal center of his own cosmos. *"Je suis devenu Dieu!"*

If, in the dialectics of intoxication, egocentricity and depersonalization remain interlocked, so do the opposing notions of passivity and control. This, too, is directly relevant to the poetic activity. The rubric of passivity under induced ecstasy is of course telling: will is lessened ("amoindrie"); the subject becomes unfit for action ("incapable de travail et d'énergie dans l'action"); time disappears; the mind suffers from inexorable "evaporation." The very measure of temporality is abolished. Yet the rubric of control is no less impressive. The drugged subject retains the power to observe himself ("la faculté de vous observer vous-même"—339); some forms of inebriation actually "exalt will" (342). More important, the "trip" toward the unknown appears in fact as a volitive act: "Vous l'avez voulu" (356). The absolutist aim is implicit: "Les yeux visent l'infini" (364). If the addict stares into his own Narcissus face, it is not only out of self-gratification, but because of the workings of a measureless proud will. In the last analysis, control itself induces a sense of drunkenness. The "free exercise of the will," appanage of the genuine poet, imposes the dreamer-somnambulist as his own magnetizer (343). In such power lies joy. The *absolute* lyric mode implies an "absolute divinization" of the poet; this joy involves a tension between enthusiasm and the analytic spirit. In this tension, in this "état mixte," Baudelaire sees the essence of "modern" poetry. These lyric dissonances, in turn, make of irony the pivot of the modern poetic experience. And irony, in a contextual image that yokes the active and the passive, is defined as the vengeance of the vanquished—"cette vengeance du vaincu."[2]

IN "LA Chevelure," this particular ironic tension is operative throughout. More specifically, the dialectics of passivity and desideration, summed up by the inverted metaphor "amoureuse d'ivresse," function as early as the first stanza.

O toison, moutonnant jusque sur l'encolure!
O boucles! O parfum chargé de nonchaloir!
Extase! Pour peupler ce soir l'alcôve obscure
Des souvenirs dormant dans cette chevelure,
Je la veux agiter dans l'air comme un mouchoir!

The poem opens with the vocative "O," repeated twice in the second line. This triple exclamation imposes the ecstatic mode (here suggesting at first adoration); it prepares indeed the word "extase" which, verbless and accompanied by only an exclamation point, appears at the beginning of the third line much like a fourth vocative interjection. The passivity (or implied submissiveness) of the ecstatic mood is further stressed by the rather rare word "nonchaloir" denoting indolence, and the reference to the "sleeping" memories.

Yet the first stanza simultaneously proposes a clear volitive strand. The first signal comes in the third line: the intentional preposition "pour," followed by the infinitive "peupler" (the verb itself suggests an active multiplication and, more specifically, procreation or even creation), announces the unambiguous volitional statement of the first stanza's closing line: "Je la veux agiter" ("I want to wave it"). These signals of intentionality, implying movement as well as a project, are further intensified by semantic elements suggestive of departure: "moutonnant" refers to the hair, but by indirection also to the waves of the sea; this double image is further developed or modulated by the preposition of spatiality "jusque," the adjective "chargé" (implying the load or cargo of a vessel), the waving of the handkerchief associated with leave-taking and—perhaps most important—the very first substantive of the poem, "toison" (fleece), referring to the hair, but immediately also, by means of the allusion to the mythological fleece, to the notion of an exotic voyage, of a quest.

These dual strands of passivity and intentionality become part of a larger network in the rest of the poem. The ecstatic and indolent strains of the opening stanza are echoed by the opening note of the next stanza (the adjective "langoureuse"), picked up by the nonactive "presque défunt" of line 7, continued by the more ambiguous "voguent" of line 9, and brought to a full evocation of passivity by the "infinis bercements" and the "féconde paresse" of the fifth stanza. On the other hand, the semantic field is equally rich in volitional elements. "J'irai là-bas" ("I shall go there"): the decisive future of line 11, applied to the elsewhere, obviously echoes the "Je la veux" of the first stanza. This desiderative note is further strengthened by the imperative in line 13 ("soyez"), related in turn to the verb of movement "enlève" (though this verb also implies the passivity of the passenger being carried away). The beginning of stanza V repeats the attack of stanza III: "Je plongerai" ("I shall dive")—another future of intentionality, itself echoed by the "saura" of line 24, as well as by the verb "retrouver" denoting a search. In the last stanza, the sense of an intentional projection becomes explicit by means of the conjunction of purpose "Afin que" ("So that") and the subjunctive compounded by a categorically imperative negation "tu ne sois jamais" ("you never be").

The dual strands of the poem, though in steady transformation, remain in a state of tension until the end. This tension is in large part made secure by one of Baudelaire's key images, the port, here revealingly located at the precise center of the text. The port, place of refuge and reverie, is also the place of departure—or, more precisely, the place of reverie about departure. Ideal Baudelairean locus of controlled dreams, of a dandyish equilibrium between movement and stability, the haven ("séjour charmant," as he puts it in the well-known prose poem) opens up while locking in. Not surprisingly, this central stanza is also the one most heavily laden with quasi-religious images: "âme," "or," "vastes," "gloire," "ciel pur," "éternelle chaleur."

"La Chevelure" is not the only poem associating sea images with the apparently conflicting experiences of inebriating indolence and artistic control. "Le Beau Navire" overtly describes the bewitchment of the "molle enchanteresse," as she lazily glides by ("Suivant un rythme doux, et paresseux et lent"), and majestically displays her body rich with precious intoxicants. "Armoire à doux secrets, pleine de bonnes choses, / De vins, de parfums, de liqueurs . . ." Yet the bewitching experience is, from the start, held in check by the opening volitive structure: "Je veux te raconter," repeated word by word at the beginning of the fourth stanza, and twice echoed within the two stanzas by the slight variation of the third line: "Je veux te peindre . . ." Desire itself seems to be kept at a distance, the spell exorcised and held under control by these volitional structures and incantatory repetitions.[3] The variation is equally revealing: the substitution of the verb "peindre" (to depict) for the verb "raconter" (to tell) clearly places the sensuous experience under the metaphoric supervision and discipline of art.

Such a framework of explicit artistic control appears as a recurrent pattern in Baudelaire's work. The opening piece of *Tableaux parisiens,* which must be read as a sort of introduction, provides another telling example. The first line affirms the artistic intention: "Je veux, pour composer chastement mes églogues . . ." This is strengthened by the future construct of line 6, "Je verrai" (repeated in line 13), the "Je fermerai" of line 15, the "je rêverai" of line 17, by the unequivocally intentional "Pour bâtir" of line 16, and brought to a logical conclusion through the glorification of artistic will: "Car je serai plongé dans cette volupté /

D'évoquer le Printemps avec ma volonté" (lines 23–24). Not only is the very notion of dreaming placed under the patronage of a future "creative" tense (I shall dream, I shall decide when and how to dream, I shall shape and dominate my dreams), but "volupté" represents here emphatically not that which art describes: it proposes itself as the very definition of *artistic will*. The analysis of this inversion, which in its own terms parallels the metaphoric structure "amoureuse d'ivresse," casts light on the concluding remarks of "Le Poème du haschisch," which glorify the "permanent nobility of intention" in the context of an essay devoted to the allurements and dangers of intoxication.

Baudelaire's ambivalent fascination with inebriating experiences, reenacted in "La Chevelure," is translatable into synonymous or metonymic images. There are indeed other words for this attraction, which is also a fear. Baudelaire himself, in referring to the phenomenon of evaporation associated with drug addiction, speaks of a "transposition": the pipe-smoking is experienced as a smoking of oneself (365). But evaporation, in association with a sensuous spell, is precisely the devil's aim in his subversion of human will. "Et le riche métal de notre volonté / Est tout vaporisé par ce savant chimiste." Baudelaire's work is colored by this fear, but also by the project to bring into a balanced, creative juxtaposition the passive delights of ecstasy and the prerogatives of the individual's self-control. Ultimately, *will* itself—especially the artistic will—is conceived as a type of intoxication. "L'inspiration vient toujours quand l'homme le *veut*" ("Inspiration always comes when man *wants* it"). However, it is a problematic inspiration, as the end of the sentence implies: "mais elle ne s'en va pas toujours quand il le veut" ("but it does not always vanish when man so wishes").[4] Only two sentences earlier Baudelaire speaks of those supernatural moments when time and space are boundlessly extended; and a sentence later he refers to "sorcellerie évocatoire" ("evocative witchcraft")—thus clearly suggesting that it is the very function of poetry to live out this tension between intoxication as experience and intoxication as method.

"Le Cygne": The Artifact of Memory

The interpretation of this poem depends in large part on the reading of the first line. Is it an invocation or an observation? "Andromaque, je pense à vous!" The poem begins with a proper name that links history, legend, and literature. The poet's voice, addressing this transcendental figure situated at different levels of the past, speaks in the present indicative. Past and present converge yet remain distinct. On the syntactic level, the sentence seems unified and self-contained (the second-person plural leading us back to an immanent Andromache), while on the rhythmic level it separates the *vous* from the first person through a vocative structure that suggests the difficulties of maintaining a link at a distance. How indeed should one read this first line? Does it imply a mere juxtaposition, a coincidence: someone happens to have thought of Andromache? Is it that certain sensations or impressions evoke the figure? Or is there an effort involved, a summons, hence an intentionality? Does the figure of the poet in the midst of the Parisian cityscape seek consolation or hope by invoking the royal widow?

From the outset, nothing justifies opting for one or the other of these readings. The first line proposes a delicate tension between present and past, between resignation and the effort needed to overcome it. *Here* and *there* all at once. The ambiguity of the demonstrative pronoun ("*Ce* petit fleuve"), referring to the Seine as well as to the counterfeit Simoïs river ("Simoïs menteur"), confirms the dialectics of separation and dependence.

The chronology of the poem implies seemingly contradictory structures of stratification and circularity. Behind the present of the evocation ("je pense") lies an experience belonging to a recent past ("Comme je traversais"); and behind this memory of a Parisian stroll, which also recalls the regretted metamorphoses of Haussmann's urban renewal ("Le vieux Paris n'est plus"), there is another time, that of a *jadis* (a former time) of a now disappeared menagerie from which a swan escaped. Present indicative, *passé composé*, imperfect, preterit, pluperfect—all the tenses unfold, progressively separating us from the moment of the evocation / meditation, and bringing us ever closer to the evoked time. Behind nineteenth-century Paris, behind the "old" Paris now vanished, one glimpses the shadow of Andromache—first, unavoidably for a French reader, the Racinian one, but surely also the Virgilian shadow, the one Aeneas meets in Book III of the *Aeneid*.[1]

Yet even in Virgil's epic, the episode is in the past; it is relived through a narration, as a return to a former time, a "flashback." Aeneas describes to Dido his encounter with Andromache: "falsi Simoentis ad undam"—the very words Baudelaire had at first used as an epigraph to his poem. Moreover, Virgil's Andromache herself belongs to three distinct places and historical moments: as Hector's wife in proud Troy; in exile, as a captive ("vil bétail") of Pyrrhus; living in illusory freedom as Helenus's spouse. And just as Baudelaire's poem projects several chronological Andromaches, so also it accumulates several Troys: the real one (before and after its destruction); the false, "imitation" Troy reconstructed in Epirus ("parvam Trojam"); the new Troy (Rome) which it is Aeneas's mission to found; and, beyond these Troys of antiquity, all the modern Troys of which Paris, huge and vulnerable, is the contemporary figuration. Finally, behind the archaeology of the city, the glance of "l'homme d'Ovide" (a memory of the *Metamorphoses*) represents simultaneously an ironic commentary on man's dereliction under the "cruelly blue" sky of exile and a reminder of the "historical" moment of his creation. At every level, the poem illustrates a nostalgia for the past, or rather an essentially hopeless effort of retrieval which—as Baudelaire himself seems to suggest—determines the allegorical process.[2] Fall or exile: the present implies a distancing, as well as a telescoping of the *before* and the *after*.

Through its rhetorical and thematic structure, "Le Cygne" is both a poem of time gone by and of simultaneity. "My beloved memories are heavier than boulders" ("Et mes chers souvenirs sont plus lourds que des rocs"). This line sums up the characteristic mixture of fugacity and permanence. The temporal organization of the poem works in a similar manner. After an early succession of tenses in the indicative whose broad range corresponds to fragmentary incidents and episodes (the jumbled "bric-a-brac"), the second part of the poem tends to immobilize the experience. The opening lines of part II give the signal: "Paris change! mais rien dans ma mélancolie / N'a bougé!" ("Paris changes! But in my melancholy / Nothing has stirred"). In a sense, it is this fixating tendency that Baudelaire associates with the allegorizing intentionality: "tout pour moi devient allégorie." The sovereign tense of this second part is the present. As for the central stanza of this section—perhaps the most justly famous of the poem—it is characterized by a total absence of verbs and a preponderance of adjectival forms stressing plastic immobilization:

> Andromaque, des bras d'un grand époux tombée,
> Vil bétail, sous la main du superbe Pyrrhus,
> Auprès d'un tombeau vide en extase courbée;
> Veuve d'Hector, hélas! et femme d'Hélénus!

Slave, widow, and wife—all are telescoped in one image. The stanza, in its powerful figuration of pain, mourning, and beauty, immobilizes a statuesque Andromache in a pose that continues into an eternal present. The experience is transmuted into an attitude.

But does such a hieratic metaphor retrieve the fragments? The mythical elements doubtless blur the distinction between past and present, but also partially restore their integrity through a poetization of triviality. The modern ring of heroic life and the heroic aspect of modernity are worked out through a system of analogies that propose the equation tubercular negress = Andromache as the simplest expression, and exile as the central motif. This system of analogies functions most intensely at the level of literary references and echoes. It is significant that Aeneas, through whose eyes we see the majestic widow in Virgil's text, is himself in exile; that Baudelaire's poem is dedicated to Victor Hugo, in self-willed political exile; that the allusion to Ovid echoes another poem of *Les Fleurs du mal* where he is described as "driven from the Latin paradise"; and that the last stanza begins with the image of the forest associated with the idea of a spiritual exile ("la forêt où mon esprit s'exile")—a double image, in fact, which unavoidably brings to mind the opening of Dante's *Commedia*.

Do these literary authorities suffice to exorcise fragmentation and recompose an order out of heaps of half-shaped columns ("chapiteaux ébauchés") and sundry bric-a-brac? Decomposition and reconstruction, dispersion and unity, represent the dialectical tensions of this poem which cannot be grasped through strictly mythical referents. Only a close textual analysis might cast light on the underlying intentionality. We must return to the first line.

A VOICE is heard. But *who* speaks, and *to whom?* One might ask: What is the status of the subject of enunciation? An "I" thinks and sees; not a solipsistic "I," but one relating to a "you" (lines 1, 3, 36). The poem thus begins with a relation between a self and a second person who, from the first sentence on, assumes a preferential role. The unfolding of the poem involves a steady enlargement of the perspective, a progressive *opening*, as the "you" and the "I" are soon blended into a collective and reassuring "we" that ultimately takes the form of a "they" or an anonymous "one": the "whoever" ("quiconque") of line 45 obviously corresponds to "those" ("ceux") of the following line. One might say that the writing process tends here toward the impersonal pronoun.[3] And this no doubt is the significance of the indefinite article "un" in the second stanza:

> Le vieux Paris n'est plus (la forme d'une ville
> Change plus vite, hélas! que le cœur d'*un* mortel)

> The old Paris is no longer (a city's form
> Changes more quickly, alas, than the heart of *a* mortal)

At this syntactic level, the solitudes experienced by the one who evokes and the one who is evoked merge in a common destiny. The capitalized / allegorized words also function in terms of a collective drama. The abstract term "Sorrow" ("Douleur") of the penultimate stanza universalizes the plural but still individualized "douleurs" of the first stanza. Yet sorrow is seen from the beginning as fertile (the tear-filled river has "fécondé" an already "fertile" memory). The sad river becomes the mirror of Andromache's grief, as if that grief were a prestigious ornament. The structure of the sentence, moreover, attributes the "immense majesty" not to the widow herself, but to her suffering. As for the river, it swells ("grandit"), literally and metaphorically, because of all the tears that pour into it.

This liquid imagery immediately establishes an antithesis of aridity and fertility, justifying the metaphor of the Simoïs / Seine rivers that connect past and present sorrows. On the one hand, there is the suggestion of a barren world deprived of life-giving waters: the stagnant puddles, the dry stones, the waterless gutter, the dust in which the swan tries to bathe his wings, the yearning for rain ("Eau, quand donc pleuvras-tu?"), the avid beak of the thirsty animal, the mud through which the consumptive negress tramps, the grim wall of fog, the orphans of the metropolis withering like neglected flowers. But there is also the emergence of a desire which is transfigured by means of wasteland images into hope and even a somber joy. The tears which, at the end of the poem, quench the thirst of those who shed them recall the fecundating tears of the opening stanza. Even more suggestive is the image of Sorrow (the allegorization becomes quite explicit) suckling the estranged humanity of the modern capital like the legendary she-wolf. It is a somewhat comforting image. The allusion to the founding of Rome (the new Troy), integrated into the order of History, proposes a reassuring continuity.

The processes of Memory ("le Souvenir") thus help account for Sorrow ("la Douleur"). The redundancy of the words "fécondé" and "fertile" referring to memory is not merely a Latin construction justified by the thematic context. It suggests the salvational nature of recollection. Proust, at the beginning of *Combray*, was to write of memory as a grace coming from above ("un secours d'en haut") to free us from nothingness and restitute out identity. "Le Cygne," by means of the "mémoire fertile," sets up a collective identity / identification ("quiconque," "ceux qui") that implies the denial or reclaiming of an absence. The image of Andromache is essentially a symbol of fidelity. The widow's *ecstasy* as she stands grieving over an empty tomb is figuratively a *stasis*. Through the metaphoric mediation of the poet's mind, her communion with her own past is contrasted with the instabilities of the ordinary human heart, "le cœur d'un mortel." The ceremonial pose of the exiled royal widow conveys a ritualistic attitude fixed as though in marble. The cult of the husband is but the objective correlative of a cult of the past that liberates the present from its own fragmentary and contingent nature. The present indicative of Part II imposes itself as the time of eternity, the time of salvation. Only in that sense can one speak of the progression of the poem, whose pivotal stanza is situated at its precise center, at the beginning of Part II which confronts the preceding themes of evanescence with a proclamation of immutability: "nothing in my melancholy / Has stirred". Similarly, the sound of the horn in the last stanza signals sadness and distress, but also the solemnity of a heroic call, and hope in the face of disaster. Significantly, it is none other than Memory that sounds the horn with the very "spirit" ("plein souffle") of poetic inspiration. Creation and re-creation are intimately wedded in the verbal and thematic structure of the poem.

Without violating the meaning of the poem, is it possible to speak of a thematics of conceptual design *(ébauche)* and of the struggle of artistic elaboration? The half-shaped unfinished columns ("chapiteaux ébauchés") of the third stanza would seem to refer to work in progress. The poem's allegorical trinity, whose third term—after Sorrow and

Memory—is Labor *(Travail)*, is consonant at various levels with the topos of the city. For the word "Labor," with all the contextual intimations of contempt and guilt, is in fact specifically associated with the word *voirie* (street sanitation, garbage removal), and therefore with the streets of Paris and images of refuse. The modern city, which, according to Walter Benjamin, so poetically traumatized the poet, imposes complementary images of construction and demolition.[4] Its "stone landscape" dramatically juxtaposes notions of change and duration. The "black majesty of the most disturbing of capitals,"[5] another image of queenly mourning, looms like a threat. In Baudelaire's poetic consciousness, creation and disintegration are ineluctably coupled. Any artistic effort is necessarily re-creation, if not anti-creation; it depends on the principle of undoing, and is activated because all "real" forms are evanescent. The design or *ébauche* on the canvas, as the famous stanza in the poem "Une Charogne" reveals, can be textured and completed only by an ideal operation of memory.

With memory at the service of the design, and this design dependent on the process of disentegration, it is easy to see that the meaning of the poem extends to the drama of culture itself, a drama based on the dialectics of dissolution and continuity. Facing the monuments of the past, Baudelaire in his moments of anguished lucidity also sees only "moss-covered stones" and "jumbled bric-a-brac." Much like T. S. Eliot, whose *Waste Land* owes so much to *Les Fleurs du mal,* Baudelaire proposes an inventory of the "withered stumps of time." And much like Eliot, he discovers in the very fragmentary cultural experience a protection against nothingness, a basis for possible salvation. "These fragments I have shored against my ruins . . . "

Lyricism and Impersonality:
The Example of Baudelaire

> . . .a suggestive magic containing all at once the object and the
> subject, the world outside the artist and the artist himself.
>
> Baudelaire

> Poetry . . . is not the expression of personality, but an escape from
> personality.
>
> T. S. Eliot

Baudelaire does not believe in chance. "Every literary composition, even criticism, must be written and controlled with an end in mind. Even a sonnet. Imagine the labor!" The labor in question is all the harder, since Baudelaire also sets out to deny the imperatives of subjectivity. He declares that the "free exercise of the will," the privilege of true poets, must impose an economy on means and ends, and abolish all factitious barriers separating the object from the subject.[1]

No poem by Baudelaire illustrates better than "Spleen" LXXV—precisely a sonnet!—this effacement of boundary lines which makes it possible for the subject to disappear in the object. It is a poem of liquidity and liquidation, a poem of the time of death—but of a death that also implies a posthumous glance. Above all, it is a poem of absence, quite specifically the absence of the *subject*.

Pluviôse, irrité contre la ville entière,
De son urne à grands flots verse un froid ténébreux
Aux pâles habitants du voisin cimetière
Et la mortalité sur les faubourgs brumeux.

Mon chat sur le carreau cherchant une litière
Agite sans repos son corps maigre et galeux;
L'âme d'un vieux poète erre dans la gouttière
Avec la triste voix d'un fantôme frileux.

Le bourdon se lamente, et la bûche enfumée
Accompagne en fausset la pendule enrhumée,
Cependant qu'en un jeu plein de sales parfums,

Héritage fatal d'une vieille hydropique,
Le beau valet de cœur et la dame de pique
Causent sinistrement de leurs amours défunts.[2]

Pluviôse: this term is given privileged status by its position at the beginning of the opening line, its isolation due to the unusual displacement of the caesura, as well as to the absence of punctuation in the rest of the quatrain. Semantically, the term is loaded, and contains all of the poem's functional connotations. The sonnet begins under an aura of pervasive humidity made all the more so by the adjective "entière" at the end of the first line. Two temporal schemes are established from the outset: the time of the rain and the time of the year designated by the month of the revolutionary calendar. We are at the heart of winter. Pluviôse, situated between Nivôse and Ventôse, stands at the center of the "dead" season. The revolutionary calendar inaugurated by the Convention in 1793 is moreover associated with the reign of destruction and death metaphorically concretized by the funereal attribute of Pluviôse—the urn. But the reign of terror and violence (hence of activity) is now but a pale memory. The real time in this poem of temporality is the time of loss and anachronism. The republican calendar, abolished by Napoleon in 1805, harks back to a past that is now completely gone, though a recent past. Baudelaire was born only some fifteen years later. The anachronism is moreover operative on the historical and political levels. At the time the poem was written, revolutionary thinking, supposedly forward-looking, increasingly looked to its own past. The sonnet reflects the sense of an irretrievable world, but also of an outdated, antiquated world suggested, from the very beginning, by the neoclassical image of the month accompanied by its decorative and vaguely mythological urn.[3] Pluviôse also suggests a malevolent divinity lavishing not life, but death.

All the threads of the thematic network originate in the poem's first word. The overwhelming image is one of liquefaction: the polyvalent urn, the dark "flood" of funereal gloom, the verb "verse" (pours) associated with a syntactic inversion, the adjective "ténébreux," the "gutter" of the second quatrain, the "rheumatic" clock and the rancid "perfumes" of the first tercet, the old "dropsical" woman in the second tercet. This last image, connoting the morbid accumulation of serous fluids, is related to the semantic complex of pathology. Announced as of the first quatrain by the verbal adjective "irritated" and the substantival adjective "cold", underscored by the ambiguous use of the adjective "pale" which leads to the word "mortality" of the following line, this motif of illness emerges fully in the second quatrain—"litter," "agitates," "without rest," "thin," "mangy," "shivering" ("frileux")—is carried over into the tercets with "lamenting," "sniffly" ("enrhumée"), and leads to the "fatal inheritance" ("héritage fatal") left by the old dropsical woman, thereby suggesting a hereditary defect, a congenital and incurable disease. This theme of illness, because of the adjective "fatal," is obviously linked with the central image of death: the self-enclosed structure of the poem, which has the last word ("defunct") tie in with the first word ("Pluviôse"), stresses the funereal thematics. After the urn that pours out icy gloom, and the deathly pallor of the sepulchral city's "inhabitants" (an ironic term in the context of the graveyard metropolis), the semantic signals become even more specific: "cemetery," "mortality," "wandering soul," twice-unreal phantom (for it exists in line 8 merely as a term of a simile)—not to mention less explicit elements, such as the "carreau" of line 5 (to remain "sur le carreau" means to be dead or seriously wounded) or the symbolic queen of spades in the penultimate line. The "fatal" inheritance does however convey a particular perspective on death—not that of absolute nothingness but, as the word "héritage" implies, a notion of survival more desolate perhaps than death itself. The sonnet seems ultimately to speak of posthumous gloom: the spiritual condition evoked would seem to be that of a post-mortem dejection, a permanent state of mourning. Life has settled at the heart of death, and is held in its thrall. The key terms of the poem (the "urn" containing and celebrating death, the "cemetery" enclosing the only available life) celebrate the cult of death and proclaim its omnipresence. This life / death contamination fully justifies the appearance, at the center of the poem, of the "fantôme" or ghost, signaling an absence / presence come to haunt a world that is neither alive nor totally dead.

This shuttle between the two worlds of the living dead also accounts for the juxtaposition and interference of the different temporalities of the poem: the times of weather and of seasons, of the clock, of history, of burials and the buried, of mourning, and finally of the last line's timeless discourse ("causent sinistrement") which affirms the open-ended nature of the poetic structure in spite of the sonnet's formal self-enclosure.

The first word of the poem, an abstract personification, also announces a rhetoric of abstraction and generalization. The sonnet illustrates a poetics of vagueness. "La ville entière"—all of the city—and the peripheral "faubourgs" (fors + bourg = outside the town limits) suggest an urban cluster that cannot be confined or defined. The first stanza in particular is remarkable for its abstract virtuosity: "mortalité" rather than "mort," "froid ténébreux" (the adjectival substantive enlarges and invades) rather than "ténèbres froides." The metaphoric equivalence and lack of differentiation between town and cemetery further blur and erase all sense of boundaries. An error in the 1868 edition—a misprint that Jacques Crépet was curiously fond of—gives "vie" (life) instead of "ville" (city). In a sense, the two are interchangeable in the context. Yet the notion of the city is fundamental in the poem, as it is in the rest of Baudelaire's work.

But what kind of city is it? No picturesque character distinguishes Baudelaire's city. Traumatic and anaesthetizing at the same time, the urban complex remains anonymous. Many of Baudelaire's texts project the image of a topographically undifferentiated and "unanimist" Paris. The poet-stroller—the *flâneur*—claims to find his inspiration in the "frequentation of huge cities," indulges in "baths of multitudes," seeks "universal communion" in the masses, chooses to establish his domicile "in numbers," and dreams of "marrying the crowd." Everything suggests a desire to abolish the limits between the self and others, between *moi* and *tous*. Baudelaire is explicit in *Fusées*, speaking of the "religious inebriation" of great cities: "Panthéisme. Moi, c'est tous; tous, c'est moi." In *Le Spleen de Paris*, he writes about the crowds: "Multitude, solitude: termes égaux et convertibles pour le poète actif et fécond."[4] This taste for universalization, for the undefined if not the undefinable, is conveyed in "Spleen LXXV" by a rather impressive accumulation of indefinite articles: "*un* froid ténébreux," "*une* litière," "*un* vieux poète," "*un* fantôme frileux," "*un* jeu," "*une* vieille hydropique"—presenting the individual in an undetermined form, defining him as a type.

Is there in fact a definable subject—either topical or grammatical— in the poem? Even assuming that one of the thematic networks relates to a central *topos*, it would be hard to find a clear correspondence between such a hypothetical focal subject and the elusive grammatical subjects of the poem: Pluviôse, the cat, the soul of the ghost-poet, the lamenting bell, the smoking log, the knave of hearts and the queen of spades— the latter being the only double subject, and implying the only form of dialogue in the poem. The other voices come from disembodied or absent agents (the soul of the defunct poet) or from inanimate objects (the bell, the log whose falsetto hissing accompanies the hoarse clock). There is no communication whatever between the different grammatical subjects, with the exception of the cards' dialogue. But it is a dialogue of the dead, and their subject is death. In all the multitude of subjects only the cat *exists* within the poem. But it is not the cat that speaks.

Some*one* does speak in the poem. But who and where is this voice? The only first-person pronoun appears in line 5, and it refers to the cat (the only animate being in the poem). The other personal pronouns all apply to inanimate figures (Pluviôse, the playing cards). By various means, the text works out a displacement toward a strangely absent *third person*.[5] But is this "absent" figure not precisely the figura of the poet? The fact is that the disappearance of the personal pronoun "mon" in line 5, through the mediating image of the cat, plays in favor of the "old poet" whose soul wanders on the roof.

A structural analysis would confirm that the true subject of the poem is the poet, and precisely in his relation to death and to survival. The exact center of the sonnet (lines 7–8) represents a unit, line 7 offering the briefest and simplest syntactical unit / statement of the text. "L'âme d'un vieux poète erre dans la gouttière / Avec la triste voix d'un fantôme frileux." All the basic elements are in place: the poet-ghost seen in his decrepitude but also his venerability, his tragic roaming *(errance)*, his expressive activity: *the voice* ("la triste voix"). And this voice occupies, so to speak, a privileged position in this pivotal line, as a sonorous monosyllabic word strongly punctuating the caesura, and coinciding with just about the perfect center of the sonnet. As for the opening and concluding lines, which answer each other through the first and last words of the text ("Pluviôse" and "défunts"), they wed images of death and funereal persistence, and suggest the notion of incomplete demise (stressed by the expressions "sans repos" and the verb "erre"), as well as that of a verbal expression reaching beyond death.

Aesthetic distance serves the posthumous experience. In this perspective, the subject of the poem can be said to be the relation between death and poetic expression in an anachronistic and artificial framework where even a deck of cards becomes an emblematic presence. The two central lines, because they are heavily loaded with literary allusions, confirm moreover that the poet and poetry are at the heart of the sonnet. The echoes of Saint-Amant and of Gresset detected by source hunters,[6] far from devaluing these lines, confer upon them a truly Baudelairean significance. In the macabre and alchemical context of Saint-Amant's poetry, the soul of his ancestor—"l'ame de [son] ayeul"(an immaterial ghost, a "Fantosme leger")—speaks up in a "plaintive voice," resurrecting various poets in the shape of homeless cats "in the gutters." As for Gresset, who makes use of some of Baudelaire's key words ("bonheur," "fausset," "urne," "fantôme," "gouttière"), he provides a parade of "ingenious bards" ("chantres ingénieux") covered with laurels.[7] The reverent play of allusion clearly suggests a communion with the poets of the past. The "vieux poète" of "Spleen LXXV" ironically and movingly belongs to a timeless literary guild.

The sonnet's system of metonymic transfers shifts and converts the various motifs. The most notable shift affects precisely the relation between an elusive and invisible self and the soul of the equally absent poet. The following equation seems to be proposed: my cat = the soul of the poet. This equation becomes even more interesting, since the poet has been substituted for the cat in the latter's traditional place in the French language: *la gouttière*. If one were to press these chiasmatic equivalences (cat relating to poet), the possessive pronoun "mon" could be shown to belong to the substantive "âme": what would be involved is *my soul*. Such a hypothesis is hardly far-fetched, and would seem to be confirmed by the example of another poem, "Brumes et pluies"—also a poem about the wintry, funereal fog ("linceul vaporeux")—where the evocation of a hoarse weathercock (once again an image of an external reality situated on the roof) leads abruptly to "mon âme." The first quatrain of "Spleen LXXV" moreover provides the signal of this system of transfers. Life and death are from the outset seen as interchangeable; it is the cemetery that contains the "inhabitants," while mortality settles in the crowded city districts. In a broader perspective, the system of transfers leads to decentralization and dispersion. Jean Prévost remarked quite justly that Baudelaire's gloom tends to "spread to surrounding objects."[8] In autobiographical terms, it is quite conceivable that the mental and physical states suggested by the sonnet refer to Baudelaire's own discomforts: irritation, sense of sterility, skin disease, depression, cold, laryngitis, disgust with his own being, pitiful memories. But that is not what the poem is about. What is important, in artistic terms, is that the "I" disappears by multiplying and fragmenting itself, by shifting, and by writing itself into a vacancy, a no-man's-space. Referring in one of his prose poems to the poet's "incomparable privilege," Baudelaire comes up with an image and with terms that are directly applicable to "Spleen LXXV": "Like those wandering souls in search of a body, he penetrates into anyone's persona whenever he wishes. For him alone, everything is vacant."[9]

This tendency of the self to shift and camouflage itself raises a broader question. It has been observed that many a poem by Baudelaire, after a generalized opening (sometimes the point of departure is a reference to a work of art), displays in the second part a return to the persona of the poet, a return to the first-person singular, quite specifically in its emphatic form: *moi*. Often it is a cry of anguish or an ironic interrogation coming right after what T. S. Eliot was to call an objective correlative: "Vois! je me traîne aussi!"—"Mais moi, moi qui de loin"— "Moi seul j'étais triste"[10] The most striking example can no doubt be found in "Un Voyage à Cythère," which ends with an accumulation of possessives: not only the sorrows that are "mine," but "my teeth," "my flesh," "my image," "my heart," "my body." Still, there is another characteristic and perhaps even more significant Baudelairean movement toward the indefinite pronoun *on,* toward the general, the collective, the depersonalized universal. "Le Cygne," as we have seen, which begins with an initial "I" subject to the presence of the Other, does not impose itself in a solipsistic fashion, but is conceived in relation to a "you," ultimately merging with an anonymous and impersonal "whoever."[11]

Between the two extremes—the poem which begins with a specified self leading to the general ("Le Cygne") and the one which moves from the general toward a powerful sense of selfhood ("Un Voyage à Cythère")—lies an aesthetic middle ground which allows the artist, according to Flaubert's famous formula, to be present everywhere and visible nowhere. From that point of view some observations could perhaps be made about the sequence and architecture of *Les Fleurs du mal.* "Spleen LXXV," for instance, is placed between two poems illustrating opposing tendencies of the *je* / *moi* dialectics. "La Cloche fêlée," at first entitled "Le Spleen," begins with a generalized "There is . . ." ("Il est . . .") referring to a type of happiness from which the poet is excluded, and leads to the tragic diagnosis of his own cracked soul ("Moi, mon âme est fêlée"). On the other hand, the "Spleen" poem following "Pluviôse . . ." begins with the first-person singular "I have more memories . . ." ("J'ai plus de souvenirs . . .") and moves on to an overwhelming and abstract figure of dejection *(ennui)* which assumes "the proportions of immortality."

If the self, in "Spleen LXXV," disappears into the larger texture while affirming itself metonymically, this is in large part, as we have seen, because of the invasiveness of the indefinite article. A closer scrutiny shows, however, that the place of honor goes to the definite article, but a definite article whose value is indeterminate, exemplary, symbolic. The two structurally and thematically pivotal lines of the poem speak of the poet's soul, *the* voice. The grammatical link between the two words gives additional value to the term *voice.* The function of the definite article is in fact double throughout the poem. It is collectivizing ("*la* ville," "*les* faubourgs") but also allegorizing, that is, tending toward abstract figures: "*la* mortalité," "*le* bourdon," "*la* bûche," "*la* pendule," "*le* . . . valet de cœur," "*la* dame de pique." In either case, the effect is one of depersonalization.

THE sonnet's analysis brings out certain psychological features. The unpeopling of the urban space, the muffling of sorrow, the retractile movement toward enclosure, would seem to suggest avoidance of a brutal confrontation. We are far indeed from the wish expressed in "Un Voyage à Cythère" to find the "strength" and the "courage" to contemplate one's body and soul without disgust. (Interestingly, "Un Voyage à Cythère" stresses rather the first- and second-person singular: "*tes* cultes," "*tes* douleurs," "*tes* membres," "devant *toi;*" "pour *moi,*" "*mon* image," "*mon* cœur," "*mon* corps.") The major themes of "Spleen LXXV" begin to emerge: death-in-life, condemnation to a vacant spiritual space, but also the reassuring possibility of assuming a posthumous stance and a posthumous perspective. In the broader context of Baudelaire's work, the poem also deals with the fundamental nature and possibilities of his lyricism.

For it is certain that Baudelaire conceives of the poet's work precisely in terms of the dialectics of personality and impersonality. "Genius wants to be *one.*" "Glory consists in remaining *one.*" But also: "The distinctive characteristic of true poets . . . is to know how to come out of themselves." The much admired "dandy" lives and sleeps in front of a mirror; the true hero entertains himself ("s'amuse tout seul"). Yet the persona of the poet in the prose poems is proud of "having lived and suffered in others." Elsewhere, Baudelaire is even more explicit, as when he speaks of the soul's "holy prostitution." The privilege and mission of the poet, for whom all is "vacancy," is to find communion—that is, to develop the art of being at will "himself and the other."[12]

T. S. Eliot, an attentive reader of Baudelaire, stretched the notion of depersonalization further still in developing his "impersonal theory of poetry." Maintaining that the difference between art and the event is always absolute, Eliot went so far as to claim that the poet, a "medium" and "catalyst," should aim at "continual extinction of personality."[13] Baudelaire's views are more nuanced. On artistic as on psychological levels, he seems to respond to conflicting demands. The desire to "come out of the self" is hardly innocent. Is it not, in one of the prose poems, the temptation of a sexually ambiguous Satan?[14] And if suffering exists at both poles ("I will no longer suffer except in myself"—"proud of having lived and suffered in people who are not me"), it may be that emerging from the self represents for Baudelaire an alibi, a refuge, an escape from that which attracts and terrifies him most: "the horrendous marriage of man to himself." Two remarkable statements tersely express this contradictory attraction. The first describes the painter of modern life: "He is an *I* hungering for the *not-I*" ("C'est un *moi* insatiable du *non-moi*"). The other is more autobiographical, and Baudelaire gave it the value of an epigraph. *Mon Cœur mis à nu* begins with this declaration: "The dissipation and the centralization of the *Self*. Everything lies in that," ("De la vaporisation et de la centralisation du *Moi*. Tout est là.")[15]

No matter how inadequate a psychological interpretation may be when it comes to discussing the poet's achievement, it cannot be altogether neglected. Baudelaire is particularly fond of the word *multiplication*. He loves the crowds because they provide him with the pleasure of numbers—"la jouissance de la multiplication du nombre." Conversely, regarding the multiple within the individual: "Inebriation is a number" ("L'ivresse est un nombre").[16] This inebriation brought about by the splitting of the self casts light on the almost triumphant bitterness that characterizes the masochistic "L'Héautontimorouménos" and on the somber joy of the specular self-confrontation in "L'Irrémédiable." Multiplication for Baudelaire is like a drug, while the drug itself provides him with an elating feeling of self-multiplication. It is quite explicitly in these terms that Baudelaire evokes the delights of "artificial paradises." The subtitle of "Du Vin et du hachish" refers to the "means for multiplying individuality." The quest for such a multiplication evidently implies that the individual sees himself as the center of the universe; at the extreme limit, nothing remains but himself. It also implies the disappearance of personality. "De temps en temps la personnalité disparaît." (The sentence that follows mentions the "objectivity" of certain pantheistic poets.) In another passage of the same essay on intoxication we find: "Sometimes it happens that the personality disappears." The remainder of that paragraph once again refers to "poetic objectivity" and to "evaporation." The 1860 preface to *Paradis artificiels* places this absence / presence in a posthumous context that might serve as a commentary to "Spleen LXXV": "I would willingly write only for the dead." At the conclusion of his first essay on wine and hashish, Baudelaire translates these preoccupations into aesthetic and volitional terms which he attributes to a "theoretician" of art: "Great poets . . . are beings who by the pure and free exercise of will reach a state where they are at the same time cause and effect, subject and object . . ."[17]

Such an ideal can hardly be surprising in a poet so locked up in his own consciousness. Condemned to a dialogue with the self, Baudelaire—much like Flaubert, though in a different register—develops an aesthetic of impersonality. "The lyric soul," he explains in a key text on lyricism and modernity, not only transforms the specific setting into a symbolic and hyperbolic *décor,* but translates personal experience into universals. This ideal of depersonalization expresses itself more sharply in an article on one of his contemporaries whom he blames for not having sufficiently veiled the "personal note." "Behind his mask, the poet can still be seen." Flaubert comes to mind, tirelessly repeating that impersonality is a sign of strength, that one must *not write the self.* Such a stance evidently foreshadows one of the main tenets of Modernist aesthetics as summed up in the well-known dictum of T. S. Eliot, who remained convinced all his life that only the life of the poem mattered: "Poetry is . . . an escape from personality."[18]

Erosion and Discontinuity
in Flaubert's *Novembre*

According to Sartre, *Novembre* signals the "impossibility of living," experienced by the adolescent Gustave, and at the same time his desire to change his being. In the background, there is willfully accepted neurosis. This youthful work foreshadows Flaubert's medical and psychological crisis of 1844. Behind the double confession of the narrator and the prostitute, one can decipher what Sartre calls the "radicalization of passivity" whose chronic symptom is onanistic and trans(inter)-sexual imagery. Flaubert, we are told, dreams of being a woman possessed by a strong male because he does not recognize that his secret desire is to be a passive male violated by a woman. This androgyny would imply the desire to surrender to a dominating female. "His original desire is not so much to be penetrated by a man's organ as to swoon under the caresses of a woman who fondles him."[1] In many of Flaubert's texts, this secret desire for a sexual transposal is translated into the inverse image of a woman who desires to be a man. Long before Emma Bovary parted her hair and wore a tortoise shell lorgnette, "like a man," Emilie in *La Première Education sentimentale*, with her somewhat "cavalier and virile" bearing, dreamt of being a man.

Flaubert was not unaware of the importance of *Novembre*. To his mistress Louise Colet, he wrote: "This work was the closure of my youth." Yet this same letter, almost in the same sentence, seems to contradict this idea of a break with the past. Immediately before speaking of closure, Flaubert underlines the text's value in terms of continuity. *Novembre*, he claims, provides a key to his innermost self. "If you have listened carefully to *Novembre*, you must have guessed a thousand unsayable things that may explain what I am." Two expressions problematize the sentence: *unsayable* ("indisables"), because it suggests unavowable secrets, a private thematic network, the difficulty of communication, the drama of language; *what I am* ("ce que je suis"), because the present indicative goes against the idea of a cleavage. Flaubert seems indeed aware of the conflict between discontinuity and persistence. The sentence that follows, by means of the restrictive conjunction "but," attempts to reconcile them. Referring to his past youth: "What remains of it is very little, but it holds fast" ("tient ferme").[2]

Flaubert was preoccupied throughout his life by the double question of repetition and continuity. In 1850 he informed Louis Bouilhet that he had in mind three literary projects: *Une Nuit de Don Juan,* the story of *Anubis,* and a "Flemish" novel about a provincial girl who becomes a mystic and dies a virgin in a provincial town. But the profusion of subjects was deceptive. Flaubert felt troubled about the thematic resemblances among the three subjects. After going over the outline of the "Flemish" novel, he added: "What bothers me is the closeness among these three projects."[3] This worry about repetition and sameness was an old one for Flaubert. It is thematized in *Novembre,* where two passages are quite explicit. Before his first visit to the prostitute, the narrator observes: "The same holds for certain ideas with which one has lived too long; one would like to be rid of them forever, and yet they flow within one like life itself." And after his first sexual experience: "the second woman that pleases you almost always resembles the first . . . Notice also how writers eternally speak about the same women, whom they describe a hundred times without ever getting tired."

It would seem that *Novembre* was conceived from the double obsession with sameness and with unavoidable hiatus. On the one hand, there is Flaubert's fear of merely copying the already-written; on the other, the awareness of a gap. This double preoccupation is at the heart of Flaubert's work, and appears as a symptom of the larger crisis of the "sign." In *L'Entretien infini,* Maurice Blanchot concluded that the co-existence of encyclopedic information (that is, a maximum of substance) and the notion of nothingness engendered an intransitive work.[4] In an article on "Flaubert and the other," Pierre Bergounioux more recently interpreted Flaubert's juvenilia as works of closure and senescence. The glut of subjects, the overabundance of materials, would seem to bespeak inflation. Since his earliest writings, Flaubert lived with the specter of the already-said, and aimed at expurgating the stereotype. Long before Jacques Derrida, the young author of *La Première Education sentimentale* denounced the assumed anteriority of the to-be-said, observed the elusiveness of every center, pointed out the collapse of the transcendental signified. He did so by insistent enumerations of semic and cultural paradigms.[5] Jonathan Culler, who places himself in the tradition of

Blanchot and Bergounioux, sees the end of *Novembre* as a radical questioning of the act of communication.[6] The principle of a break is indeed explicitly settled in the text: "The manuscript ends here, but I knew its author." For this rather conventional retrieval by an editor-friend leads not to an effect of authenticity, but to a stylistic warning ("He was a man who indulged in the false and the unintelligible, who greatly abused epithets") and to an overt affirmation of fictionality ("which must be tolerated in a novel, out of love for the fabulous"—"par amour du merveilleux").

Camouflage or Parody?

The documentary, autobiographical significance of *Novembre* is undeniable, not because of the facts narrated but because the perspective totalizes an adolescent's sensuous experience. Gustave enjoys erotic and autoerotic fantasies ("Her soft, moist hand ran over my body . . . I felt her warm, quivering skin under me"), and he evokes the loss of virginity. (The prostitute joyfully observes, "So you are a virgin, and I deflowered you?") He indulges in the phantasm of a double defloration, that of the adolescent as well as that of the prostitute Marie: "I am a virgin! Does that make you laugh?" But *Novembre* is also a mini-anthology of Romantic commonplaces: feigned contempt for life, blending of cynicism and tenderness, taste for ruins and the distant past, ennui, vague longings, indulgence in suffering, death wish—nothing seems to be missing. The story refers explicitly to Goethe, Chateaubriand, Byron, Vigny. But what is the relation between these bookish topoi and the very intimate personal experience? And how precisely is one to understand the adjective *unsayable* ("indisable") which Flaubert himself italicizes? One hypothesis is that the literary code was to serve as a form of camouflage, making it possible to insert private obsessions in an established tradition, and thus to hide and reveal them with supposed impunity. Such a strategy depersonalizes the onanistic passages despite the first-person singular. "I stretched out on the ground, on my stomach . . . Ah! how I wanted to enfold something in my arms, to smother it with my heart or, better, to split myself, to love this other being and merge with it." The strategy of the cliché also makes it psychologically easier to indulge in narcissistic and solipsistic reveries: "I would have liked to be a woman for the sake of beauty, to be able to admire myself, to be naked . . . to see myself reflected in the flowing waters."

But another hypothesis is possible. The context may well be bookish because the confession is an imaginary one, and the favorite literary motifs had to be elaborated and protected within the framework of a parodistic structure. The real difficulty of *Novembre* stems from the fact that the metaphoric texture covers a borderline zone where private obsessions and literary tradition blend, where the already-said asserts itself as the only available arsenal for a literature-to-be-written. The inventory of themes plays ironically with tired literary conventions, yet also prepares the thematics of the novels to come: eroticism linked with failure, the sadness of the flesh, the double face of woman, the temptation of adultery (the very word "adultère" has aphrodisiac powers for the young hero), multiple incarnations, attraction to the double notion of infinity and nothingness. *Novembre* seems to provide a catalogue of specific images, themes, even episodes that will reappear meaningfully in Flaubert's major novels: the young girl's early reading experience, the farmer's daughter's vocation for the role of courtesan, the cutting of the lock of hair, the disenchanted friends, the weight of dreams, the lover's complaisance toward the husband, the metaphor of the narrow and oppressive house ("Ma maison me pèse sur les épaules"). The "closure" Flaubert refers to is doubtless also an overture.

Overflow and Vacuity

To some extent the paradox can be explained as a thematization of discontinuity which appears at various levels and in various ways: in the subtitle ("Fragments de style quelconque"), in the multiplicity of narrative points of view (the first persons of the protagonists, the third person of the editor-commentator), in the interruption of the narrative flow which, despite its brusqueness, hardly interrupts the movement of the narration. Flaubert even thematizes the grammatical shifts and displacements in perspective. "Feelings must have few words at their service; otherwise this book would have ended with the first person." The principle of disruption is also felt at the stylistic level. The judgmental third person takes exception to the confessional mode and to the literary exploitation of the first person, questions the metaphors, hyperboles, "and other figures," points out the noxious literary models ("He fed on very bad authors, as can be seen from his style"), and denounces pretentious turns and the abuse of epithets. But the deepest and largest rift is produced by temporal discontinuities, by the separation of "instants," that is, by the problematic relation between being and time. "Every moment of my life is suddenly separated from the next by an abyss." The accumulation of instants, the very profusion of experience, only increase the impression of disruption and void.

Novembre conveys an even more disturbing paradox than the apparent incompatibility of literary clichés and intensely personal motifs. Inflation is seen as a principle of vacuity. This anguish of emptiness functions in relation to a sense of surfeit. In more ways than one, *Novembre* sets up the literary problem that will continue to haunt Flaubert. The relation between overabundant subjects and artistic paralysis is explicitly stated in the last chapter of *La Première Education sentimentale,* where Jules remarks that the plethora of topoi in the postrevolutionary era, and the extraordinary turmoil of ideas and ideologies during the first half of the nineteenth century, do not at all imply the freedom of the artist ("de cette surabondance de matériaux résulte l'embarras de l'art"). In *Novembre,* the dialectical relationship between overflow and vacuity reveals itself at the level of metaphor. Images of plenitude, often translated in sexual terms, are countered by images of hollowness: the "empty fields" ("prairies vides") of the first page; the staved-in barrel ("tonneau défoncé"), emblem of sadness and futility; the abandoned temple; the vacant heart, symbol of death. Ultimately it is thought, or rather thinking, itself that evacuates the subject of its substance: "it seemed to me that my thought alone would finally dry up this subject, and empty it by steadily feeding on it."

The Stale Bed

The *already-written* or *already-said,* so dear to modern criticism, looms heavily over Flaubert's texts. All interpersonal relations seem condemned to incommunicability. Henry and Emilie in *La Première Education sentimentale* will experience this profound malaise more overtly: "She had no further confidences to make to him or intimate stories to tell him. Everything indeed had been said, and said again, repeated a hundred times. Language became useless" (Chapter 24). It is the metaphorization of this drama of language that makes *Novembre* so interesting. The dream of double virginity is intimately wedded to the problem of verbal expression, which in turn explains the insistent exploitation of the image of the virgin-prostitute. Belonging to all and everyone, at the service of the many who take turns on her bed, she experiences a powerful attraction to the *unique.* As she explains it, her vocation is precisely this expectation and this search. "I hoped that one day someone would come—it surely had to happen, considering the large numbers—

someone bigger, nobler, stronger." This obsession with numbers relates Marie, the prostitute, to Don Juan. Does she not confess to the desire to be a man in order to "climb up to windows at night?" But she is obviously an inverted Don Juan, whose expectation of the unique and of the impossible through the multiplication of the same seems to be fixated on the repetition of language. "Every night, I read the love letters of the day in order to find some fresh expression coming from some heart constituted differently from the others, and made especially for me. But all are alike. I knew ahead of time the end of their sentences." The narrator suffers in a similar, though specifically literary manner. Believing himself to be a poet, he is distressed to find in others his most beautiful conceptions and expressions. "I thought myself their equal; I was merely their copier!" The image of the beaten path is literalized by the metaphor of the Roman road whose trace can still be seen, even though it is no longer in use.

The most striking feature of this network of images is the intimate association of writing, prostitution, and the public thoroughfare. The association between the street and the bed is of course logical. Both are places of transit. The first evocation of the prostitute establishes the figural link. "At the time I was still a virgin, I enjoyed contemplating the prostitutes. I walked along the streets where they live." The metonymic shift is quite expected. In French, one says "faire le trottoir," just as in English one refers to "streetwalkers." But behind the metonym lurks a metaphor. For it is not only the prostitute who brings up the image of the street. The street conjures up the image of prostitution. "I walked in the streets and on the squares. Women walked by me—many of them." These feminine images are from the outset images of proximity and multiplicity. They soon become images of solicitation and provocation. "Leaning out of their carriages with their coats of arms, duchesses seemed to smile at me and invite me to silken loves." The erotic suggestion becomes more precise: "On their balconies, women wearing scarves moved forward to see me and tell me: love us! love us!" The almost dreamlike walk has an aim after all. "I knew where I was going: to a house." We know of course to what kind of house, to what special "maison," he directs his steps.

The metaphor behind the obvious contiguity (street-streetwalkers-house of prostitution) harks back to the notion of wear and tear. Marie's bedsheets are still warm from all those who "passed" through them. She refers to her bed as the "common pallet" ("grabat commun") through which crowds have "passed". The repetition of the verb *passer* is a further reminder of the public thoroughfare. This thoroughfare is a "passage" which, in the context, implies fatigue, erosion, and profanation. The rug next to her bed is "worn at the center"; the fringes of her bed hangings are "worn". But this wearing out also concerns language. The billets-doux which the prostitute examines in the hope of finding something new and unique are clearly symbolic. For language belongs to the others, that is, to everyone. Hence Marie's dream of places that are not public (that is, not commonplaces) but that might "belong to us," and that would not be soiled by the presence or even the glance of the "others." Words are not virginal; they have been used before. But how is one to cure oneself of the desire for purity? Diderot's allegorical image of the language-castle in *Jacques le Fataliste* comes to mind. This castle carries a frontispiece that reads: "I belong to no one and I belong to everyone. You were here before you entered, and you will still be here after you have left."

No Word, No Form?

The figure of the prostitute thus implies far more than profanation and cynicism. What is involved is the erosion of linguistic signs. Flaubert's originality stems in large part from an attitude toward language which is experienced as an anxiety and an obsession before it is turned into a literary theme. The young Gustave is hypnotized by words precisely because they appear to him as heavy with overuse. During his Egyptian journey, lying next to the sleeping courtesan Kuchiouk Hanem, the young man dreamt of all the others who had lain in her bed. Words have the same effect on him, particularly those referring to love. A sentence in *Novembre* can serve as shortcut: "From then on, one word among human words seemed beautiful to me: adultery." The word is personalized, and capable of arousing him. "Some words deeply stirred me, above all the words *woman, mistress*." But it is noteworthy that these words derive their disquieting force from their literary context. The narrator seeks their explanation "in books," just as it is "in books" that he studies the passions he yearns to experience. Yet the books in question imply the notion of other books behind them, and ultimately a father-text that remains beyond reach. The self can be conceived only in terms of a model.

The binding of authenticity and dependence raises multiple problems. The conditional form ("Those passions I would have liked to experience") underscores the difficulty of unmediated desire. On the one hand, the very existence of a model is oppressive. The reading of books has a depressing effect: "I threw them away in disgust." But above all, it is communication that remains ambiguous and doubly difficult. The absence of spontaneous desire implies the devaluation of the signified, while the use and unavoidable abuse—or prostitution—of language implies the indignity and inadequacy of the signifier. Exhaustion, whether that of the senses or of language, is thus present from the start.

This hesitation between two insufficiencies is summed up in one sentence which brings out the problematic relation among *thing, word,* and *form:* "I vaguely desired something splendid which I could neither formulate by word nor give form to in my mind." Are we dealing here with the futility of experience or the futility of writing? Flaubert's lifelong drama in literary terms—*Novembre* is thereby an exemplary text—is uncomfortably situated between his rejection of the subject and his discrediting of expression. On the one hand, as modern criticism tends to stress, there is in his work the parody of the interpretive act. The metanarrative signals serve to subvert the sense of unity as well as the unity of any sense. The subtitle announcing fragmentation, the multiplicity of points of view, the instabilities of the text, the denial of any reassuring order—all these features of *Novembre* play in this direction. Yet it is also true that in this text as elsewhere Flaubert stubbornly continues to believe that he has, or rather that there *is,* something-to-be-said. Many years before conceiving the character of Emma Bovary, he understood that feelings have "few words at their service." Torn between two opposing temptations of silence,[7] Flaubert intuited early in his career that his task would be to dramatize repeatedly their link to each other and their fundamental incompatibility.

From *Novembre*
to *L'Education sentimentale:*
Communication and the Commonplace

"I loved to lose my way in the vortex of the streets," says the narrator of *Novembre* (XVII, 175).[1] This going astray is of course figurative as well as literal. The young man's wanderings inevitably lead him to the prostitutes, to the streets which they themselves "walk". City sidewalks, *les trottoirs,* remain a permanent temptation for Flaubert's characters. Henry, in *La Première Education sentimentale,* who likes to be dizzied by street crowds, walks on the boulevards of Paris "to see the whores" ("pour voir les catins"—XVIII, 4). These immersions in the multitude unleash imaginary pleasures that are both predictable and fleeting. The hypnotic effect of repetition and fugacity, a constant feature of Flaubert's reverie, is thus linked to the double image of the street and the prostitute. A quarter of a century later, Frédéric Moreau still feels this "longing for the boulevard" as soon as he is away from Paris.[2] The fact is that young Gustave himself claimed to know nothing more beautiful in Paris than the street, when the gaslights are lit and prostitution displays itself shamelessly. In a letter to his friend Ernest Chevalier, he explains: "I feel a galvanizing contraction in my feet arising from the pavement, where every evening so many whores loiter in their rustling dresses."[3]

But there is another image that complicates the metaphor of the street. The narrator of *Novembre,* while yearning for the prostitute's caresses, compares this adolescent passion, as we have seen, to a Roman highway on which consular chariots once sped—a highway long abandoned, and now overgrown and crossed by new paths, but whose trace has not altogether disappeared. The very banality of the image heightens its meaning in the context. The memory of chariots driven along the Roman highway connotes public use. This indirect reminder of Marie's profession is further significant because Flaubert and his contemporaries readily associated the image of the whore and the whorehouse (the *lupanar*) with the decadent mores of the late Roman Empire. In another letter to Ernest Chevalier, Gustave observed that the rue de Grammont and the rue de Richelieu, during the most tempting evening hours, made him dream of antiquity.[4] More significantly, the image of the covered yet visible or legible trace of the highway is like a palimpsest, suggesting an "archaeology" of the writing process. This link between beaten track and linguistic communication is textually verifiable, since the subsequent paragraph in *Novembre* insists on the sameness, redundancy, and erosive effects in (and of) the act of writing. It would seem that the image of the Roman road, coupled with that of the prostitute thirsting for the impossible absolute of love, signaled the metaphoric association between public life, prostitution, and writing.

The Parisian street was to retain its special appeal and functional value in *L'Education sentimentale*. The street represents the point of intersection between individual and collective destinies. For Frédéric, daydreaming as he walks along the street means surrendering to chance or fate, indulging his passivity. He feels vaguely adrift, carried by his inclination, or rather by the "incline" of the broad sidewalk—"le large trottoir, descendant." The street means absence of will, merging with the crowd, "getting rid of oneself";[5] it means wandering in order to escape. But the self cannot so easily be denied or forgotten. Roaming about in the capital unavoidably brings Frédéric face to face with his bad conscience.

The solipsistic stroller may also have unexpected and unwanted encounters with the larger spectacle of history in the form of public gatherings, mob scenes, and riots. The spectacle of political street activities does in fact bestow its full significance on the image of the street as river. The human flow of the street which carries Frédéric along provides him with the same sense of spectacle and of a spectator's passivity as river navigation, at the beginning of the novel, when he stands motionless on the boat and watches the banks of the Seine glide by. Spectator by temperament, Frédéric thus remains sensitive above all to the theatrical elements of the events of *1848*: festive streets, carnivalesque rejoicings, the wounded and the dead who do not seem to be really wounded or dead. But he is also aware of something larger and almost solemn: the "magnetic nature of enthusiastic crowds."[6] Flaubert himself, despite his contempt for political utopias, was capable of being moved by what he describes in a letter as the immensely inebriating spirit of revolutionary days.[7]

The sidewalk of course also signifies the hope of a devoutly wished encounter. It is in the hope of a chance meeting with Madame Arnoux in the streets of Paris that Frédéric goes on endless errands. The street is the privileged locus and the emblem of this chance on which Frédéric relies. The operations of chance in the more titillating quarters of the great city, where crowds anonymously brush against the stroller, spread a latent eroticism. Paris never seems more seductive than on those sultry summer days when Frédéric observes, in the women who pass by, the langorous expression in their eyes and the camelia tones of their skin.[8] In the midst of the city's diversity and contrasts he is keenly aware of similarities that only intensify the eroticism of the streets. For the prostitutes he notices under the gaslamps unfailingly remind him of Madame Arnoux.

The image of gaslight brings to mind not only the prostitutes of *Novembre* but Flaubert's important letter of 1 June 1853, in which he associates the figure of the prostitute with his monastic yearnings and his vocation as a writer: "I could never see any of those women in low-cut dresses walk by under the gaslight in the rain without feeling my heart beat faster, just as monks' robes with their knotted cords tickle my soul in some deep and ascetic corner. There is such a complex intersection in this idea of prostitution: lust, bitterness, nothingness of human relations . . ."[9] This nothingness of human relations, which he ironically tries to communicate to his mistress, Louise Colet, is the substance of *Novembre*. And who knows if it is not for this very reason that, in another letter to her quoted earlier, Flaubert insisted on the biographical importance of a text he was determined never to publish ("If you have listened carefully to *Novembre*, you must have guessed a thousand unsayable things that may explain what I am.")[10] The metonymic associations, as we have seen in the previous chapter, are in fact revealing. The streets haunted by the narrator, streets inhabited and frequented by prostitutes, carry him with the logic of dreams toward that other dealer in artifice, the actress—the woman who appears only under a special light, who instills in everyone the fever of desire and the illusion that she can be possessed.

But this network of images (street-prostitute-actress) constitutes what the narrator calls "the barrier of illusion" (XVII, 168). The street spectacle, much like the spectacle in the theater, inhibits communication. The prostitute's bed, the theater, the street scene are all places of display and of transience which exclude the unique, the authentic, the unmediated. The dizzying procession of female figures in the street brings about an *accelerando* that allows no respite. Promiscuity seems to be a function of multiplicity. The street is transformed into a bazaar of the senses, an open-air bordello. Images of provocation and solicitation abound. We have seen how the male narrator of *Novembre* imagines, as though in a dream, that all the ladies in the street invite him to luxurious love-making. But before entering the bordello, he already knows that the vast variety of female "forms" conveys the sadness and even the despair of monotonous heterogeneity. This relentless resemblance in multiplicity in confirmed by the prostitute herself: "The uniformity of pleasure made me despair" (XVII, 197, 224).

This vision of the street implies, moreover, a mobile perspective that needs to be better defined. The movement is in fact a *gliding* movement. The passers-by on the sidewalk are "gliding by one after the other like shop signs seen from a carriage" (XVII, 175). Not only is the moving carriage viewed from the outside, but the human eye, observing from within the vehicle, becomes a vehicle in its own way, thereby merging in characteristic Flaubertian fashion the movement of the spectacle with that of the spectator.

Reveries of vehicular mobility, implying the illusion of motion and the reification of the spectator-become-spectacle, recur in the frequent associations of the cab *(fiacre)* with sexuality. Henry and Emilie, in *La Première Education sentimentale,* surrender in their cab to what Flaubert describes as the "rocking" ("balancement") of the old "painted box" along the boulevards (XIX, 126). Young Emma, still exalted by a novel she has been reading secretly in the dormitory of her convent, dreams of love as she listens to the distant sound of a cab rolling along the avenue late at night.[11] And it is precisely in a cab transformed into a jolted box that, together with Léon, she takes part in this obscene though concealed exhibition of the sex act through the streets of Rouen— a scene which Sartre has admirably interpreted as the dehumanizing caricature of love-making. Sartre is no doubt right in thinking that even more traumatic than this "fall" into the automatisms of sex is the memory of Flaubert's own fall associated with his first epileptic seizure in 1844, which occured while he was holding the reins of a carriage. According to Sartre, this seizure was both a symptom and a symbol of a psychological conversion to passivity. On that winter night on the road to Pont-l'Evêque, Gustave willfully *chose* and radicalized the passivity which would allow him to settle with impunity into the unreality, or rather irreality, of Literature.[12]

If *L'Education sentimentale* seems to be an intensely personal novel, this may be due in large part to the many variations on the motif of vehicular passivity. On the first page, the reader learns that Frédéric has chosen the slowest and longest way to return to his home and to his mother. The author deliberately chose to make his unheroic hero a passive passenger on a boat which, though in motion, is itself a prisoner of the meandering river. Frédéric, immobile on the deck, daydreams as he watches the riverbanks glide by like two wide ribbons that are being unwound. In much the same way Flaubert himself, reclining on a couch in his felucca, had watched the banks of the Nile slip by.[13] In this opening scene of *L'Education sentimentale,* Flaubert ironically attributes the passengers' expansiveness during this very ordinary river trip to the unexpected pleasure of a "maritime excursion." Nothing could be less maritime or oceanic than this banal experience, this collective upstream voyage along a familiar river-highway with predictable stops. The river / road metaphor recurs from chapter to chapter. The floodlike rains are such that the street-torrent rushes between the spokes of the wheels. Later, the lines of carriages returning from the horse races move on the large "riverlike" avenue.[14] The carriage is, moreover, seen as the analogue of the boat. Henry, on his way to Paris in *La Première Education sentimentale,* surrenders to the movement of the stagecoach "which rocked gently like a boat" (XIX, iii).

This passivity, associated with both the river and the street, is given full ironic treatment in the opening scene of Part II describing Frédéric's arrival in Paris after he has come into some money. While Frédéric remains engrossed in his hopes and projects, the stagecoach passes through flooded neighborhoods. The perspective becomes kinetic. The vehicle rolls along the street, but it is the street that seems to be in motion, ironically projecting into Frédéric's consciousness a series of subliminal images: sickly trees, dirty puddles, heaps of garbage, a sordid pub—and above all, signs and posters (a pair of crossed billiard cues, a huge tin cigar, a bonneted matron representing a midwife). But this sobering reality has no hold on Frédéric's consciousness; it simply glides by. We have already seen that in *Novembre* the heads of the passers-by glide by "like shop signs seen from a carriage" (XVII, 175). In both texts, but in particular in *L'Education sentimentale,* such perceptions of street mobility correspond to a de-realization—that is, to an unwillingness to make any responsible connection with reality. Nothing can displace the dream which, in the human form of Madame Arnoux, Frédéric has substituted for reality. The procession of sordid images and crass commercial signs only emphasizes his vision of "two eyes" shining behind the curtain of rain and fog.

The same de-realizing passivity is evident somewhat later when, on a whim, he decides to visit Madame Arnoux in Creil. This time the setting is the train, and the perspective that of the train window. But the movement and the sensation are by now familiar: "Green fields stretched out to the right and to the left; the train rolled along; the tiny station houses glided by like stage sets; and the snowy puff of smoke from the locomotive, always wafting toward the same side, danced on the grass for a little while, then scattered and disappeared."[15] All the images and suggestions of the novel's first scene return: effects of gliding and unwinding, movement attributed to an inert landscape, inertia of the passenger, unreality of the setting, the hero's passivity, dispersion associated with smoke.

The principle of loss will remain associated with the image of the vehicle. At the end of the novel, the recognition that his life has been a fiasco coincides with Frédéric's refusal to climb into Madame Dambreuse's carriage after her despicable behavior at the auction. The fiasco is personal, but also political and collective, associating hopelessness with the image of the city street. It is on this same page that the worker on the boulevard tells Frédéric in no uncertain terms that he refuses to fight for the Republic.

This passage has more than one funereal resonance. It sets up the end of the chapter when Frédéric—still on the boulevard!—witnesses the death of Dussardier, killed by a policeman. And it is in this same chapter that Frédéric, "lost among the ruins of his dream,"[16] has but one remaining desire: to find in the peaceful setting of the country and in his mother's house a sleepy life ("vie somnolente") that would be both a return to the womb and the analogue of death.

Here, too, the novel displays a remarkable thematic unity. The street scene, with its flow and dispersion, is often the setting for noncommunication, loss, and mourning. The feeling of desertion experienced by Madame Arnoux—one of the rare moments when we are allowed to penetrate her consciousness—is heightened by images of cabs passing by, of a packer nailing up a crate, of tall houses blocking the sun.[17] And toward the end of the novel, we follow Frédéric and Madame Arnoux as they wander and reminisce in the dark streets of Paris, engaged in an almost posthumous stroll, moving like two ghosts amid the crowd and the city noises as though walking on a "bed of dead leaves."[18]

Even the Seine, the great channel of communication, is far more than a décor for passive reverie. "A happy, lustral presence" according to Bernard Masson, the river is also, according to Albert Thibaudet, the pretext for liquid images of life in the process of decomposition.[19] Sorrow, desolation, loss, death, mourning—these are indeed the permanent associations with the river. The derogatory suffix *-âtre* gives the Seine a sordid color. Its waters are "verdâtre" and "jaunâtre"; its quays, covered with foam from the sewers, are "grisâtres." The river flows on, cruel and indifferent to human suffering. "An old man in shirt sleeves was crying at an open window, his eyes raised to the sky. The Seine was flowing by peacefully."[20] These two sentences immediately precede the account of the brutal mistreatment of nine hundred prisoners locked up under the terrace of the Tuileries.

More precisely, the Seine is a backdrop for despair and a temptation to suicide. Wandering aimlessly through the streets of Paris after the Alhambra ball, Frédéric reaches the Concorde bridge. Leaning over the parapet in a moment of utter dejection, he thinks he sees his own floating corpse.[21] Once again, *Novembre* works in a prefigurative way. The young hero stops on the Pont-Neuf, looks at the "greenish" river, and thinks of all those who came to that spot in order to make an end of it (XVII, 187). The riverbed—another commonplace—becomes for him a pauper's grave, a "fosse commune." Similarly, it is on a bridge that Jules, in *La Première Education sentimentale,* feels tempted by the idea of suicide (XVIII, 142). This intertextual contamination underlines the ironic ambivalence of the brief episode when Frédéric, stopping on the same Pont-Neuf, feels shivers in his very soul which he attributes to love and hope.[22] Yet the tolling of the bell should be a warning.

Ambivalence, or rather polyvalence, serves as a still deeper warning. The image of land and water communication, because it seems to communicate too much (dreams, desire, movement, hope, symbolic itineraries, displacements, gliding effects, floating shapes of death), ultimately fails to communicate a clear meaning. The thoroughfare thus becomes the channel for the incommunicable. The cliché, which has such pathetic and poetic value in the work of Flaubert, always says too much and not enough. All of his literary efforts are thus marked by the disturbing discordance of language and image.

Novembre is in this respect exemplary. The metaphoric link between the public place, prostitution, and language has already been observed. The narrator is hypnotized by words which, because of their overuse, have become heavy, opaque, almost independent realities. At times, it is the invisible and unheard of word, hidden behind things, which he desperately tries to discover—the word "which others did not hear"

(XVII, 173). And he is not the only one to be disquieted at the same time by the overabundance and the inadequacy of language. The prostitute Marie is struck, as we have seen, by the erosive sameness of expression. In the amorous missives she receives she finds nothing but eternal redundancy.

The erosion motif occurs with remarkable frequency in Flaubert's early writings. The narrator of *Novembre,* when he arrives in Paris, settles in a furnished room whose pieces have been "worn down by others" (XVII, 248). Henry, at the beginning of *La Première Education senti-mentale,* finds himself in a hotel room whose furniture is likewise "worn down by everyone" (XVIII, 2). Interestingly, however, erosion is not just observed and painfully experienced; it is cultivated and thematized. "I like to wear things out" ("J'aime à user les choses"), Flaubert writes to Louise Colet.[23] This statement must not be read lightly. For the writer, it is the erosion of the signifier rather than of the signified that matters. If Flaubert, lying beside a snoring Egyptian courtesan, thinks of all those who have shared her bed before him—an almost timeless image—it is because words, which have also been "used" for so long and by so many, have a similar exotic and poetic effect on him. The prostitute herself, we have seen, is aware of the trodden paths of language, and deplores the ubiquity of the already-spoken. All her lovers repeat the same formulas. But much like the poet who suffers from and through language, she yearns for "fresh expression" (XVII, 223), for a linguistic space unsoiled by the crowd.

The dual specter of multiplicity and sameness provokes a specifically Flaubertian form of anguish—that of a felt emptiness related to excess. The proliferation of matter, including subject matter, becomes a principle of sterility and paralysis. But it would be wrong to conclude that Flaubert proclaims the bankruptcy of the literary topos. Much has been made of Flaubert's desire, stated in a letter to Louise Colet to write "a book about nothing" (16 January 1852). It would be just as easy to quote the many passages in his correspondence where Flaubert maintains that verbal expression can never live up to the lived experience. Already in *Mémoires d'un fou,* begun when he was fifteen years old, he wrote: "Pitiful human weakness! With your words, your languages, your sounds, you speak and you stammer"—while the genuine experience can never be put into words. Not even a crude experience can be translated into words. "With all your language, you cannot express the pleasure given you by a naked woman . . . or a plumpudding!" (XVI, 540). Once again, is Flaubert stressing the triviality of the experience or the futility of writing? And must one really choose between these two inadequacies simply because there is a hiatus between the expression and its subject? Flaubert's lifelong struggle is somehow situated between his conviction that artistic expression must be self-sufficient and the equally strong belief that the artist has something important to communicate. All through his life, the writer who called his sentences his only adventures felt there was such a thing as a literary *subject*. And though he propounded a theory of impersonality, he believed that good subjects corresponded to the writer's temperamental needs. "Let me find a subject fit for *my voice* and I will go far," he wrote to Louise Colet. And to Madame Roger des Genettes: "The secret of masterpieces is the harmony between the subject and the temperament of the writer." He then goes on to explain that a subject is a matrix from which all the rest follows.[24] There can be no doubt that Flaubert believed at the same time that there is nothing to be done but to *copy* (in this respect, Bouvard and Pécuchet are decidedly living out the fate of writing) and yet that there is something important that deserves to be given literary form.

The image of the public thoroughfare—*voie publique*—takes on its full meaning in the light of this contradiction. The highway or byway trodden by the many is the very model of the commonplace. But this commonplace, this trampled and defiled passage, is also the only available way that remains. It represents both the threat of defeat because of endless repetition, and the opportunity for an exalting challenge. According to Flaubert, only mediocre temperaments avoid the commonplace. "The commonplace is handled only by imbeciles or by the very great."[25] To be the great innovative poet of the cliché is the aim and also the achievement of Flaubert. This is why *Novembre* is not only such an interesting text, but why the expression "unsayable things" ("choses indisables"), which he applies to this piece of juvenilia,[26] is so crucial to an understanding of his work.

Idyll and Upheaval
in *L'Education sentimentale*

Flaubert is a subtle landscape painter, and his landscapes always have a purpose. Sometimes they function metaphorically. Charles Bovary, in his student room facing the "sordid little Venice" of his neighborhood in Rouen, dreams of unknown happiness in a distant place, thus experiencing *bovarysme* in his own limited register even before Emma appears on the horizon.[1] At other times, what Flaubert gives us is a complex of images suggesting the sensations of flatness, expansion, contraction, and torpor: a characterless landscape, a gray, monotonous surface provoking indeterminate reverie and moral anesthesia. The imperfect tense—the typical tense of description—takes precedence over the perterit, the tense of will and action.

Landscape descriptions can of course be part of the psychological structure and the dramatic progression. The Norman gardens, which in early April seem to dress up for the summer's festivities, have a dual importance: not only are they the appropriate setting for Emma's feverish coquetry (fanned by the warm breeze), but their description ironically precedes her visit to the priest—a scene of pathetic misunderstanding in which her vague spiritual longings find no human echo.

More interesting than such contextually functional landscapes are the structured descriptions which offer simultaneously a thematic tension and a commentary on that tension, illustrating in typical Flaubertian manner the nature of a literary language which turns into its own interpretation and critique. The description of the Rouen that Emma sees on her weekly trips to meet Léon appears at first like painting or an engraving of the town and its immediate surroundings: the town laid out in the form of an amphitheater, the nearby countryside, the river, the boats, the little islands.[2] Yet it is all filtered through Emma's consciousness. She sees what she wants to see and what she can see. Her desires determine form, movement, and color. Her anticipation and yearnings metamorphose the provincial city into an entrancing and disquieting Babylon filled with danger and promise. The spatial imagery (the fields, the sky, the boat, the brown smoke belched by the factory chimneys, the clouds carried away by the wind) creates a sense of enlargement, of soaring, but also of blurring and confusion. What is more, the landscape which seems "motionless as a painting," immobilized into an artistic construct, suggests that for Emma the aim of reverie is to recapture a *model,* and that this attempt inevitably leads to failure. Nothing really moves in the static totality. Even the clouds which seem to float like "aerial waves" break up against a cliff.

The pseudorealism of a passage such as this is only a screen. Even the apparent transfer of a character's state of mind to a particular landscape is less important than the interplay of language. In this description of Rouen, the verbal construct participates in the tension between movement and immobility which is a central thematic inspiration for Flaubert. The landscape seems to be in motion, but the verbs of movement *(descendre, s'élargir, remonter)* obviously do not alter the fact that it remains static. Other verbs of motion *(s'envoler, s'emporter)* are also in evident contradiction with images of immobility: the anchored ships, *(ship* and *anchor* in themselves are terms that provide a tension), the islands which are compared to motionless black fish *(poissons* and *arrêtés* imply another contradiction), the high cliff which stops and breaks up the clouds. Escape is impossible; the dream is hopeless. And not just for Emma—it is Flaubert's own sensibility that is involved. The landscape described is where the problematics of the character and the profound themes of the book converge.

In *L'Education sentimentale,* Flaubert perfected the techniques of this convergence and of this hidden auctorial presence. In general, landscape descriptions in that novel link the idyllic mode to a sense of catastrophe. Beginning with the first scene of river navigation when the two banks unfold before the passive and unheroic hero, the gliding landscape, inaccessible and tempting, provokes an idyllic reverie which excludes any possibility of actualization. "One could distinguish vineyards, walnut trees, a mill surrounded by greenery. Beyond, small paths zigzagged across the white rocks which seemed to touch the sky. What bliss it would be to walk up side by side with her, with his arm around her waist, while her dress swept the yellow leaves!" But this bliss is imagined precisely because Frédéric knows that between him and the woman he met in this briefest of encounters there is an "abyss," that he will lose her "irrevocably" without even having come close to her, that only a cosmic upheaval might bring about the fulfillment of his dreams. "Budging the sun" would be easier![3]

The trip to Paris at the beginning of the second part, which repeats the travel images of the novel's overture, also takes place in a climate of passivity. Once again, the imagery associates landscape and mobility through effects that look forward to the cinematographic technique known as *traveling*. Whereas at the beginning of the book the dominant note is the expectation of happiness (the weather is radiant), the return trip to Paris takes place in the middle of winter, in a heavy downpour, amid flooded streets, in merciless view of a desolate suburban landscape. The key passage begins with a sentence that sets the tone: "The chaotic plain had the appearance of vague ruins."[4] The "plain" is no longer countryside; the ruins are not yet the city. These ruins have nothing prestigious about them; they are not the vestiges of former glory, but the ineffectual outline of that which is fated to abort. The no-man's-land Frédéric crosses suggests a transitional space between human activities and the activities of nature. "Here and there, a half-finished stucco shack stood abandoned." The rickety, branchless trees, sapped of their strength by the pollution from nearby chemical factories, confirm the themes of sterility and abortion. These themes are further stressed by the midwives' signboards. Other signs play an important role in this passage (a huge tin cigar indicating a tobacconist's shop, two crossed billiard cues between the windows of taverns, various posters covering the walls of houses) and point to a world where advertisement determines desire, where publicity and artifice are all-powerful.

Love in the Parisian style, to which the hero feels destined, is discredited in advance by this sordid peripheral cityscape. The midwives' signs, showing a bonneted matron dandling a baby, hardly correspond to Frédéric's expectation of exalted eroticism. And yet the rain-drenched landscape, the grim setting, the commercial solicitations of a society ruled by inauthenticity do not succeed in discouraging him: "a fine drizzle was coming down, it was cold, the sky was pale, but two eyes which were to him as precious as the sun were shining behind the mist." Only here, the devotion to his dream is presented in a minor key, as an invincible yet foolish stubbornness.

It is in the Fontainebleau episode that the art of the landscape as symbol and commentary reaches its high point.[5] Ambiguity operates simultaneously on two levels. On the first, the notions of serenity and idyllic experience come into conflict with images of violence and cataclysm; on the second, we witness contradictory moral and intellectual judgments, as the political upheavals—which the protagonists try in vain to forget—intrude again in their urgent ubiquity and perfect insignificance. Frédéric and Rosanette decide to spend a honeymoon in Fontainebleau, in part because Frédéric wants to enjoy intimacy with his mistress, but largely because he is eager to "abandon" revolutionary Paris. The fact is that Rosanette increasingly irritates him during their stay in Fontainebleau, particularly during their visit to the château. But the interest of these pages lies not so much in the growing malaise between the lovers, nor in Rosanette's ignorance and basic stupidity revealed in any number of inept comments. It is rather in the "particular melancholy" that emanates from this royal residence loaded with history, and which powerfully conveys "the eternal misery of everything."

On first impression, all seems calm and restful. The idle strollers in the street, the murmur of the fountain to which the lovers fall asleep, the vast silence during their walk in the forest—everything predisposes to what Flaubert calls a "gentle inebriation" ("ivresse tranquille"). From the outset, however, these elements of repose and delight are dialectically bound to the notion of upheaval. The local inhabitants appear idle because Frédéric and Rosanette still have the vivid memory of the political turmoil in Paris. And the not-so-distant reality of this turmoil reasserts itself through the unwelcome arrival of travelers from Paris with news of bloody battles in the capital.

The longing for a shelter grows even stronger as a result, and the forest of Fontainebleau seems to satisfy this need. It is an ideal place of escapism. Yet it is also the setting for a fake enchantment, and ultimately it provokes renewed anguish. At first, everything is delightfully bucolic. Pigeons are cooing. The sunshine lighting the edge of the woods creates a "purple mist," hangs "silvery drops" on the tips of the branches, projects "patches of gold" on the dead leaves. In short, the forest is the perfect place for lovers' walks, and the language describing this sylvan vegetation is in itself—at least at the beginning—erotically charged. "The beeches, with their smooth white bark, mingled their foliage; ashes languorously curved their grayish-green boughs." These tactile suggestions, these effects of gentle clasping and intertwining, correspond to a pervasive and stylized sensuality with recognizable literary overtones. The pine trees seem to sing, and the delicate birches are bent "in elegiac attitudes."

Eroticism soon intensifies, however, to the point of urgency, even brutality. "Huge gnarled oaks . . . embraced each other . . . " The verb Flaubert uses for the image of the embrace—*étreindre*—suggests sexual embrace, but also the wrestler's grip or clasp. It can serve as a verb for love as well as for struggle and anger. Its pivotal double meaning is clear in this single sentence, which in fact ends on a new note. In their interlocked position, the enormous trees are described as "sturdy on their trunks, similar to torsos throwing out their bare arms in desperate appeals and furious threats, like a group of Titans immobilized in their anger." Imperceptible at first, and then with all the evidence of a revelation, the tone has shifted from gentleness to violence. It is as though the key words *(désespoir, menaces, furibondes, Titans, colère)* were there to remind the two lovers who have escaped from the city that a terrible and crucial battle is being fought there at that very moment, that their escape is illusory, that one cannot escape from events and deny history, that lack of solidarity and the refusal to participate only lead to guilt. Though Frédéric feels "contemptuous pity" for the rebels, he ultimately blames himself for "not being there with the others."

The description of the idyllic and threatening forest offers Flaubert an opportunity for even greater complexity. It allows him to play even more fully on the notion of revolution by opposing not merely peace and war, but *political* and *geological* revolution—that is, two very different forms of upheaval, conceived in totally irreconcilable moral, metaphysical, and temporal contexts. Here is the description of the Fontainebleau rocks as seen by Frédéric: "They became more and more numerous, at the end filling the entire landscape, cube-shaped houses, flat like paving blocks, propping one another up, piled up on one another, merging together like the unrecognizable and monstrous ruins of some vanished city. But their frenzied chaos evoked rather images of volcanoes, floods, great unknown cataclysms." Two features—both of them ambivalent—characterize this passage. At one level, we witness the further development of the antithesis between peaceful and convulsive nature—an antithesis that underlines the impossibility of escape since the forest becomes, ironically and mythically, the mirror and echo of the revolutionary agitation in Paris. But at another level, precisely because myth settles at the core of the text, the analogy between Nature and Revolution—that is, the incongruous juxtaposition of two unrelated forms of cataclysm—brings out the meaninglessness of political change and of all the fleeting sound and fury, thus implying the profound futility and absurdity of the revolution.

The author's presence in this specific landscape becomes palpable. Certain reactions are quite personal. In order to document himself, Flaubert visited the forest of Fontainebleau on several occasions. In his notebook, he jotted down the following: "Nature at the same time melancholy and joyful . . . Solitude incites to rebellion—rebirth of the instinct of savagery." But observations such as these, while confirming the link between bucolic elements and the themes of violence, are less important than the revelation of the author's latent anguish in the face of action, and his awareness that it is impossible to remain outside events. In this sense, the meaning of this passage transcends the specific case of Flaubert. It expresses a more general intellectual malaise in confronting the seductions and imperatives of history.

Flaubert and the Articulations
of Polyvalence

Ils se racontèrent leurs anciens jours.

"They spent the afternoon watching the mob in the street from their window." Part II of *L'Education sentimentale* ends on this image of indolent political voyeurism, typical of Frédéric's and Rosanette's aloofness from historical events. We are at a turning point. Part III begins with the noise of gunshots. These are the preliminaries of the revolutionary action. In the meantime, cozily settled near the window as in a theater box, the two lovers watch the street spectacle with sensuous delight.

Desire and voluptuousness are the dominant mood. Frédéric and Rosanette are in fact about to make love, though not without titillating delays. She has already let herself be pushed onto the divan, and has laughed under his kisses. They are now looking forward to a gastronomic interlude. While the mob, as Frédéric bluntly puts it, prepares to kill off "a few bourgeois," he takes her to an elaborate dinner at Les Trois-Frères-Provençaux. A brief sentence sums up their total indifference to the political events. "The meal was drawn out, delicious." The comma, substituted for the more usual copulative conjunction, transforms what might have been mere objective information (lengthy *and* delicate) into the suggestion of an exquisite duration.

The following sentence also carries a grammatical commentary: "Ils s'en revinrent à pied, faute de voiture" ("They came back on foot, since there were no carriages"). The adverb *en* preceded by the reflexive pronoun is a French turn which weakens and transforms the simple indication of an origin and a direction, and suggests a pleasant stroll. The street itself is invitingly festive, the thoroughfares illuminated by Venetian lanterns as if it were carnival time. But the holiday atmosphere is deceiving; the noisy, swarming crowd is ominous. Bayonets gleam against the somber background. Already the rattle of the first fusillades can be heard. Rosanette, her teeth chattering, holds tightly to Frédéric's arm. Even fear creates a semivoluptuous shiver. In one of the rare direct authorial intrusions in the text, Flaubert signals his own critical stance: "There are situations in which the least cruel of men is so detached from all others that he would watch the whole human race perish without feeling his heart quicken."

But there is worse than this indifference and this fear, neither of which is attuned to revolutionary hopes. Their first night of love means failure and profanation for Frédéric. It is Madame Arnoux he has wanted all along, but she has failed to show up at their rendezvous. The theme of profanation could not be clearer: with masochistic refinement he takes Rosanette to the love nest prepared for the "other woman." Only a few pages earlier we have seen Frédéric arrange the little apartment on the rue Tronchet, where he was to receive Madame Arnoux, "more devoutly than somebody adorning an altar." If he now sobs after making love with Rosanette, it is because he knows the extent of his personal disaster. Sexual and nervous release are accompanied by gunfire in the distance. The shame of having betrayed his great love is made worse by an untruth which does not even have the honesty of an outright lie. When Rosanette asks him why he is sobbing, he can only answer, "I'm just too happy," adding "I've wanted you too long!" These are the last words of Part II. Part III begins with the sound of shooting. The articulation between the two parts of the novel is clearly meaningful. The revolution seems condemned from the outset to failure, to betrayal and shame, to the defeat of all its aims and ideals.

This articulation is of course totally planned. In this novel where chance seems to reign supreme (encounters, disappearances, opportunities, and missed opportunities), there is in fact no room for chance. Henry James, who read it as "an epic without air" observed that it "all hangs together," that all its pieces are "strongly sewn together."[1] Flaubert himself used another image. He spoke of *emboîtement* (fitting, jointing, interlocking)—which is the same as articulation. For this was Flaubert's precise ambition: to write at the same time the story of a sentimental education (the life-apprenticeship of a young individual), the "moral history" of an entire generation, and a historic account of a pivotal moment in French history. The project was awesome. At every point Flaubert had to face questions of priority. What was to be in the foreground? And what if there was none? In a letter to Alfred Maury, he remarked that the milieu in which his characters were moving was so teeming with life and activities that there was "a risk they might disappear in it." And in a letter to Jules Duplan, he identified the joint between Parts II and III as particularly troublesome: "I have much trouble fitting [emboîter] my characters into the political events of 1848. I am afraid that the background will devour the foreground."[2]

Problematic joints, parallelisms, and ironic links are especially noteworthy in Part III, which ends with Chapter 5 (the brief Chapters 6 and 7 constitute a double epilogue taking place sixteen years after the main events). This third and last part of the book, which begins on a note of profanation, comes to a close on a note of multiple failure. Frédéric's refusal to get into the carriage with Madame Dambreuse (a refusal which is part of an entire cluster of "sentimental" failures) is echoed, on almost the same page, by the refusal of the worker to fight for the Republic—that is, the ultimate failure of the 1848 revolution. " 'What! Isn't there going to be any fighting?' Frédéric asked a workman. The man in the smock replied: 'We're not so stupid as to get ourselves killed for the bourgeois! Let them settle their own affairs!' " These parallel fiascoes—human, political, historical—leave no doubt as to the thematic focus of the novel. Yet redundancy also enigmatizes the theme. The shuttle from level to level, the reversals and multiple elaborations of the image, are such that nothing is more difficult to determine than the exact nature of the failure in question. Which one serves to illumine which other? Which one is at the heart of the novel? Where, in other words, is one to situate the metaphor? In such a tight metaphoric structure, can failure even be considered the subject?

Sartre reproached Flaubert for having been a retrospective spectator of the events of 1848, and later a frightened and silent bystander of the events of the Commune. Choosing to live life as though it were already posthumous, Flaubert, according to Sartre, missed out on his time. Lukács's critique is equally severe. Speaking of *Salammbô*, Lukács deplores Flaubert's preference for spectacle over participation and commitment, his separation of human tragedy from political action. In a sense—and despite all appearances—this divorce is even greater in *L'Education sentimentale*. For paradoxically, the parallel themes developed in the different contexts (the individual, the group, the historical events) set up a barrier between the private and the collective sectors. Articulations do not produce meaning. Redundancy seems to serve negativity. What indeed is the relation between the street riots and the betrayal of love dreams? What unifying link is there, beyond the basic principle of betrayal, degradation, and disintegration? But that is precisely the point. The principle precedes and determines the event, condemning it in advance to ridicule and ignominy. Is Flaubert's novel apolitical or antipolitical? One thing is clear: he seems determined to discredit the events of 1848.

Three episodes which Flaubert treats with obvious care can be read as a thorough critique of the revolutionary movement, as well as of those who opposed it. The sack of the royal palace, at the beginning of Part III, debunks the myth of the People, who are represented as a malodorous, stampeding mob carried away by a frenzy of destruction. The second episode is the visit to one of the revolutionary "clubs"— the "Club de l'Intelligence"—amid "clouds of stupidity" and orgies of inept political eloquence. The third episode is by far the most atrocious. It is the hallucinatory description of the nine hundred political prisoners locked up under the Tuileries, crowded together in their own excrement and surrounded by corpses, the victims of a merciless spirit of vengeance—an uncanny foreshadowing of the twentieth-century concentration camp nightmare. On both sides, there is cowardice, savagery, and betrayal. Nothing better defines this collective degradation than the way Flaubert sums up the life of Monsieur Dambreuse, who loved power with such intensity that "he would have paid for the privilege of selling himself."[3] The image of political prostitution could not be given a more emblematic formulation.

Does *L'Education sentimentale* amount to a vast statement of cynicism and negativity? Some critics never thought otherwise. When the novel appeared, the *Journal des Débats* accused Flaubert of desecrating everything, of being indifferent to morality. Taine, though appreciative of the novelist's irony and "objective art," reproached him for his radical detachment from everything. "Won't you some day come to a conclusion, a personal belief?"[4] But that is just the point: Flaubert hates conclusions. For him, to conclude is the essence of stupidity. This refusal to conclude, which in *Bouvard et Pécuchet* will logically lead to the image of the two clerks continuing to "copy," accounts for the circular structure of *L'Education sentimentale*. There is no end, no resolution; everything recurs and returns to the beginning. The river trip at the beginning of the novel is upstream. The boat does not transport to Paris a hero bent on conquest, as it might in a novel by Balzac: it brings him back to his mother. The opening of the novel prefigures the final pages, where Frédéric longs for a sleepy life in his mother's house in the country, a return to the womb. The sentence suggests a desire for death-in-life: "he longed for the freshness of the grass, the quiet of the country, a somnolent existence in the shadow of the house where he was born." (435). The circular as well as the regressive movement of the novel is confirmed by its twice-repeated final statement ("That's the best time we've had"), which recalls the beginning of the book, or rather that which at the beginning is already a memory: the visit to the bordello, which heralds the ubiquitous theme of prostitution.

Does history then—not of individuals, but of the group—compensate for the erosion of private dreams? Lukács argues somewhat elliptically that *L'Education sentimentale* presents redemption through temporality. Yet the same Lukács stresses the negativity of this novel, its discontinuous substance that juxtaposes fragments of reality in order to bring out their incoherence and isolation. According to this view, Flaubert's novel exemplifies the problem of nineteenth-century fiction. For this is the paradox of *L'Education sentimentale*, according to Lukács: the book that best describes modern alienation *(Entfremdung)* is also, because of that, the one that expresses the greatest longing for an impossible unity. *L'Education sentimentale* is therefore the narrative poem of ironic tension and discordance between thought and reality, yet also of a deeper irony which somehow relates a transcendental quest to real duration. It thereby mediates between experience and desire, reaffirming a wholeness that in the end cannot be qualified as ironic.[5]

This notion of a triumphant time, a time of hope because it implies the reclamation of "lost time," is surely suggestive. It might apply to the work of Proust. But does Flaubert allow us to put the problem of time in those terms? Has he not multiplied the temporal schemes in *L'Education sentimentale* as though to set them against each other? There is the time of history, a linear time extending over almost thirty years (from 1840 to 1867); but there is also a circular temporal structure implying a duration leading back to the beginning. There is the time of the flowing river, the time of dissolution, drifting, gliding—the time of a generation adrift, unable to sense its place in history. There is the time of revolution, which is also the time of anachronism, as the participants in the events of 1848 try to imitate the models of 1789. There is the larger time of the history of France, which is also a time now devoid of relevance, as illustrated by Rosanette's ignorance and inept remarks at Fontainebleau. Finally there is the time of prehistory, geological time: the huge rocks in the forest of Fontainebleau associated with ancient cataclysms make the Paris fighting seem insignificant. This time from which man is excluded is extremely ironic, but not in Lukács nostalgic and, so to speak, positive sense. Flaubert's deeper irony has to do with the ultimate divorce between Time and History. It is the supreme irony of the negative absolute, the one Flaubert no doubt had in mind when he referred to God's big joke ("tout n'est peut-être qu'une immense blague"), or when he talked of the artist's "impersonality" as a way of seeing things "from the point of view of a *superior joke,* that is, as God might see them from above."[6]

The most revealing episode in this regard may well be the excursion to the forest of Fontainebleau. In it are juxtaposed, with no possibility of merging, the time of the protagonists who wish to escape from history, the time of history which does not allow for any escape, and, beyond these conflicting times, the time of a fundamental, nonhuman Order or Dis-Order. The description of the forest, as seen by the two characters, conveys an eroticization of nature which is quickly transmuted into images of violence (the gently curving beeches, the embracing oaks reminiscent of titanic wrestlers)—ironic reminders of revolutionary violence. This irony is further complicated because it involves a condemnation of Frédéric's selfish indifference to history in the making, as well as a judgment on the significance of historic events in the face of cosmic upheavals. The nightmarish proliferation of rocks leads Frédéric to make the utterly banal remark that they have been there "since the beginning of the world." But the banality is part of the grander irony. For is this not precisely the way the hypothetical Flaubertian God might see the world, as an enormous joke—*une blague supérieure?*[7]

The circular structure of *L'Education sentimentale* is part of the overall ironic strategy. The end echoes the beginning. Flaubert in fact wrote *two endings,* two consecutive concluding chapters, as though to draw attention to the post-mortem nature of the epilogue. Distance and temporal discontinuity are also stressed, since this double epilogue is separated from the rest of the novel by the famous "gap" Proust admired so much—a gap of sixteen years just before the penultimate chapter. There is, moreover, an evident parallelism between the elements of this double ending: both chapters (6 and 7) focus on conversations which are assessments of the past, the first between Madame Arnoux and Frédéric, the second between Frédéric and Deslauriers—Frédéric thus establishing at the same time the link and the difference between these terminal chapters.

A double epilogue points to the importance and complexities of the conclusion. Three letters to different friends confirm Flaubert's concern over the novel's ending. To Jules Duplan: "What's so terrible about this book is that everything has to be finished before one knows what it is all about" ("pour savoir à quoi s'en tenir"). The second comment is in a letter to George Sand, and refers to the choice of a title and to his own uncertainty about the central idea of the work: "I have a great desire to read you the end." (This desire is interesting, as it implies a trajectory linking the end to the first signal of the text, namely its title.) The third letter casting light on the importance of the double epilogue was written to Turgenev some ten years after the publication of the novel, when Flaubert was still smarting from the incomprehension of critics and readers. "Without being a monster of pride, I believe that this book was unfairly judged, especially the end. For this I hold a grudge against the public."[8]

The problem of endings goes obviously beyond the Flaubertian context. In *The Sense of an Ending,* Frank Kermode implied that the preoccupations and fictional techniques of a writer like Flaubert correspond to broader theoretical issues. According to Kermode, the time of fiction, different from the time of Tragedy and the time of the Bible, is not of an apocalyptic nature. There is no ultimate revelation in the novel. In order to cast light on this novelistic temporality, which is neither that of pure contingency nor of eternity, Kermode invokes a third temporal category: neither *nunc stans* nor *nunc movens,* but that which Thomas Aquinas, referring specifically to angels, calls the *aevum.* This duration, essentially of a spatial nature, implies no finality but proposes a mode "in which things can be perpetual without being eternal."[9] In other words, the notion of apocalypse, which is based on the belief that different times meet in eternity, is here replaced by the notion of the *sempiternal*—that is, a kind of endless, chronic time-space. The world simply continues, outliving itself. Life, like *la bêtise,* which so fascinated Flaubert, is literally in-finite, interminable. That is why *Madame Bovary* does not end with Emma's death, but shows us Homais triumphant. Viewed in this light, the epilogue provides the opposite of a tragic ending. While subject to the artifice of form, such a manner of concluding a novel denies any possibility of revelation.

The epilogue of *L'Education sentimentale* is even more complex because of its binary structure and because both final chapters are systematically ambivalent. A retrogressive analysis beginning with the ultimate sentence of the book allows one to follow in an almost schematic fashion the oscillations between a "positive" and a "negative" reading. The famous last words ("That's the best time we've had") refer, as is well known, to a visit to the local bordello. But the apparent cynicism of this final assessment is perhaps not so cynical after all. For what is remembered is not a banal stop at a brothel, but the almost mythical memory of an adolescent adventure. The apparent cynicism is thus tempered and even transformed by the prestige of tender memories, specifically the memory of innocence. The remembered expedition to the house of "la Turque" is that of two young boys. To speak of loss of innocence is nonetheless to evoke it by preterition. But what stresses innocence (rather than the loss of it) is that nothing in fact happened during the visit. Overwhelmed by contradictory emotions at the sight of so many assembled women, Frédéric simply ran away, and Deslauriers followed suit. Yet amusingly, the outcome is hardly reassuring. The flight in question can be interpreted in almost opposing ways. Frédéric's paralysis and escape serve the theme of innocence, but they are also symptomatic of what lies ahead: his lifelong passivity, lack of willpower, evasiveness.

The same ambiguity prevails in the paragraph preceding the hasty retreat from the bordello. It all took place on a Sunday when everyone was at vespers. The hour of serenity and of prayer seems hardly the proper moment to take off for la Turque's establishment. In fact, the two boys set out somewhat tremulously. The "long detour" they take can be attributed to their not wanting to be seen walking in that direction. But it also corresponds to their secret apprehension, to their unavowed desire to delay the moment of the fearful initiation. The "detour," moreover, has a symbolic, prefigurative value pointing to a lifetime of meandering. Discussing the reason for their failed ambitions (dreams of love, dreams of power), Frédéric gives as the principal cause "le défaut de ligne droite": they did not steer a "straight course."

The flowers picked by the two friends on their way to la Turque's special "house" have a particularly ambiguous status. For these flowers, which Frédéric presents "like a lover to his betrothed" (an ironic image of purity, but also of naïveté), have been picked in Madame Moreau's garden. The mother is thus associated with the bordello in Frédéric's mind: he seems unable to free himself from her, yet feels driven to desecrate her image. This "place of perdition," as the good women of Nogent-sur-Seine call it (fearing for their maids and for their husbands!) is also a place endowed with an exotic poetry confirmed by the name "Turc" (the real name of the madam) and the hoarse voices of these ladies heard singing or humming. But the place of poetry is also, for Frédéric, the place of paralysis. He is so upset by the many available women (a prefiguration of the paralyzing choices in his private life) that he remains, typically, "standing without saying a word." It would seem that everything in this last chapter is to be read in an ambivalent, undecidable manner.

Similar ambivalences affect the other panel of the terminal diptych, the one describing the last meeting with Madame Arnoux, the venerated madonna-mistress. More sentimental at first glance, this penultimate chapter, immediately followed by the bordello evocation, contributes very largely to the anticlimactic ending. In many ways, this scene is even richer in ambiguities. On the positive side, her visit (her "last act as a woman"), ending with her maternal kiss on Frédéric's forehead and her gift of a lock of her white hair, provides them both with the happiness of evoking the past and the almost atemporal experience of cherishing that which might have been. No longer does he regret anything. "His former sufferings were redeemed." As for her, she is enraptured by the adoring words Frédéric addresses to the woman she no longer is.

And yet how can the reader not be aware of the disturbingly ironic and even negative aspects of this scene? For the adoring words "inebriate" the one who pronounces them. Frédéric, we are told, "began to believe what he was saying." Everything he says and does, from the moment he becomes aware of her white hair, indicates bad faith and becomes a lie. The declaration of love he makes to the woman she has ceased being is filled with empty rhetoric and clichés. And even worse, along with Frédéric's vague fear of incest, is his cowardice. For if he suddenly suspects Madame Arnoux of having come "to offer herself" to him, is it not because he can already predict the ensuing disappointment, boredom, and difficulty of getting rid of her? "Another fear restrained him, that of being disgusted by her later. And anyhow, what a nuisance it would be!" There is supreme irony in what follows. As Frédéric turns on his heel (signal of his retreat) to roll a cigarette, she attributes this facing the other way to his exquisite sensitivity and considerateness. Gazing at him in utter admiration as though he were quite unique: "Comme vous êtes délicat! Il n'y a que vous! Il n'y a que vous!" His movement and her words illustrate the most profound misunderstanding.

The ultimate ambiguity of the chapter is to be found in the closing sentence. Madame Arnoux has just climbed into her carriage, and now the carriage has disappeared. At that point Flaubert writes this simple sentence, setting it apart as a one-line paragraph: "And that was all" ("Et ce fut tout"). This totalizing and at the same time empty *tout* sums up in a single expression the poetry of the unrealized, the theme of insignificance, the beauty of the retrieved dream. For this terminal *tout*, this "all" of final loss that keeps echoing in the reader's mind, refers to the great "nothing" of the protagonists' relationship; yet it is precisely this nothing, this lack, that is being given supreme value. Nothing becomes everything here. This is what Madame Arnoux seems to assert by means of a striking cliché: "Never mind, we will have loved each other well" (N'importe, nous nous serons bien aimés").

Has Flaubert deliberately avoided giving a "meaning" to what he considered so important an ending? What significance is the reader to find in the double ambiguity of the two final scenes, beyond a lesson in the equivocation of any statement? Perhaps the meaning should be sought in what may be the common denominator in these two dissimilar scenes. They do indeed share two features. Both of them deal with an exchange of memories and an evaluation of the past. In both chapters, the interlocutors become the narrators of their own existence. Two authorial statements echo each other from chapter to chapter. The story of Frédéric's and Deslauriers's visit to la Turque becomes narration: "Ils se la contèrent prolixement" ("They told each other the story at great length"). As for the last encounter between Frédéric and Madame Arnoux, it is likewise translated into narrative: "Ils se racontèrent leurs anciens jours" ("They talked about bygone days"). The parallelism and repetition *contèrent / racontèrent*) suggests moreover that these bygone days are now immobilized at a great distance. This past is now dead. The characters, though still alive, already see themselves from a post-humous perspective. Do Frédéric and Deslauriers not "exhume" their youth? Do Madame Arnoux and Frédéric not walk like ghosts in the streets as on a "bed of dead leaves"? To be sure, Frédéric and Madame Arnoux continue to live, or rather to outlive themselves. But that is not the point. The remarkable fact is that the recapitulative formula in the future perfect ("we will have loved each other well") must also be read as an anticipatory statement, predictive of an ultimate backward glance. It is like an epitaph projected toward a hypothetical future situated at the frontier of life (or threshold of death), at the line of demarcation between the temporal and the atemporal. From that ideal vantage point the past becomes a privileged vision, even though life continues to unfold in its imperfection. The future perfect fixates this vanished past in the lasting order of death. The time of death thus appears as the time of hope, the time of salvation, since the point of view of immortality is, so to speak, granted to the consciousness still ensnared in the act of living.

"N'importe, nous nous serons bien aimés": the statement made in the present embraces at the same time that which was and will be forever, placing the speaker at the precise point of intersection where life and fiction converge. The future perfect can be said to be the very time of optimism, since it claims the possibility of an ultimate assessment no longer subject to change.

This sentence coming like a sigh after a long musical silence illustrates in almost paradigmatic fashion the notion of a *perpetual* duration that is not to be confused with the absolute of eternity. This notion of the endlessly enduring, grounded in the inadequacy of lived experience, might even be seen as a prime cause of Flaubert's radical option for art over life. In such a perspective, fiction converts the flux of life into the stability of a posthumous order that alone is capable of canceling nothingness. "Never mind, we will have loved each other well"—the sentence begins with a negative exclamation: "N'importe . . . " To choose such a perspective means replacing with a single sentence the inadequacy of existence that Emma Bovary already bewailed. It means preferring a text, as well as producing it. It is indeed a text fabricated by Frédéric and Madame Arnoux that they *tell each other*. Having become the listeners (or readers) of their own lives, they play out within the novel Flaubert's own imaginary transfers from life to art. It is appropriate to recall that, precisely in a letter to the woman who was the model for Madame Arnoux, Flaubert refers to his quiet, monotonous life as one in which only "sentences are adventures."[10] This idea of the adventure of writing casts additional light on the references to "love passages in books" made during the last conversation between Frédéric and Madame Arnoux. Having become the readers of their own existence, they transmute into a lasting order what is otherwise banal, ironic, and sadly definitive in the final statement ("And that was all"), which falls like a heavy curtain at the end of the chapter. Their collaboration in the use of the future perfect blends with that of the reader (and author) of the novel. What they experience is the artifice of form, the illusion of an artistic order, a time scheme which gives value to the all / nothing by creating what the poet Yeats called the "artifice of eternity."

It is hardly surprising that, in this double elaboration of two final chapters apposing the author's and the characters' texts, it is memory that is elevated to the dignity of a "meaning." If the failure that is life weaves the web of fiction, it is because in the weaving that serves to veil an emptiness, the substitute construct of memory provides significance.[11] It is a distorting and transforming operation capable of changing the moment into an epiphanic instant. It is a *choice* that becomes vision. Flaubert's cult of memory at times verges on fetishism. "With me, nothing is effaced," he writes to his niece Caroline;[12] and at the end of *L'Education sentimentale:* "That's the best we've had." All one need do is transpose the past tense into a future perfect—a transposition carried out in the penultimate chapter—in order to measure and fill the huge gap which throughout Flaubert's work separates the disconsolate assessment of existence from the stubborn belief in a possible transcendence.

The Temptation of the Subject

"Les plus grands . . . reproduisent l'Univers."

"Oh! les *sujets,* comme il y en a."

From Constantinople, during his travels in search of near-Eastern exotica, Flaubert announced to his friend Louis Bouilhet that he had found three literary subjects: a night in the life of Don Juan that would blend worldly and mystical love; the story of Anubis, the woman who wanted to be embraced by a god; the life of a young Flemish virgin who vegetates, dreams, and masturbates in her prosaic provincial setting.[1] Alert readers of Flaubert will recognize germs of *Salammbô, Un Coeur simple,* even *Madame Bovary.* The range seems impressive. Yet interestingly, what worries Flaubert, as he explains to Bouilhet, is that the three subjects are fundamentally one and the same. This sameness annoys him ("ça m'emmerde considérablement"), but also appears to him as an unavoidable law. "One does not choose one's subjects; they impose themselves," he explains to George Sand a number of years later.[2]

Two important ideas emerge from these letters separated by almost twenty years: the *unity* as well as the necessity of a literary project—which is another way of referring to the inner, intimate configuration of a work. Not the least of Baudelaire's achievements as critic is to have perceived, immediately upon the publication of *Madame Bovary,* that there existed a powerful thematic link between this novel and a work as apparently dissimilar as *La Tentation de Saint Antoine,* which he described, with uncanny acumen, even though he knew only the published fragments, as the "chambre secrète" of Flaubert's mind.[3] Baudelaire's very positive stress on resemblance and sameness must have reassured and delighted Flaubert. The diversity and multiplicity of subjects were seen to serve a thematic center. Baudelaire was in a sense answering Flaubert's anxiety expressed in the letter to Bouilhet—an anxiety that corresponds to the deeper search for his literary self during the Oriental journey. "Before I begin tilling, I must know the quality and limits of my terrain."⁴ The concern for the three subjects is part of a more lasting concern for the very nature and function of a literary subject.

It is perhaps time to dispel some misunderstandings that have affected recent discussions of the author's attitude toward the concept of the *subject*. Overstatements, if not downright distortions, have indeed invaded a certain criticism bent on viewing the author of *Madame Bovary* not only as the direct ancestor of the *nouveau roman*, but as one of the fathers of literary "modernity."⁵ The status of the subject is of particular import, since it affects the notion of referentiality, the production of meaning, and the possibilities of symbolic interpretations.

Contemporary criticism is fond of quoting Flaubert's proclaimed desire to write a book with hardly any subject, a book about nothing at all ("un livre sur rien") that would be held together through sheer power of structure and style. A number of other sallies or paradoxes have been found useful in this effort to enlist Flaubert in the cause of modernity. "One can write anything at all as easily as whatever one likes," Flaubert affirmed to Louise Colet whom he liked to impress with his literary extremism. Or: "I would like to create books which require only the *writing* of sentences." It is almost as though Flaubert coined the by now commonplace chiasmatic opposition between the story of an adventure and the adventure of a story. Did he not, in speaking about his own uneventful life, describe the act of writing as the real drama, "in which the adventures are the sentences"?⁶ All this feeds the prevailing notions that Flaubert is interested above all in form; that he engages, as an *experimenter,* in a game of literary structures; that his fiction, projecting the bad conscience of the traditional novel, is committed to the ultimate disappearance of the characters; that he is the first of the nonfigurative novelists, that his books reflect essentially the problematics of textuality.

On the occasion of the hundredth anniversary of Flaubert's death, *Le Monde* (25 April 1980) ran a short article entitled "Le Premier Ecrivain moderne." The article, signed Gérard Genette, sums up the modernist doxa: Flaubert, though choosing the medium of the novel, attempts to escape from the tyranny of storytelling; he not only subverts narrative movement but eludes meaning, and aims at undecidability; he reaches toward the essence of literature, which perversely is its own disappearance. His is the tragedy of a vocation which ultimately tends toward a spoken silence. Genette thus usefully synthesizes what various recent critics have chosen to find and to stress in Flaubert: Maurice

Blanchot, the intransitive nature of the literary work; Pierre Bergounioux, the elusiveness of the center of meaning; Claude Burgelin, the
self-referential nature of the text; Jonathan Culler, the fundamental
questioning of the communicative act. And even Sartre, though he
continued until the last to believe in intentionality and meaning, saw
Flaubert as one of the original Knights of Nothingness.[7]

All this is not sheer critical fantasy and willful (or wishful) reading.
Flaubert's literary habits and pronouncements, even if one discounts
the consciously playful or aggressive nature of some of the paradoxes,
do provide more than a hint of the essentially ironic, perverse, and
aporetic nature of his literary idiom. The dogmas of impersonality
("One must not *write oneself*"), of the autonomous value of art, of the
priority of language (words precede experience)—all seem to undermine the conventional notions that literature is *about something* and
that the subject is centrally important. Here again Baudelaire's article
anticipates the most recent assessments. Flaubert, according to him, set
out to prove that all subjects are indifferently good or bad, that everything depends on literary prowess. This observation, made in 1857, is
the more remarkable since Baudelaire could not possibly have known
Flaubert's correspondence, and since the latter never expressed his theoretical views in print (though he may, of course, have communicated
some of his ideas in unrecorded conversations). But for us, who read
his finest letters as rich theoretical texts on the art of the novel, Baudelaire's insight seems to be almost too obvious. For throughout his
correspondence, Flaubert repeatedly questions the prestige of the subject and appears to deny the mimetic function of literature.[8]

He affirms the insignificance of the subject not merely as a challenge
to the vulgarian and utilitarian thinking of the *caboches épicières,* but as
axiomatic: "In literature there are no beautiful artistic subjects." Style,
form, and point of view (they are often interchangeable) are all that
count, and their efficacy and prestige grow in inverse proportion to the
deflation of subject matter, "style by itself being an absolute way of
seeing things." Increasingly, it would seem, Flaubert moves toward the
aesthetics of formalism. In a letter to George Sand, in 1876, he wonders
why a book, independently of what it purports to say, could not produce
the same architectural effect as a Greek temple, through the precision
work of its articulations, the texture of its surfaces, the harmony of its
structure—thus reaching out toward a form of abstract perfection. But
even much earlier, at a time he was still at work on *Madame Bovary,*
he could assert that from the point of view of "pure Art" one might
say that the subject did not exist.[9]

Such statements amount to a declaration of independence of art. If Flaubert irascibly maintains that the word "subject" is without meaning ("ne veut rien dire"), it is because long before Edouard in Gide's *Les Faux-Monnayeurs,* he is convinced that the truly great works are those that are least dependent on an external reality: "The most beautiful works are those containing least subject matter." The creative pride behind such affirmations casts light on the provocative final sentence of *La Légende de Saint Julien l'Hospitalier:* "Et voilà l'histoire de saint Julien l'Hospitalier, telle à peu près qu'on la trouve, sur un vitrail d'église, dans mon pays." ("And that is the story of Saint Julian the Hospitaler, more or less as it can be seen on a stained-glass window in a church in my part of the country.") Not only is the referred-to reality here a work of art in its own right (the stained-glass window of the Rouen cathedral), but between text and what it refers to no true mimetic relation exists. Flaubert in fact comments revealingly on this fake relation and on the importance of the discrepancy. In a letter to Gustave Charpentier, he imagines with delight the puzzlement of the reader had an illustration of the cathedral window been added to the text: "Comparing the image to the text, one would have said: 'I don't understand anything. How did he get this from that?' "[10]

Of course, Flaubert abhorred the very idea of having his books illustrated. And the gap between text and referential reality, as he sees it, not only serves the prerogatives of art but intensifies the power to perplex and bewilder. The combination of ironic and poetic mystification is a potent temptation for Flaubert. He repeatedly stated that the loftiest works, the ones that unleash the power to dream, are also *imcomprehensible.* Hence the lasting ambition to conceive works that would puzzle and even madden the reader. Two years before his death, he put it explicitly: "This is my (secret) purpose: to astound the reader so much that it drives him crazy." The aim was already formulated years before he published his first novel. In a letter to Bouilhet, he dreams of a text so written that the reader would not know "whether he is being made fun of or not."[11]

Since this particular declaration of intent relates to the projected *Dictionnaire des idées reçues,* one might wish to read it as indicative of a satirical thrust. But much as he admired Voltaire, and despite many satirical elements in his work (Homais, the Club de l'Intelligence, Bouvard and Pécuchet—who, it is worth recalling, are at their most inept when searching for a method to discover literary subjects!), despite telling satirical gifts, one should pay heed to Flaubert's affirmation that he never set out to write satire intentionally. The resistance to his own satirical vein is no doubt, in part, a form of resistance to sociopolitical encroachments. If Flaubert had an almost visceral aversion *(dégoût physique)* to newspapers, if he found "militant" writing nauseating, this is a sign of a general retreat from the notion of engaged literature. Satire is always, in some form or other, concerned with, and committed to, the problems of the "real" world.[12]

But there is another reason for the fact that Flaubert, as artist, almost instinctively mistrusted and eluded satire. And this has to do precisely with an underlying fusion of poetic and ironic objectives—the desire to enigmatize the poetry of his vision. Irony inverts, subverts, camouflages, dissimulates, and recreates, ultimately producing an elegant self-conscious code. Even when communicating, it remains strangely private. Satire on the other hand, pretending to repudiate the Muse for the sake of the public weal, is openly indignant, denounces visible vices and follies, and explicitly or implicitly affirms the permanence and priority of a social reality.[13] Viewed in a certain perspective, satire and irony (though one may occasionally serve the other) are hardly compatible in their essence.

The antirepresentational, antimimetic bias of Flaubert is further sustained by an early conviction that art and life are distinct, even antagonistic, realities, and that the former is clearly superior to the latter. From his earliest texts on, he repeatedly suggested that life cannot measure up to books. He openly declared his preference for a factitious existence ("vie factice"). Hence the advice given to Louise Colet to indulge not in real debauches, but in those of the imagination. "One must create harems in one's head, and palaces with one's style." Writing is perceived, all at once, as derivative, legitimate self-defense, and as a hostile substitute for life. Nonliving becomes, as it were, the precondition of the artist's vocation. Conversely, nonwriting appears as a form of death: "My nonwriting weighs heavily on me," he confides to Jules Duplan in a depressed mood. More dramatically still, in a letter to Mlle Leroyer de Chantepie: *"In order not to live,* I immerse myself in Art in my despair."[14]

Statements such as these help us to understand why Flaubert's aesthetic bias so often takes the form of the very opposite of what his contemporaries, perhaps because it suited them, chose to praise as his "realism."[15] For Flaubert's peculiar love-hate relation to reality nurtures his antimimetic stance, making him at times stress the unbridgeable hiatus between art and life ("Art is not reality . . . One has to choose"), at others point to the need for transcendence: "Reality, in my view, should be only a springboard." Not only is "exact narration" considered impossible and undesirable, but literature's superiority over the plastic arts is largely attributed to its nonreferential status. One might ponder the following declaration in a letter to Duplan: "A drawing of a woman looks like a woman, that's all . . . whereas a woman described in words makes one dream of a thousand women."[16]

One could go on and on marshaling evidence. From where we stand, a century after his death, Flaubert can only too easily be made to loom as a prophet of modernism. There is, however, something partial and selfserving in this critical perspective. To be sure, Flaubert the "homme-plume," as he called himself, lived out the writer's craft as a total vocation; he approached each work as a new problem, as a new challenge; he sought, in the literary experience, the essence of literariness. And between this literariness and the subject matter there existed for him a fundamental gap. Art he always saw as a matter of *excess:* that which could not be made to correspond. He was, at the same time, haunted by the specter of repetition, the paralyzing and silencing effect of any linguistic act, the fear and consolation of being no more than a redundant scribe. Much like the budding poet in *Novembre,* who discovers that he is only a *copyist,* much like Frédéric, who is discouraged by the numerous literary echoes he detects in his own writings, Flaubert himself is plagued by the pervasiveness of the *déjà-dit.* Only with him, this self-consciousness turns into an ironic and parodistic strategy that blurs genres and becomes, one might say, creatively deconstructive. And the case for Flaubert's modernity is further strengthened by his deliberate view of himself as a transitional figure, preparing and anticipating the literature of the future. With arrogant humility, he liked to see himself as achieving "that which is most difficult and least glorious: the transition."[17]

Yet there is something simplistic and downright falsifying in a critical position that sets up Flaubert as the progenitor and exemplar of modernity. His fascination with the past, his allegiance to classical culture, his reverence for those he calls the "pères de l'Art" are demonstrably keener than any of his attitudes toward the to-be-created future. Homer and Shakespeare are literally referred to as coworkers with God: they are the conscience of the world. Throughout his life, and increasingly so as his own art matured, he felt that only the classics deserved to be read and studied. "Devote yourself to the classics . . . Do not read anything mediocre," he advises Amélie Bosquet. "Read the classics . . . You have read too many modern books," he admonishes another correspondent. As a first rule of literary hygiene, he urges the daily reading of great texts of the past: "Every day . . . read a classic for at least one full hour." More significantly, as Sartre so well put it, Flaubert saw himself, while alive, as already posthumous, as integrated into the free-masonry of all the great dead writers of the past, as writing uneasily not for the future (and even less for the present) but for all those readers who already have, or will have, their place in the vast cemetery of culture.[18] One might add that, temporally speaking, the future perfect *(futur antérieur)* is the symbolic tense of Flaubert's literary calling.

It could be argued, perhaps too cleverly, that a particular type of uneasy relation to past culture is precisely a characteristic of modernity. But such an argument would hardly dispose of deeper contradictions. Flaubert, it should be noted, was quite aware of some of them. "Il y a en moi . . . deux bonshommes," he declared: one is in love with lyric outbursts or *gueulades,* the other is determined to observe reality, to seek out and analyze the truth ("qui fouille et creuse le vrai"). He himself diagnosed the compartmentalization of his mind, allowing the most scabrous contradictions to coexist: "I live by pigeonholes; I have draw-ers, I am full of compartments." Flaubert's correspondence, so justly praised for its theoretical interest, is in fact a fascinating web of con-tradictions, of confusing overlaps and blurrings. The key notions of *representation* and *reproduction*—at times opposed to each other, and others almost interchangeable—are shifting in meaning and context. The notion of illusion is ill defined, and the concept of truth, whether in the guise of "vrai" or "vérité," remains thoroughly inconsistent. "From the moment something is true, it becomes good," he writes late in life to George Sand, echoing an early conviction that all great works do reveal a truth ("la vérité qu'elles manifestent et qu'elles exposent"). But his reaction to Zola's *L'Assommoir,* which he qualifies as "ignoble" to the Princess Mathilde, has another ring to it. "To produce reality [*faire vrai*] does not strike me as the prime condition of art." And pondering the poor reception of *L'Education sentimentale,* he comes up with an altogether ambiguous statement: "It is too real and . . . is lacking the distortion [la fausseté] of perspective."[19]

Granted that some of these inconsistencies have to do with changing contexts and changing interlocutors, it remains true that Flaubert's theoretical pronouncements, unless one systematically represses the ones that do not "fit" into a system, seriously complicate the task of defining his critical position. This is especially so if one examines Flaubert's unsteady and constantly shifting attitudes toward the priorities of art and experience. On the one hand, the inferiority of experience is posited as a precondition of art: it is the poet's voice, not lived life, that is to provide the raw material for reverie. But on the other hand, experience is considered ineffable, too overwhelming to be spoken. In Beirut, looking at the sea and snowcapped mountains, he scorns the nerve ("toupet") of those who dare write descriptions. The one literary lesson of his Oriental trip, he claims, will have been to discourage him from ever writing a single line on the Orient. The impossible mimesis: again looking at the sea, he muses on how radically false any attempted artistic "reproduction" would be. The vanity of art in the face of reality impressed him during his earliest literary efforts. "What vanity art is," he writes in *Mémoires d'un fou,* "to want to portray man in a block of stone, the soul in words, feelings through sounds, and nature on a painted canvas." The Unsayable haunts the young writer, struck by the inadequacy of language. "Pitiful human weakness! With your words, your languages, your sounds, you speak and you stammer"—while the essence of the experience cannot be expressed.[20]

This inexpressible experience, often defined as the *Idea,* is thus surprisingly perceived as beyond words, indeed as independent from words. Flaubert goes so far as to suggest—and this may seem strange in our era of linguistically oriented criticism—the existence of a style without words. The narrator of *Mémoires d'un fou* has learned Byron by heart—in French. The fact that it was a translation does not seem to matter. "The flatness of the French translation disappeared in the face of the ideas themselves, as though these had a style of their own, independent of the words." The corollary of this wordless style is obvious: an experience that lies beyond words, beyond art. "I vaguely yearned for some splendid thing which I would not have known how to formulate in any words or define in my mind in any form . . ."[21]

The problematic relation, in this sentence, between the words "chose," "mot," and "forme" does point to a wavering between two fundamental frustrations: the unattainability of unmediated experience and the futility of the mediation of writing. Flaubert's drama as writer will somehow remain situated between two opposing negations: the denial of the subject and the discrediting of linguistic expression. The ambiguity outlasts his adolescence. While writing *Madame Bovary,* he observes, in a manner that seems to displace *bovarysme* from the character to the act of writing: "We have too many things and not enough forms." Just as Emma's dreams are too big for her house, so Flaubert suffers from a sense of oppressive limitation. The overabundance of available subject matter ("oh! les *sujets*, comme il y en a") becomes as crushing and as paralyzing to the anguished writer as the endless cortege of heresies in *La Tentation* is to the anguished saint. Already in *La Première Education sentimentale*, which he completed when he was twenty-four years old, Flaubert had commented on the relation between wealth of subjects and artistic paralysis. The nineteenth century, with its revolutionary background, its Napoleonic saga, its collapsing and reborn regimes, its ideological fermentation, provided a dizzying marketplace of topics. But this wealth itself strikes the young Flaubert as a threatening plethora: "The overabundance of subject matter causes the difficulty of art."[22]

We are compelled to return to the central issue of the subject and its status. For if it is indeed tempting to draw up a catalogue of Flaubert's pronouncements deflating the import of the subject, thus lending support to the declared ambition to write a book "about nothing," it is possible also to come up with a no less telling list of conflicting statements, all of which proclaim the subject's centrality. "Everything has to come out of the subject," he peremptorily informs Louise Colet. It is hard to imagine a more categorical statement. What Flaubert means is that the literary devices, in a viable work, derive from the conceptual thrust of the subject. The subject as matrix: we are far removed from the notion of the generative power of language and rhetoric. Flaubert says as much in a colorful letter to Louis Bouilhet. Literary know-how (the *ruses*, the *ficelles*) and sophisticated self-consciousness are not enough. Masterpieces are conceived only when there is an organizing central principle, which Flaubert defines as "the heart of the matter" and more specifically as the "very idea of the subject." And he pursues this with a series of bold erotic metaphors to stress his misgivings about a literary virtuosity that remains impotent: "Nous gamahuchons bien, nous langottons beaucoup, nous pelotons lentement, mais baiser! mais décharger pour faire l'enfant!"[23] ("We're good at sucking, we tongue a lot, we pet for hours; but—the real thing! Can we ejaculate, can we engender a child?")

The conviction that there exists an original bond between subject matter and creativity lies behind countless comments on the importance of the subject. When Flaubert writes that the secret of masterpieces is the concordance between the subject and the author's temperament, when he repeatedly hopes to find a subject suitable for his own particular temperament ("a subject in *my register*"), when he flatly states that for a book to be oozing with truth the author must be pregnant with his topic ("bourré de son sujet"), what is involved is the belief in the generative power of the subject. He could not be more explicit about this than in a letter of 1861 to Mme Roger des Genettes: "A good subject for a novel is one that comes all in a piece, a single shot. It is a matrix that gives birth to all the other ideas." The belief in the subject's matricial virtue would explain why, in flagrant contradiction to the claim that there are no "beautiful" subjects, that all subjects can be indifferently good or bad, Flaubert nonetheless remains stubbornly faithful to the notion that the African desert is more inspiring a subject than a vegetable garden or the even more pedestrian *trottoir*. And this would explain why he can get angry with his friend Feydau for supporting precisely the paradoxical notions he himself so often advocated: "Why do you insist on getting on my nerves by maintaining that a cabbage patch is *more* beautiful than the desert?" This disputation with himself has its fictional projections. Thus, Pellerin, in *L'Education sentimentale,* whose ideas echo Flaubert's own pronouncements yet seem to mock them, at the same time rejects the doctrine of realism ("leave me alone with your hideous reality!") and reaffirms the priority of the subject's intrinsic value: "Better . . . the desert than a sidewalk."[24]

The reaffirmation of the subject's preeminence would also explain why, despite disclaimers, Flaubert never gave up an interest in satire, why topicality remained a steady temptation, and why, far from signing the death warrant of the fictional character, he continued to believe in the independent, nontextual reality of his own characters.

The satiric impulse goes back to preliterary days, when Gustave and his Rouen schoolfriends invented the pre-Ubuesque figure of the Garçon, at once mocker and mocked, an early embodiment of Flaubertian laughter. The Garçon, vulgar and parodistic, seems to undermine and negate. This negation itself is, however, a program; it corresponds to the explicit identification of the roles of thinker and demoralizer: "If ever I take an active part in the world, it will be as thinker and demoralizer." Jules, the artist as a young man in *La Première Education sentimentale,* feverishly collects satirical topics, *matière à satire:* Academicians, police officials, Fourierists and Saint-Simonians, nouveaux riches, Victor Cousin and Pierre Leroux, the platitudes and the hypocrisies of the day. Jules even considers the caricature of caricature, while the author himself parodies the tone of Montesquieu's *Les Lettres persanes.* Quite deliberately, Flaubert accepts, via Jules, the challenge and topicality of the satirical tradition, as he observes that the Turcarets of the Stock Exchange, the Diafoirus at the School of Medicine, and the Brid'oison at the Palais de Justice are still powerfully alive. The desire to focus satirically on the sociopolitical reality of his own period also comes through in many a letter. Not only does the nineteenth-century bourgeois appear to the young writer as a most tempting enormity ("Qu'est-ce que celui de Molière à côté?"), but the political utopias of his day strike him as a particularly fertile comic terrain. "Il y a là-dedans des mines de comique immenses, des Californies de grotesque." And it is worth recalling that at the end of his life, as a sequel to the historically rooted *L'Education sentimentale,* Flaubert had in mind projects *(Napoléon III, Le Préfet)* dealing with life under the Second Empire.[25]

Equally noteworthy is Flaubert's continued belief in the extratextual reality of his characters. In a letter to Taine, he makes a revealing comment about the unwritten presence of his characters: "There are many details that I don't write. For instance, Homais is slightly pockmarked." The unwritten physical detail matters, however, less than the pretextual or extratextual, psychological individuation. Flaubert, in his early thirties, speaks of himself proudly as "an old psychologist." He will continue to view the creative effort of the novelist as an inductive process leading to the reconstruction or reproduction of a psychological reality which has a preexistent, independent status. He in fact congratulates himself precisely on this psychological intuition and reconstruction. *"Bovary* will be . . . the summa of my psychological knowledge"—and, as he explains to Louise Colet, "n'aura une valeur originale que par ce côté." Even more telling, for it clearly denies the priority of formalistic concerns, is the following appraisal of his achievement in *Madame Bovary:* "The reader will not be aware, I hope, of all the psychological labor hidden under the literary form, but he will feel its effect." This notion of form as hiding a deeper truth certainly does not give much support to linking Flaubert's name to the generation of the *nouveau roman,* a generation that so scornfully denounced what Robbe-Grillet called "the old myths of depth."[26]

Thus, Flaubert himself places curious difficulties in the way of any attempt to canonize him as an apostle of a formalistic, self-referential, intransitive literature devoted to the problematics of its own textuality, a literature whose subject, as Jean Ricardou wants us to believe, is "the functioning of the book" and nothing else.[27] And the greatest difficulties Flaubert places in the way of a post-mortem conversion to this brand of fashionable "modernity" have to do with his insisting that the prime function of literature is to *reproduce* and *represent.*

Reproduction and representation are, of course, far from the same thing, though they tend to overlap in Flaubert's usage. The greatest poets, Flaubert asserts, reproduce the world ("reproduisent l'Univers"). But with equal axiomatic assurance, he declares that the greatest geniuses have never done anything but *represent*. Though the two notions blur, their distinct meanings for Flaubert can be traced. When he refers to reproduction, it seems quite obvious that he means something both more precise and more limited than a totalizing of experience, a *speculum mundi*. The reproduction is, first, that of material reality. His literary self, as he puts it, wants "the things he reproduces to be felt almost materially." The outer physical reality must come into focus; it is the objective: "The external reality must become part of us . . . in order to reproduce it properly." And Flaubert not only advocates but practices close observation of the model. While at work on *Un Coeur simple,* he kept (ironically?) a stuffed parrot on his desk, "so as to paint from life."[28]

Three images—the eye, the mirror, and the mime—preside over the Flaubertian doctrine of reproduction. Seeing sharply comes first. For anything at all to become interesting, it is enough, he is convinced, to look at it for a long time. Beyond the "voluptuous sensation" that comes with the contemplation of the object, the steady gaze has to do with the conception and delineation of the object as subject. If Flaubert is so pleased to have what he calls a "myopic" vision ("I see the very pores of things, the way the nearsighted see"), it is because he is convinced that all great works depend on the abundance of functional details ("détails intrinsèques au sujet"). This reaffirmation of the subject's centrality, and of the detail's specific role in the larger economy of the work, suffices to cast strong doubt on Roland Barthes's somewhat hasty contention that the concrete detail in Flaubert, serving only the illusion of reality ("l'effet de réel"), remains resistant to any structure or meaning.[29]

Flaubert's symbolic myopia is in fact the prerequisite for a larger vision. Flaubert speaks of the need to become the eye of the world ("être oeil, tout bonnement"), to lose oneself in the subject, much as Saint Anthony dreams of becoming matter. "Staring at a pebble, an animal, a painting, I sometimes felt myself becoming part of them." The great literary artist, in turn, provides his reader with a supreme ocular and specular experience. Upon reading Shakespeare, "one is no longer a person but an eye." The mirror image serves indeed as a mediation between the visionary eye and the spectacle of external reality. "Let us be magnifying mirrors of external reality." Appropriately, the transition between the reflecting eye and the spectacle is provided by the metaphor of the imitative actor, and more specifically the *mime.* "L'artiste doit contenir un saltimbanque," states the aging Flaubert. But the imitative process depends first of all on the ability to observe. "To be a good mime, one must . . . first of all *see* people, be imbued with them."[30]

But this mimetic function of art, precisely because of the mediating specular and theatrical metaphors, does not really imply a *reproduction* of a fixed reality. Here, the other key term, *representation,* serves not as a contradiction but as a corrective. Art, says Flaubert, is representation: "We must think of nothing but representing." Yet even in order to "represent" such immaterial realities as "les passions" or as "humanity of all times," Flaubert feels driven to the most painstaking documentation: on agricultural fairs for *Madame Bovary,* death by thirst for *Salammbô,* the symptoms of croup for *L'Education sentimentale,* provincial sites for the setting of *Bouvard et Pécuchet.* Flaubert's principle remains invariable: "to know things before describing them." That, of course, includes books. The powerful attraction to erudition is, however, not a mere yearning for a sheltered life spent counting "fly specks": it corresponds to the conviction that only encyclopedic knowledge can give literary mastery. "In order to write, one should know everything." And Flaubert stresses the encyclopedic nature of this literary documentation: "Books that have given rise to entire literatures, such as Homer and Rabelais, are encyclopedias of their time." What lurks behind this respect for knowledge and its fecundating power is not only the potential of caricature (and self-caricature), which Flaubert was to exploit fully in *Bouvard et Pécuchet,* but the conviction that no matter how omnipresent the specter of eternal redundancy, there is a worthwhile something-to-be-written, that the subject exists, and that it can be communicated—though perhaps only in an enigmatic or, as Flaubert puts it, "incomprehensible" manner. This indeed, for Flaubert, is the paradox of the subject: "I have a need to say incomprehensible things."[31]

Flaubert himself provides the qualifier to his perplexing relation with the "subject." In the same sentence that prominently features the word *sujet,* the word *illusion* appears as the ironic companion. Literary form, he explains, is achieved only when "we are obsessed by the illusion of the subject." Illusion may even be seen to achieve priority in Flaubert's theory of mimesis. "*Illusion* is the first quality and aim of Art." Though he boasted that *Madame Bovary* would make his fellow Normans roar with indignation because of the absolutely lifelike *couleur normande,* Flaubert was obviously not a dupe of the mimetic fallacy. Writing to

Léon Hennique, shortly before his death: "Do you take me for enough of a fool to be convinced that in *Salammbô* I created a genuine reproduction of Carthage, and in *Saint Antoine* an accurate depiction of the world of Alexandria?" Raymonde Debray-Genette has very shrewdly made the point that when Flaubert speaks of reproduction, the verb "to reproduce" comes heavily loaded with connotations of craft and artifice. What is to be imitated is not nature itself but its devices. It is because of this *artistic* imitation of nature that art appears as a second nature, an analogue. Or rather, it is nature itself that here functions as the metaphor for artistic creation: "Let's get used to seeing the world as a work of art whose devices we must reproduce in our works." The verb "reproduire" is thus emphatically linked to literary technique *(procédés)* rather than to a fixed reality.[32]

Mutability is indeed of the essence. Transmutation, recasting, transformation, metamorphosis are the key images associated with the creative act. "I wish . . . to transform through Art everything I have felt." Or again: "I am presently devoured by a need for metamorphoses. I would like to write everything I see not as it is, but transfigured." One might justifiably claim that the profound and unifying *subject* of Flaubert is not this or that character in a given setting, but the struggle against the very conditions of existence by means of what he himself defines as the "plastic and total recasting through Art."[33]

Raymonde Debray-Genette makes another important point: the *structures imaginaires* are indeed far more significant in a given textual space than the imperatives of the so-called subject.[34] But it should be added that such structures are the precondition for thematic unity, that elaboration of the themes represents the real subject of the work. To be sure, this thematic subject, ultimately the organizing principle of the writer's total vision, is harder to define; it always partly eludes both reader and writer, camouflaging its powerful singularity behind a surface variety. Hence Flaubert's bafflement at the fundamental resemblance of the three widely different topics he describes in his letter from Constantinople. Hence also his uncomfortable yet exhilarating feeling that what he has to say must necessarily remain unsayable, *indisable*.

And this precisely is the merit of thematic reading and thematic criticism when, at their best, they focus on textual strategies: they decipher, through a careful reconnaissance of linguistic and figural patterns, the *hidden subject* of the work. This "other" subject, which, in the case of Flaubert, centers on the superiority of artifice and imagination over life, cannot be reduced to what has come to be known as textual self-referentiality. Just as the book "about nothing" is not the same as the book about pure textuality, so the writing of fiction is a self-projecting as well as self-transposing activity: "A book is for me a special way of living." And more clearly still: "I have always put myself into everything I have written. It is I who am in Saint Anthony's place."[35]

It is most revealing that Flaubert, in his fiction, avoided the portrayal of the artist as hero. This figure makes only the briefest appearance—in a work Flaubert refused to publish. Jules, in *La Première Education sentimentale,* achieves a kind of salvation through suffering, solitude, and the struggle with the demon of Art. But even in this novel, the artist hero appears only in order to disappear. The priority of art implies, it would seem, the death of the artist. "The more I detach myself from artists, the more enthusiastic I become for art." If Flaubert confesses to having disseminated himself in his works ("mon moi s'éparpille . . . dans les livres"—"j'ai toujours péché par là"), this only strengthens the latent hostility to the artist hero.[36]

Yet it could be argued that, in the deepest sense, all of Flaubert's writings extol the artist. Even the caricatures of Pellerin and of Bouvard and Pécuchet deal—perversely, to be sure—with ideals and ideas dear to the author. And "bovarysme," that yearning for the unattainable, that confrontation of dream and reality, is certainly not Emma's monopoly. Baudelaire once again was uncannily perceptive when he identified Emma, in pursuit of the ideal, as the "poète hystérique." Of course, Emma's flaw is that she uses art to feed her dreams, instead of placing her dreams in the service of art. In a subtle way, Frédéric and Madame Arnoux move closer, if only by preterition, toward an aesthetic possession of their own existence. During their last encounter, we have seen, they become the narrators of their own past ("Ils se racontèrent leurs anciens jours"). Abstracted from their passion, they place themselves at the supreme vantage point of a transcending future anterior: "N'importe, nous nous serons bien aimés." Albert Thibaudet, as perceptive a reader as Flaubert could have hoped for, went so far as to hint at Frédéric's and Madame Arnoux's status as protonovelists: at the end they possess their dream instead of being possessed by it. The *livre sur rien* may well turn out to deal latently but powerfully with a subject and with meanings that go beyond intransitivity and the sophisticated playfulness of a nonsignifying signifier![37]

Flaubert himself, for those who care to listen, provides ample warning against the abuses of reductive and dogmatic criticism. The first warning relates to his belief in genius, and calls for humility. It is a great sin indeed to be "without veneration for genius." The second warning has to do with the tyranny of all systems that would bend masterpieces to their arrogant theoretical dictates. Because he is convinced that every genuine work projects its own poetics, he develops a "complete contempt for all the poetics in the world." The third warning is perhaps the most important. There is no substitute for fair, sensitive, and intelligent reading: "cela demande tant d'esprit que de bien lire."[38]

Stendhal, Reader of Rousseau

> But those beautiful sentences moved me in spite of myself.
>
> Stendhal, *Vie de Henry Brulard*

"Don't believe anyone blindly." This eminently *beyliste* advice given to Lucien Leuwen by his father might have been offered by Stendhal to his future critics. Young Henri Beyle's enthusiasm for Rousseau is well known. Even better known are the dismissive comments with which the adult Beyle-Stendhal lumped together Rousseau, Chateaubriand, Madame de Staël, and Salvandy among the masters of flowery language. But is one right in concluding, as has been done consistently, that Stendhal underwent a real "evolution," that he rebelled against the idol of his childhood? Between 1803 and 1806, young Beyle was converted to what is known as *l'Idéologie*. Biographers like to claim that he thereby liberated himself from a model he henceforth considered harmful to his happiness and intellectual growth. According to Paul Arbelet, Rousseau ends up being "one of the authors Beyle hates most."[1]

There is, of course, good reason to stress the importance of the Idéologues. As of 1802, writing from Paris where he hopes to shed his provincial background, Stendhal offers a systematic correspondence course on Idéologie to his sister Pauline and his cousin Gaëtan.[2] Not even Mélanie Louason, the second-rate actress who became his mistress, is spared his pedantic discourses. Young Beyle suffered serious indigestion from his consumption of Helvétius, Maine de Biran, Cabanis, Pinel, Destutt de Tracy. Some of his new masters are today almost completely forgotten. Such is the case of Lancelin (the author of the *Introduction à l'analyse des sciences,* 1801–1803), who for a while filled Beyle with delight.

But biographers should be cautious. By stressing the impact of the Idéologues during those formative years, there is a risk of constructing an image of Stendhal no less misleading than the one he himself loved to fabricate when he claimed that the language of the statute books (le Code Civil) was his stylistic model. Despite his sallies and mental pirouettes, Stendhal never became the intolerable cataloguer of human passions that his private notes, the *Filosofia Nova,* seemed to announce. Though he would always be tempted by "methods," "systems," and psychological strategies (a taste derived from Laclos's novel *Les Liaisons dangereuses* as much as, if not more than, from Helvétius!), it is evident that Stendhal is first and foremost a poetic novelist, and that the Idéologues are not exactly models of lyricism.

It might be useful to reconsider the role of Rousseau in Stendhal's development and in his writings, for despite his resolve to undergo an "ideological" therapy, Stendhal never ceased to read and admire Rousseau, and to feel his powerful, at times oppressive, presence.[3]

I

On 30 April 1805 (he is twenty-two years old, and for two years has absorbed impressive doses of Idéologie), Stendhal complains in his *Journal* of a "strange state of madness," an "exaltation" of the sensibility which according to him has become his "habitual state" and of which he would like to cure himself.[4] He feels that this "madness" ("folie") and this "exaltation" condemn him to be unhappy and unsuccessful. It is like an illness he seeks to diagnose; the name of this illness is an "exaltation of Rousseau."

This entry in the *Journal* is particularly precious because autobiographical texts such as *Vie de Henry Brulard,* written some thirty or forty years after the events, are not altogether reliable. But in this case the *Journal* and *Henry Brulard* agree. Young Henri Beyle is a fervent disciple of Rousseau's fictional hero Saint-Preux, both in Grenoble and in Paris, where Henri has recently arrived.

Stendhal first read *La Nouvelle Héloïse* secretly. His father, while admiring the book, apparently considered it irreverent or irreligious— "impie. This was a good enough reason to want to steal it from the paternal bookshelves. It is true that young Henri was at that time specializing in such thefts (Mathilde de La Mole, the young heroine of *Le Rouge et le Noir,* will also steal forbidden books from her father's library). Young Henri Beyle even tried to read furtively several articles in the *Encyclopédie.* But the *Encyclopédie* bored him. What were those rational texts compared with *La Nouvelle Héloïse,* which he read in bed, first locking his door, in a state of sensual ecstasy "impossible to describe"? The "transports de bonheur et de volupté" must have been quite powerful, since they hardly diminished even after the young victim of Abbé Raillane's Jesuitic tyranny began to feel that Rousseau had the "double defect" of praising priests and religion. Neither the discovery of Paris nor the pleasures of army life were to dampen his youthful enthusiasm. In June 1802 he writes to his friend Edouard Mounier that he reads and rereads Jean-Jacques all the time.[5]

These readings had a decisive influence on Stendhal's imagination. It is as a real pilgrim that he was later to visit the supposed home of Rousseau in Geneva. "When I arrived in Geneva, I was crazy about *La Nouvelle Héloïse*," he writes toward the end of *Henry Brulard*, as he evokes his unforgettable first descent into Italy with Bonaparte's army. His mental inebriation is at every point associated with literary memories. The view of the lake and the sound of church bells at Rolle give him a feeling of almost *perfect happiness:* "For such a moment it is worth having been alive." Even before arriving in Rolle, which is associated with the memory of Rousseau, Stendhal is "drunk with happiness from reading *La Nouvelle Héloïse* and at the thought of coming through Vevey." Crossing the Saint-Bernard pass, despite the biting cold, the dangers of the road, and his clumsy horsemanship, he can think only of living his own experience as though seen through the eyes of his literary hero. "If I was dreaming, it was about the sentences with which J.-J. Rousseau might describe these lofty snow-covered peaks." And even the yearned-for Italy—revealed to him in Ivrea by the gap-toothed soprano who initiated him into the joys of opera buffa, the Italy of the easy-virtued Pietragrua and the inaccessible Méthilde—is first and foremost the Italy of *Les Confessions*. "I told myself: I am in Italy—that is, in the country of Zulietta, whom J.-J. Rousseau met in Venice; and in Piedmont, I am in the country of Mme Basile." Stendhal was not about to forget Zulietta and Mme Basile. The two figures ultimately blend in his fiction to produce those passionate incarnations of the feminine Italian spirit: Clelia Conti and the duchess Sanseverina.[6]

Rousseau's moral influence seems retrospectively important. Saint-Preux, the hero of *La Nouvelle Héloïse,* was a model of virtue for young Henri. "The reading of *La Nouvelle Héloïse* and the moral scruples of Saint-Preux made me a profoundly decent person." (The French expression "honnête homme" points to something broader than merely "honest," to a kind of civility of heart). One can imagine Stendhal's smile years later at the thought that a book read clandestinely had stimulated tears of enthusiasm for virtue. Saint-Preux, a "virtuous" seducer, could not have had a better disciple than Henri Beyle, who, though keenly envious of Valmont's amorous success, repeatedly asserted that there was greater happiness in suffering like Saint-Preux than in conquering like Don Juan or Valmont. There is more here than a taste for voluptuous virtue. In his admiration for Rousseau's firm letter to the archbishop of Paris, Christophe de Beaumont, Stendhal also reveals his esteem for Rousseau's strength of character and sense of dignity.[7]

A glance at Stendhal's early correspondence shows that the paunchy consul, at work on his autobiography in Civitavecchia, was not twisting the truth in *Henry Brulard*. Young Henri Beyle was indeed filled with admiration for Rousseau. In a letter to his sister Pauline, he describes him as "the man who had the most beautiful soul and the greatest genius ever." He advises her to read Plutarch, because Rousseau read him and was inspired by him. Plutarch's is a lesson in fortitude and moral grandeur from which he himself claims to have learned. "[Rousseau] had on me the same influence that the Romans who nourished his youth have had on him."[8]

What is more surprising, since he was later to find fault with Rousseau's declamatory rhetoric, is to hear young Beyle praise Rousseau's style—and this at the same time he was teaching his sister the rational beauties of Idéologie. "My dear Pauline: While reading tonight Rousseau's *Confessions,* not for the facts, but for the divine style, as a trained ear is pleased to hear *divinamente suave d'un instrumento . . .*"[9] The Italian words are meant to stress the musicality of Rousseau's prose. Does that mean that to reason solidly like Lancelin and Destutt de Tracy is not enough for him? In the same letter, the young Idéologue revealingly returns to his musical comparisons. "Rousseau's second *promenade,* the story of the fall caused by the Danish dog, is a stylistic masterpiece; it has on me the same effect as Cimarosa's sublime aria in *Il Matrimonio segreto:* 'Ah! pietade troveremo / Se il ciel barbaro non è,' when it is well sung. In other words, it fills me with delicious happiness." If one considers that Cimarosa was for Stendhal almost the equal of the "divine" Mozart (his name is associated with the first "crystallization" for Italy), one must conclude that in 1805 Rousseau was decidedly in the very best of company! Young Beyle makes some concessions to his newly chosen ideological masters; he declares to Pauline that Rousseau is intellectually inferior to Tracy, Hobbes, Helvétius, Condillac, but insists that his heart is "inimitable."[10]

As of 1803, negative comments begin to multiply. Beyle criticizes Rousseau's way of reasoning. Rousseau the thinker never appealed to him. Habitually impatient with received ideas, he tends to echo the mistaken opinion (widespread still today) that Rousseau the sentimentalist cannot, when he chooses, also display a powerful analytical mind. "J.-J. Rousseau was closer to being a poet than a philosopher," Stendhal writes in one of the notebooks of the *Pensées*. (I, 149) As for Rousseau's pedagogical theories, they bore him to tears. Though he praised *L'Emile* in one of the prefaces to *De l'Amour* as a bold and thought-provoking work, his comments in *Henry Brulard* have a more authentic ring: "I stole this book in Claix, but understood nothing, not even the absurdities of the first page, and after a quarter of an hour I gave up." The "absurdities" of the first page ("everything degenerates in the hand of man") were not likely to inspire young Beyle any more than the parallel Rousseau draws between the deaths of Socrates and Jesus, which he dismisses as a piece of "mad declamation." It is nonetheless interesting that in preparing outlines for his two (unfinished) plays, *Letellier* and *Les Deux hommes,* Henri Beyle thought of Sophie in *L'Emile* as an inspiration.[11]

Rousseau the preacher irritated him even more. Moralizing always indisposed him. A chapter of *Histoire de la peinture en Italie,* which carries the impertinent title "We Have No Use for the Virtues of Antiquity," bluntly asserts his impatience with preachiness. "I will state now and forever that all moralizing bores me, that I prefer the tales of La Fontaine to the most beautiful sermons of Jean-Jacques." To be boring is the one unredeemable sin for Stendhal. He never forgave Rousseau for having been in his own way a pedant, and for having created moralizing characters. "The pedantry of Julie d'Etange bothered me in Rousseau." Despite Rousseau's humor, which has yet to be studied, Stendhal reproaches him for being insensitive to comedy. He cannot forgive him for taking himself so seriously. From Moscow, where he is with Napoleon's army in 1812, he writes to a friend that if Rousseau was unhappy in life, it is because he failed to follow the sound principles of *beylisme* which would have given him a lesson in hedonism. "The most beautiful things in Rousseau have a bitter taste for me; they do not have the Correggio-like grace that is destroyed by the slightest nuance of pedantry." The observation is not new; already in his *Pensées,* while planning his own literary strategy, he gave himself the advice to "avoid the misanthropic tone that mars the works of Jean-Jacques."[12]

Stendhal's reputation as a denigrator of Rousseau is largely based on his many sallies against his style. Here as elsewhere, however, there are qualifications and contradictions. In his *Pensées* he claims to take lessons in style from Rousseau, whereas in *Mémoires d'un touriste* he talks of

Rousseau's nefarious example. "Michelangelo said, 'My style is destined to produce many great fools'; Jean-Jacques might have stolen this idea from him." Once again, it would be unwise to speak of evolution. At the height of his period of enthusiasm for Helvétius and Tracy, Stendhal is indeed far from weaning himself from Rousseau, as his biographer Paul Arbelet would have us believe. For he compares him—and precisely in terms of style—to one of his favorite composers.[13]

It is true that almost every time Stendhal makes an unfavorable comment about Rousseau, it is aimed at his style, and more specifically at what he calls *emphase* (rhetorical amplification, noble diction). "I abhor almost equally the descriptions of Walter Scott and the declamatory tone [*emphase*] of Rousseau," he writes in *Henry Brulard*.[14] To some extent, this is a cliché of the period; in *La Peau de chagrin*, Balzac speaks of the rhetorical and affected sentences of J.-J. Rousseau. Stendhal is more specific. He blames Rousseau for wanting to force the reader to react by exaggerating his own reactions: "This net catches many fish," but mostly "small fry" ("goujons") of the commonest variety. Stendhal goes so far as to accuse Rousseau of artifice, sham, even charlatanism. "J.-J. Rousseau, who was well aware that he wanted to *deceive*—part charlatan, part dupe—had to pay utmost attention to matters of *style*. But what kind of style? A mendacious style, Stendhal would reply. Evoking the precious memory of his arrival at Lake Geneva, so dear to Rousseau, he gives himself the following warning: "Contrary to my purpose, I must reread and correct this passage for fear of lying craftily like J.-J. Rousseau."[15]

But if Stendhal is afraid to "lie" like Rousseau, if he is so obsessed with sincerity, is it not because he remembers that when he passed through Rolle he was under Rousseau's powerful influence, and that he still is under this influence when he evokes this distant memory? Paradox and irony are Stendhal's habitual modes. In 1812 he confides to his *Journal* that he dislikes *Les Confessions*. The observation is rather amusing if one recalls that these same *Confessions* are one of the three books for which Julien Sorel would gladly die ("se serait fait tuer"), and that *Le Rouge et le Noir* is rich in situations that seem to be derived directly from Rousseau's autobiography. Stendhal's most revealing literary exercise or project during his stay in Milan is perhaps that of "translating" *Les Confessions* into his "own style." "Milan, le 12 août 1814.—Traduction des *Confessions* de Jean-Jacques en style à moi." And he adds that it was an "amusing exercise" undertaken in order to develop his style ("pour me former le style").[16]

The "translation" of a work he pretends not to like is a strange exercise indeed! The true significance of this exercise is revealed by Stendhal himself in a marginal note written two days later, which demonstrates how much he is still under the influence of Rousseau's style and ideas although he claims to resist them: "One must have one's own style, which finally happens when one has one's own way of feeling. But in order not to be hampered by questions of technique [*le mécanisme*], one must study and be able to imitate the technique of others. I am still far from having this talent; I admire too exclusively what I like." (14 August 1814). Proust thought much the same way when he praised the exorcising virtues of the pastiche. The choice of words in Stendhal's note deserves to be examined more closely. What in fact is meant by "pour me former le style"? Is it that he thinks he does not yet have a style of his own? And if he has yet to develop his own style, is this—as he seems to imply—because he does not yet have his "own way of feeling?" In that case, from whose way of feeling is he trying to free himself in 1814, at the age of thirty-one?

Stendhal's well-known remark on Rousseau's style in a letter to Balzac is even more subject to caution. "Here is the bottom of my disease: the style of J.-J. Rousseau, of M. Villemain, of Mme Sand, seems to me to say many things one must *not* say, and often many *untruths* [*faussetés*]."[17] Most often this passage is read as a literary confidence to a trusted colleague. Yet the sentence presents a number of problems, the first being that we do not know the exact nature of the letter he finally sent off. All we have are three different drafts of this thank-you letter, and there is no way of knowing whether Rousseau is still mentioned in the final version. There is, in fact, every reason to doubt it. Of the three drafts, only the first mentions Rousseau, though the other two continue to inveigh against the "tortuous" style of Villemain, George Sand, and Chateaubriand. One might say that only the first version is spontaneous, having been written on 16 October 1840—that is, on the day after he read Balzac's rave review of *La Chartreuse de Parme*. But a careful look at the three versions forces one to conclude that the first is the most cavalier in tone. Written with bravado, this draft seems to aim at an impression of sincerity—"There now, I have come out with it" ("Voilà le grand mot")—but also to respond with dignity to a totally unexpected review. One senses the effort of the unappreciated, little-known novelist, elated and deeply moved by the generous article of his much more famous though younger colleague, and who in thanking him wishes above all to establish the independence of his mind. To a large extent, Rousseau is here the victim of Stendhal's pride.

II

Stendhal's derogatory remarks about Rousseau, as we see, are never unambiguous. His case would confirm Benedetto Croce's and André Malraux's notion that artists begin by imitating predecessors and liberate themselves only at the cost of flagrant ingratitude. It is as though Stendhal the adult were ashamed of his first bursts of enthusiasm, however much he enjoys recapturing his adolescent emotions. A recurrent exclamation of solidarity might serve as an epigraph for *Henry Brulard:* thus I was, thus I still am!

The evidence clearly indicates that Stendhal continued to read Rousseau even after 1803, and not only to read but to emulate him. In April 1803 he mentions the *Lettre sur les spectacles* (it must have been a recent reading, as he gives a precise page reference), and expresses his agreement with Rousseau's idea about the changing tastes of the public. The year 1803 is a year of transition, but will his tastes and reactions be so different later on? In May 1810 Beyle informs his sister that he has delayed his departure for Lyons in order to visit Ermenonville and Mortefontaine, pay his respects to Rousseau's tomb, and dream in the setting "where two tender lovers preferred to die together rather than be separated." Carried away by these bookish evocations, he sentimentalizes: "What a model!" It is true that in his *Journal* this idealistic excursion is presented in quite a different light: as a pleasure trip in the agreeable company of a certain Mme Genet, a "juicy twenty-eight-year-old nun." This pilgrimage took place, moreover, at a time when Beyle, back in Paris from the wars and intent on escaping from the chores of *commissaire des guerres,* bought himself a fashionable gig for 2,100 francs, and hoped rather prosaically to be appointed to the Conseil d'Etat. Yet the lyrical effusions in his letter to Pauline have no less genuine a ring than the cynical observations in the *Journal.* Material concerns and sensuous longings only sharpen the need for reverie. And military service, or servitude, certainly did not dampen his ardor for literature. Stendhal was the kind of soldier who carries his favorite poet to the front. From Moscow, which he was soon to watch burn, he informs his friend Félix Faure that he reads *Les Confessions* and enjoys music like Rousseau. True, he is at that point very comfortably quartered in the Academy of Medicine. But is is significant that he devotes these moments of respite from the 1812 campaign not only to "work" (on his play *Letellier,* meditations on the theater, theorizing on *ideal beauty*), but to rereadings of Rousseau. No mention, moreover, is made of the Idéologues during this period.[18]

So that if in 1814, in Milan, he works on "translating" *Les Confessions,* it is not, as might be thought, after a long period of neglect. Even when he does not actively read Rousseau, he still thinks of him. Describing the banks of the Saône in *Mémoires d'un touriste* (I, 165–166), he evokes the well-known passage in *Les Confessions* which ecstatically describes a night spent sleeping under the starry sky. For in 1837 Stendhal no longer needs to reread *Les Confessions;* he virtually knows the book by heart. "After so many years of not reading this passage of *Les Confessions,* I remember almost verbatim the words of this man so hated by soulless people."

This man so hated by soulless people . . . For the "happy few," as Stendhal himself liked to call his future readers, can there be a greater tribute? Stendhal usually reserves this tribute for the heroes of his own novels— the romantically imprudent heroes who are always the butt of "les âmes sèches," those pedestrian enemies of all poetic madness and generosity. These "desiccated souls" are often the voices of reason; they have practical common sense on their side. They are also the truly subversive advocates of a pragmatic, antiromantic morality within the novels. Stendhal is thus perfectly consistent with himself in this same passage of *Mémoires d'un touriste,* where he relegates Voltaire to the ranks of writers who are "incapable of tender feelings."

Yet things are not quite so simple. For Stendhal may not love these rational and demystifying minds, but he admires them. This admiration is not merely intellectual and distant, but takes on the form of an assimilation that affects his style. Proust was able to demonstrate in *Contre Sainte-Beuve* that Stendhal's irony was entirely in the manner of the eighteenth century, namely an elegant irony à la Voltaire, "though Beyle did not like him."[19] Indeed, Stendhal hardly ever has anything good to say about Voltaire. Despite his grandfather's veneration for the philosopher, whose bust adorned the parlor, Henri Beyle, even as an adolescent, always found Voltaire silly and childish *(puéril),* disliked him "sincerely and mightily,"[20] and even accused him of meanness and low envy. Stendhal is not the only postrevolutionary writer whose debt to eighteenth-century irony and whose love-hate of eighteenth-century values creates perplexing tensions.

What remains clear is that Stendhal stays faithful to Rousseau, that he continues to see him as a spiritual and emotional intercessor. Writing one of his many wills, in June 1836, he bequeaths to Giulia Rinieri (Berlingueri), the woman he almost married, "a beautiful volume" of Rousseau. In the same will, he asks to be buried near Montmorency, which is where he corrected the proofs of *De l'Amour* in 1822, in a setting that inevitably recalled the sentimental complications experienced by the author of *La Nouvelle Héloïse*. And he continues to express his admiration in a most unequivocal fashion. He looks up to Rousseau the man, calling him "this great man," and blaming the Swiss for their ingratitude. He values the nobility of his mind, praising his courage and his integrity even in apparently small matters. "Only Jean-Jacques Rousseau was able to remain poor and beat M. le prince de Conti at chess, while overjoyed to receive the visit of a prince." Above all, he keeps repeating—even Stendhal can be a victim of the commonplace—that Rousseau's greatness lies in his sensibility. It is to him, Stendhal explains, that we owe our love of Lake Geneva. Some remarks are more piquant. At the time that he still dreamed of becoming a playwright and a successor to Molière, he thought that he had to "begin by having a tender soul like Jean-Jacques."[21]

It would be easy to produce a long inventory of passages proclaiming the importance of Rousseau. Stendhal the *tourist* (he put the word into circulation in France) knows to what extent the name Jean-Jacques is henceforth linked to certain sites and to certain types of landscape. Time and changing fashions cannot alter this. *"La Nouvelle Héloïse* will not age in ten or twelve centuries," he pontificates in his *Pensées*. He knows, of course, that if Rousseau matters so much, it is not for having sung the beauties of this or that lake, but for having proclaimed the individual's right to the pursuit of a certain type of happiness, and for having thus proposed a declaration of independence of the human heart. One wonders whether in 1804 young Beyle already knew that the theme of "la chasse du bonheur" would become one of the leitmotifs of his own work. The future Molière, also under the influence of Alfieri, still appears to dream of being "useful to the nation" by undermining the prestige of tyrants (1804 was the year Napoleon crowned himself emperor.) We still seem to be far removed from the dynamics of escapism that will characterize *beylisme* metamorphosed into the art of fiction. But already in that year young Beyle is meditating on the lesson of Rousseau who taught him the right to seek "happiness" in accordance with one's individual temperament. "The tyranny of derision has diminished nowadays; we owe this to Jean-Jacques. A person can freely say, 'You find pleasure in going to the bois de Boulogne in a carriage, and I in going there on foot.' He will seem eccentric but not ridiculous." This predilection for Rousseauistic attitudes, or rather for what might be called *le bonheur à la Rousseau,* will only intensify with the years.

The role of Don Juan is no doubt more prestigious, he tells us, but Saint-Preux's role holds in store rarer joys that only superior sensibilities (*âmes d'élite*) know how to relish. Thus, Stendhal evokes in *De l'Amour*, as though he had made them his own, the delicious moments "Rousseau experienced in the parc de la Chevrette, beside Madame d'Houdetot," or those in Venice "listening to the music of the Scuole" and in Turin "at the feet of Madame Bazile."[22]

It is the art of Rousseau that Stendhal admires above all—his colorful accounts, his delicate descriptions, his sense of detail. In an article written for an English periodical, Stendhal quotes an entire passage ("a charming yet very truthful description of the little town of Chambéry") drawn from Book 5 of *Les Confessions*. In his *Mémoires d'un touriste*, under the heading "Chambéry," he refers with pleasure to "the famous waterfall so well described by J.-J. Rousseau." One can moreover imagine the sense of recognition with which Stendhal, who spent his childhood in the setting of Grenoble, read (even if he sometimes skipped pages) the landscape descriptions of Rousseau. "Those beautiful sentences moved me in spite of myself."[23]

What is more surprising, coming from this "connaisseur" of the human heart that Stendhal fancied himself, is to hear him praise the subtlety of the feminine portraits (the "grace" and the "lack of affectation" of Madame Bazile), the subtlety of psychological observations ("Rousseau plays with delicate and little-known truths"), and his straightforwardness in sexual matters. "One must be grateful to Rousseau for having dared describe things faithfully in a century of false decency." All this praise can be reduced to this: Rousseau's genius, whether dealing with landscape descriptions, the delicate sensuality of Madame Bazile, or shrewd observations on the "human heart," resides in the inner music of his style. In *Mémoires d'un touriste*, Stendhal observes that many of Rousseau's letters are still unpublished—one in particular, which he calls a small masterpiece: "It will prove to be one of the most beautiful texts in the French language." Through an ironic detour, we are back to Rousseau's *style*, a style which Stendhal at some point pretends to have profoundly disliked, but which he has never ceased admiring and enjoying. Even Fénelon, though "supposedly perfect" as a prose artist, is never as "moving" as the author of *La Nouvelle Héloïse*. An amusing entry in the *Journal* states that Rousseau might have become the "Mozart of the French language," had it not been for a slightly pedantic strain. In 1810, Henri Beyle obviously still judges Rousseau's style—that of *La Nouvelle Héloïse*, if not that of *Le Contrat social*—as eminently *musical*. No amounts of the Idéologie he ingested will make him give up this idea. It is Rousseau's *sentences* he loves. "On est touché par les phrases de Rousseau," he writes in 1814. From this to seeing Rousseau as a permanent model, a stylistic teacher, is no great distance. When in doubt as to the suitability of an expression, the self-styled enemy of *emphase* urges himself to consult his master: "Is this good French: *être d'un ton* for *avoir un ton d'aisance?* To check in J.-J." And why not? He puts it in the clearest possible terms: his own taste was "formed by Jean-Jacques Rousseau," and quite specifically by his rhythmic, harmonious, and "eminently moving" prose.[24]

Not surprisingly, Rousseau's presence can be felt in passages that seem to have nothing to do with Rousseau. "Imitation" is perhaps too strong a word; but certainly there are echoes and affinities promoted by a long-standing acquaintance with Rousseau's work. The two writers share many views. They both look down on French music. "The French are decidedly ridiculous when they speak of music," writes Stendhal, adding: "Everything Rousseau said eighty years ago is still completely true today." Did Rousseau not affirm, in his *Lettre sur la musique française*, that French was too dry a language to lend itself to musical expression? One can almost hear the author of *Vie de Rossini*. In general there seems to be a meeting of minds in their judgments of France, and in particular of Paris. "Provincials" both of them, they are, so to speak, exiles, outsiders—one by birth, the other by choice. Both of them find the French lacking in spontaneity and naturalness. Both deplore French "wit" (Stendhal in spite of his own dazzling talents as a quipster) and abhor the coldness of Parisian gallantry and libertinism. "I hate licentious French conversation." Or again: "The French wit one finds in the Parisian theaters almost made me cry out aloud: scoundrels! . . . scoundrels! . . . scoundrels! . . ."[25] Finally, both pass severe judgment on a society they consider physically and spiritually exhausted, a society in which the vitality of the individual and the talent of the artist are in danger of being smothered.

Whether because of affinity or influence, many of Stendhal's tastes coincide with Rousseau's. His childhood raptures during excursions near Grenoble, his dislike of flat countrysides, his disappointment with Paris ("the surroundings of Paris seemed horribly ugly to me; there were no mountains"), his idyllic descriptions of the Italian lakes—all these recall the world of Rousseau. Fabrice del Dongo's early education in the setting of Lake Como, with the beat of oars and the rhythm of the waves in the background, is "Rousseauistic." Many scenes in *La*

Chartreuse de Parme and in *Le Rouge et le Noir,* especially the nocturnal moments of reverie, convey a Rousseau-like atmosphere. The inventory could be extended indefinitely: passion for Italy, taste for memoirs and chronicles, attraction to solitude and altitude—at almost every point one hears familiar echoes.

These echoes, however, are so deep and prolonged that one can hardly speak of conscious tastes or attitudes. It is the whole imaginary world of Stendhal that is involved. Proust admirably understood that Stendhal's love of heights, for instance, is linked to the notion of spiritual life; it expresses the essence of his vision. The same might be said of other motifs and themes he shares with Rousseau: images of maternal women, dreams of chaste eroticism, communion of sympathetic souls, the notion of the "happy few," the hostility of society to the free development of the individual, the poetry of renunciation—above all, the incorrigible romantic belief in the existence of great loves which, as he explains himself, comes to him directly from Rousseau. "Jean-Jacques . . . m' a donné *the character loving and the g[reat]'s love,*" he confides to his *Journal* in his odd mixture of French and faulty English.[26]

Ultimately Stendhal's own style is influenced by assiduous contact with *La Nouvelle Héloïse.* It is no longer fashionable to assert that Stendhal has no style. He has, in fact, a style very much his own. But what has not been sufficiently recognized is how much this very personal style, with its unmistakable ellipses and impertinences, he owes to Rousseau. It is difficult to read the pages describing Fabrice's nocturnal expedition to Grianta (the sound of the bells, the oars slapping the water, the vast silence, the joy of shedding tears) without recalling any number of famous passages in Rousseau. Fabrice, deeply moved by the "profound stillness" and the "sublime beauty" of the hour, sits down on a rock shaped like a small promontory on the lake. "The universal silence was only broken at regular intervals by the faint ripple of the lake as it died away on the shore." (*Chartreuse,* Book I, Chapt. 8) The sentence seems to come straight out of *Les Rêveries* or *La Nouvelle Héloïse.*

III

Nineteenth-century readers and critics were, on the whole, more aware of Rousseau's influence on Stendhal's fictional world than twentieth-century commentators. They were themselves closer to him. Charles Monselet wrote that Julien Sorel, the hero of *Le Rouge et le Noir,* relives Rousseau's wayward youth. P. Brun also felt that Julien "bears a close resemblance to young Jean-Jacques Rousseau," for both suffer from "sacred pride" and a pathological distrust.[27] It is true that the narrator himself informs the reader, at the beginning of *Le Rouge et le Noir*, that *Les Confessions* are "the only book through which [Julien] formed an image of life and society." And in the plans for an article he sent to his Italian friend Salvagnoli, he himself insists on the filiation Rousseau–Julien Sorel: "Rousseau's youth has much in common with his."[28]

These evident links can be verified in Stendhal's lesser-known fictional works, even in his sketches. Alfred, in *Mina de Vanghel*, botanizes with a passion that "stems from the proximity of places where Jean-Jacques Rousseau spent his youth." Mina herself settles in Les Charmettes, the "country house . . . where J.-J. Rousseau says he spent the happiest days of his life." There are also the interesting manuscript pages dated 22 November 1831, entitled *Le lac de Genève: Roman de moeurs et moral—Oeuvre posthume de M. Ducray-Dumesnil*. The title of this projected novel, abandoned in the early stages, is in itself significant. But Stendhal further insists in the second paragraph: "Lake Geneva: what words for an eighteen-year-old heart! The rocks of Meilleray, J.-J. Rousseau, Vevey, *La Nouvelle Héloïse*."[29]

All this is rather explicit. More telling are the Rousseau resonances in Stendhal's novels: the arrival at Mme de Rênal's house recalls the arrival in the house of Mme de Warens; the repugnance Julien feels at the thought of eating with the servants brings to mind Rousseau's humiliations in Turin; the theological seminary in Besançon has its counterpart in *Les Confessions*; the rock from which Julien likes to survey the landscape and admire the circling bird of prey seems to come directly from Rousseau's text. As for Fabrice's chestnut tree, which was planted in his honor and which he tends at the risk of his life, is it not a new version of the famous walnut tree that Jean-Jacques and his cousin planted and watered in a rapture of joy, and which Rousseau many years later wished to see again in order to water it with his tears?

It is mainly while rereading *Les Confessions* that one is struck by any number of passages whose tone and point of view—one might say whose "vision"—foreshadow key passages in Stendhal's work. Similarities of situations and events, parallelisms of attitudes and reactions, stylistic analogies seem almost intended to bring Rousseau back to life. At times, the analogies are signaled by the narrative voice. Having read in *Les Confessions* that Mme de Beuzenval sent Jean-Jacques to eat in the servants' hall, the reader immediately makes the connection with Julien's extreme aversion to associating with the domestics. But this is in large part because Stendhal underscores the resemblance: "He drew his repugnance from Rousseau's *Les Confessions*." Most often, however, Stendhal provides no commentary. Yet can a Stendhalian read about Jean-Jacques's distress at the seminary ("What a sad home is a seminary, especially for one who has just left the home of a lovely woman!") without thinking of Julien's situation in Besançon? Can he follow him in the evocation of the double life he led in Turin ("disciple and valet in the same house," without thinking of the "double" relation Julien has with the Marquis de La Mole as secretary and adopted son? Can a *beyliste* reread the passage in which Rousseau describes his happiness on discovering opera in Venice (he "locks" himself in a box and surrenders to his emotions) without immediately recalling the boxes at La Scala, where Stendhal was to know such musical and amorous raptures?[30] And the churlish individual with the air of a "grenadier" who accompanied Jean-Jacques to Turin—does he not prefigure a certain Captain Burelvillers, who was Beyle's companion on the road from Geneva to Milan? As for the lessons in etymology which Rousseau the "lackey" gave his masters, they surely announce the remarkable recitation of the Bible by Julien the "domestic." And Jean-Jacques's nocturnal readings of love novels with his father—did they not give Stendhal the idea that it was his "bastard" of a father (a widower like Rousseau's) who initiated him into the beauties of none other than *La Nouvelle Héloïse?* Once again, as is so often the case with Stendhal, life and literature merge, so that it would be difficult to determine whether it is Stendhal or his protagonist who has been most affected by the example of Rousseau.

Certain vaguer resemblances are no less revealing. Like M. Masseron, the town clerk who bemoans the ineptitude of his apprentice, Count Daru marvels at the clumsiness and spelling mistakes of the young provincial relative who has been so warmly recommended to him. Like Jean-Jacques, who is a domestic servant but also a protected "favorite" of the family, Julien finds himself in ambiguous situations that make him vulnerable to the disdain of his masters and the hostility of the other domestics. Perhaps in imitation of Jean-Jacques, who claims to have returned chaste from Italy, [31] Stendhal likes to imagine—despite the veneral disease he brought back as a souvenir—that he too had lived a singularly abstinent life there. The poetizing of chastity in the works of the two writers would indeed be an interesting comparative topic.

But more symptomatic than such similarities are those of dreams and yearnings, the striking resemblances in affective reactions. When Rousseau describes how the boy Jean-Jacques loved to indulge in visions of glory, adventures, and mistresses, he is setting the pattern for Stendhal's account of how young Henri Beyle delighted in fantasies of love and courage such as that of saving the life of some prestigious Parisian lady and becoming her lover. Both writers are tempted to treat their childhood self as a fictional other; except that, in the case of Stendhal, the self-fictionalizing tendency is further galvanized by a process of assimilation and translation. If Jean-Jacques admires the passing troops and ardently hopes to become a soldier ("I already saw myself in an officer's uniform, with a beautiful white plume"), Henri Beyle's heart will also beat faster at the sight of regiments of dragoons; he too will dream (as will Stendhal's heroes) of strutting about in handsome uniforms. And if the young provincial Jean-Jacques suffers from appearing awkward and silly ("gauche" and "sot") at Mme de Boze's dinner table, Stendhal the adult, mellowed by age and touched by a combination of personal and literary memories, will speak in almost the same terms of the adolescent who was made to feel so inadequate in the house of Count Daru.[32]

It becomes obvious that Stendhal cultivates all possible resemblances or points of contact. Jean-Jacques is moved by the sound of bells; Stendhal will always be moved by this sound. Jean-Jacques thinks that the Borromean islands on Lago Maggiore "deserve to be described"; Stendhal will never miss the chance to praise the beauty of these sites. Jean-Jacques confesses to taking little pleasure in French poetry (he claims never to have had any talent for "elegant inversions"); Stendhal will likewise proclaim his contempt for the alexandrine, which he considers a screen for nonsense, a "cache-sottise." When it comes to money, same tune. Rousseau feels (a rather bourgeois opinion) that money should above all be considered as an "instrument de la liberté," a means of ensuring "independence." The truth is that Stendhal never thought otherwise, and his ideas on the subject in turn impressed Delacroix and Baudelaire. In assessing their professional competence, the two writers meet again; both like to describe and amplify their skills as administrators and diplomats. And both seem obsessed with the fear of being surrounded by enemies and spies. This fear comes close to madness in Rousseau; in Stendhal, it is a gentler mania, a playful stance of sorts, but which leads him to take the most childish and at times melodramatic precautions.[33]

It is probably in the way each writer conceived of his amorous life and translated it into fictional terms that one can detect the most telling affinities. When Rousseau laments his lack of success with women (which comes from "loving them too much," or remembers his fiasco with Zulietta in Venice;[34] when he confesses that he would have liked to "elude" the happiness of becoming Mme de Warens's lover, and that it is through timidity that he became "cynical" and "caustic"—one is again compelled to think of Stendhal. There are differences, to be sure. Stendhal does not suffer from the myth of a personal "fall." He cannot conceive of love without jealousy ("I loved her better dead than unfaithful").[35] He pretends never to speak of his pain and suffering to the women he loves. Above all, and unlike Rousseau, he hates to be pitied. Nonetheless, the analogies between lived and fictionalized loves in the two writers are remarkable. Both like to people their solitude with the women they have loved, or might have loved. Without being blind to their own inadequacies, they are both convinced of the generosity of their "heart," and live in expectation of a happiness which they feel they deserve. Both appreciate "honest" women. Stendhal and all of his fictional alter egos would enthusiastically endorse Rousseau's notion that "there is no pleasure comparable to the one given by an honest woman one loves." As for the "minimal demands" which, according to one critic, characterize Rousseau's amorous liaisons,[36] the expression might apply as well to Stendhal, who wrote to Métilde Dembowski: "Even if I had the talent of seducing you, and I do not think this talent possible, I would not make use of it."[37] Surely Stendhal must have meditated on the pages where Rousseau says that he was not made to enjoy love (*jouir*). For he also knew, and perhaps even sought, rejection by women. His exalted imagination made him in many cases prefer romantic inaccessibility to actual possession. "Physical pleasure . . . is only of secondary importance to tender and passionate souls," he writes at the beginning of *De l'Amour*. And in his novels, he almost always avoids the subject of physical love, as well as the perhaps more difficult subject of sensuality and tenderness transformed after intimacy.

Even the difficulties of writing provoke in both authors very similar reactions, especially as they face the challenges of autobiography. Evoking memories that still affect him, Rousseau complains that he cannot continue: "The pen falls from my hand." How many times will Stendhal have to interrupt himself before being able to continue *Henry Brulard!* "I had to walk back and forth for a quarter of an hour before being able to resume writing." Both autobiographers admit that they can get the facts wrong, but vouch for the accuracy of their affective memories.

"I may omit facts . . . , be wrong about dates, but I cannot be mistaken about what I felt," writes Rousseau in *Les Confessions*. And Stendhal: "I beg the reader . . . to remember that I lay claim to truthfulness only insofar as my feelings are concerned; I have always had a poor memory for facts." Both are in the habit of speaking about themselves in the third person: "poor Jean-Jacques." In the case of Henri Beyle, this need for self-dramatization gives rise to the numerous pseudonyms of which Dominique, Henry Brulard, and of course Stendhal are merely the most famous. Both assert that they can write only "par passion," and proclaim their essential dilettantism. Stendhal's statement that to write an outline paralyzes him ("faire un plan me glace") echoes Rousseau's statement ("Mon indifférence pour la chose eût glacé ma plume"). And both are profoundly convinced of the ineffable nature of our deeper feelings, in particular of the experience of happiness. "I have always said and felt that true pleasure [*jouissance*] cannot be described," remarks Rousseau. The sentence might have been written by Beyle.[38]

How many of Rousseau's turns, figures of speech, and expressions announce the tone of Stendhal! Referring to his first meeting with Mme de Warens, Rousseau speaks of the unaccountable "sympathie des âmes"; style and circumstances seem to look forward to the early chapter of *Le Rouge et le Noir* which carries the Goethe-inspired title "Les Affinités électives." The "disdainful" Mlle de Breil deigns to cast a flattering glance in the direction of Jean-Jacques much in the same manner as the "disdainful" Mlle de La Mole will gratify the proud plebeian Julien with her eloquent glance. As for the pages Rousseau devotes to his relation with Mme d'Houdetot, they are studded with sentences that might come directly from the writings of Stendhal. The following, for instance, about an amorous conversation during which Jean-Jacques was particularly eloquent: "It was the first and only time in my life; but I was sublime."[39] All one needs is the third-person singular to recreate the admiring authorial comments by which Stendhal, the inveterate ironist, occasionally rewards his heroes, who are often so clumsy in love.

Finally, some of Stendhal's key concepts—his *idées maîtresses*—can be traced back to *Les Confessions*. The most outstanding example is no doubt the prison theme, or rather the theme of freedom discovered in the prison cell. "I have said a hundred times that if I were to be locked up in the Bastille, that is where I would write about freedom." Elsewhere, nostalgically remembering his happiness on the island of Saint-Pierre: "I came to wish that it might be my prison for life [*prison perpétuelle*]." This carceral nostalgia will be fully experienced by Julien Sorel and Fabrice del Dongo, who will learn to love their prison cells and wish to remain there. "Is it not amusing that happiness awaited me in jail?" remarks Fabrice. For it is in prison that Stendhal's heroes experience their most exhilarating moments: love, solitude, memories, superb views, spirituality coupled with poetic fervor. The four prison walls and the panorama glimpsed through the bars become the symbol of the private world of dreams.[40]

Was Stendhal fully aware of being such an assiduous "reader" of Rousseau? Perhaps he was more conscious of the resistance he put up. There are, however, many indications that he was fully, even playfully, aware of his relationship with Rousseau. Is it not reasonable to assume, for instance, that having read Rousseau's reference to his special enemy the mayor of Verrières, M. du Terraux, Stendhal got from *Les Confessions* the name of the little town of *Le Rouge et le Noir*, as well as the idea of casting M. de Rênal—Julien's master and "enemy"—in the role of mayor? More significant is the avowed intentionality of Stendhal's autobiographical project, for it goes to the heart of his life and writing. It is in the following terms that in 1835 he announced a new book to his publisher Levavasseur: "Except for the style, they are *My Confessions*, like Jean-Jacques Rousseau's, but with more candor." The book in question, destined never to be finished, was *Vie de Henry Brulard*.[41]

Vie de Henry Brulard:
Irony and Continuity

Speaking in *Vie de Henry Brulard* of his talent for making enemies, Stendhal mentions his friend Di Fiore, through whom he hoped to discover himself, since the eye cannot see itself (535).[1] According to Stendhal, Di Fiore teased him about his "hidden, or rather poorly hidden, irony, perceptible in spite of [himself] in the right corner of the mouth" (579). Various portraits of Henri Beyle (by Sodermark and Silvestro Valeri; also the pencil drawing by Henri Lehmann) all reveal the slightly raised corner of his mouth, like a horizontal question mark, suggesting a barely contained impulse to mock. But to mock whom and what? The sentence quoted is quite ambivalent: "hidden" but also "poorly hidden" irony; "apparent" irony, but also irony perceptible in spite of himself. The mouth tends toward mockery, but what is the language of the eyes? And what could be meant by involuntary irony? Above all, how can that which is perfectly decipherable—whether apparent or transparent—be ironic?

Many pages later, Stendhal makes a qualifying statement. Once again he mentions Di Fiore, his favorite witness. Having just stressed the permanence of selfhood, the notion of sameness and stable identity, Stendhal writes: "As I was in 1799, so I still am in 1836," and he adds: "I learned to hide all that behind an irony which is not noticeable to ordinary people [*le vulgaire*], but which Fiore accurately perceived" (877). But what is "all that"? Is it his basic character, his unique identity? If so, it must be a poetic identity, since Stendhal has just evoked the figure of Torquato Tasso. Once again, how is one to understand the decipherment of irony? What was "apparent" (or evident) in the earlier passage here becomes imperceptible. Imperceptible to the "common mind," it is true—not to Di Fiore, who as a result appears as the first of the "happy few."

It is obvious that the very notion of irony, lexical as well as contextual, is here more elusive and complex than ever. We are in the habit, especially since the eighteenth century, of reading irony as a critical encoding; we understand it as an offensive weapon, albeit camouflaged. Stendhal is perhaps the great mythographer of the modern sensibility because he has taught us to read irony in its lyrical obliquity, in the service of an emotional and intellectual masquerade, of that which the masquerade hides and which cannot be spoken with impunity. This is not Voltaire's belligerent irony, but an irony that protects and defends.

Could it be that the pseudonym "Stendhal" refers to the most ironic of texts and the least ironic of men? What seems to matter to him, from the start, is to remain impenetrable to the eye of the other, "n'être pas deviné."[2] The need for the mask complements the pleasure of surrendering to romantic illusions. Stendhal himself knows full well that the themes of dissimulation and disguise are at the core of his vocation as a novelist. "I would wear a mask with pleasure, I would change my name with delight," he writes in *Souvenirs d'égotisme*.[3] His literary strategy is that of a proud and, so to speak, spiritualized hedonism; it seeks to veil the tender dreams, playing in the domain of sensations somewhat the same role that understatement plays in his rhetoric. This rhetoric of irony protects what matters most to him, while refusing to indulge in the sin of pompousness—*l'esprit de sérieux*. To read Stendhal means to follow the movement of his style, whose pirouettes, ellipses, and instabilities communicate the *vibrato* so dear to him. Such a style provokes and seduces the reader, making him the accomplice of narrative duplicities. To read Stendhal is an exercise in agility and discontinuity which continually enigmatizes the lyric impulse.

The theories of irony available in the critical marketplace are only moderately useful in dealing with Stendhal's tone and manner. From Aristotle to Schlegel, Kierkegaard, Jankélévitch, Lukács, Harald Weinrich, the deconstructors, Muecke, and Wayne Booth, truth and deception are coupled, in one way or another, in the ironic choreography. But what truth and what deception? The theory that Harald Weinrich proposes in *Linguistics of the Lie* is on the whole rather reassuring. Basing his discussion on the Socratic model of the *Euthyphro*, Weinrich suggests that the efficacy of the *eiron*, the embodiment of *Kleintun* (belittling, giving the appearance of inefficacy), implies a triangular situation and the presence of a witness who, it turns out, is none other but the reader himself.[4] But such an exercise in dissimulation, even if the intellect is in danger of becoming its own spectacle, is essentially in the service of a lesson, a disguised didacticism: *larvato prodeo*. Vladimir Jankélévitch, in *L'Ironie ou la bonne conscience,* would seem to come closer to the spirit of Stendhal: true irony can never be immobilized or petrified ("mé-dusée"). The inversions of the *pro* and the *contra,* the art of saying *yes* in order to communicate *no* (and vice versa), must not become mere automatisms. Viewed in such terms of endless mobility, irony "does not ask to be believed, it wants to be understood"[5]—or, to follow Kierkegaard to his logical conclusion, it wants to be interpreted rather than understood. Such a process knows no respite; it remains at the same time progressive and regressive—the model of a restless herme-neutic movement which never allows one to transcend the undecida-bility of the text.

One can, of course, observe in the work of Stendhal various categories identified by theoreticians of irony: *irony of situation* (Sanseverina's joy-ous outing to the Farnese tower, which will in time become the site of so much of her suffering); *irony of fate* (Julien on his rock meditating on the destiny of his model Napoleon, while in reality his sensibility carries him toward the world of reveries à la Rousseau); *irony of the absurd* (the daydreaming in the "land of ideas" which the prison becomes at the end of *Le Rouge et le Noir*). But how arbitrary such categories and classifications are! It might be more profitable to speak of the ironic questioning of all arbitrariness and all authority, including that of the author and of his text. In that, much like Diderot but in perhaps a more secretive and also more romantic manner, Stendhal remains the un-challenged master. His authorial intrusions, the playfulness of his nar-rators, his instabilities, reticences, elusiveness, usurpations, and silences all contribute to subvert the grammar of his narration, and to frustrate the reader who expects comfortable univocity.

But it is primarily at the level of structural discontinuities that Sten-dhal illustrates fictional irony as Lukács understands it—that is, as the narrative expression of a degraded epic implying the quest for a unity that is no longer possible. In Lukács's terms, the thrust of fiction as a genre is predicated on a perceived absence, and is therefore at the same time impelled toward a future, while attempting to retrieve a lost past. Such bidirectional temporality is essentially ironic. It represents con-flicting perspectives according to which "fragments of reality" remain juxtaposed in their hardness, their incoherence, their separateness.[6]

This fragmentation, these discontinuities, characterize all of Sten-dhal's works, though none more markedly than his autobiographical *Vie de Henry Brulard,* which seeks to embrace the panorama of Rome and the panorama of his life from the height of the Janiculum. But the notion of a panorama is only a pretext in this opening passage. From the beginning, the mobile glance discredits the notion of a referential subject that might be stable and static like a city map. The overview gives way to narration. Time schemes blend and blur. Historical time is juxtaposed to personal time. This gliding from one "time" to another may give the illusion that unity can be achieved under the sign of death and posterity. In reality, Stendhal plays with the possible directions of his life, of any life, and with the multiple faces of destiny. He teaches us what it may mean to treat oneself as a "character," to divide oneself in order to surprise and know oneself, not in the lived act but in the act of writing. He teaches us how to confuse chronology in order to apprehend the operations of time, how to lie in order to invent the truth. Stendhal, in other words, teaches us, by means of irony, that all biography is necessarily a fiction.

For the shift from one temporal dimension to another, the parallelism established between the history of a life and the history of a city, can only bring out the essentially unassimilable nature of lived experience, and the arbitrariness of any imposed order. The parallelism Rome / Henri Beyle lends itself to two favored figures of irony: understatement and amplification. Understatement goes with the trivialization of history ("I fell with Nap[oleon] in April 1814"—*O.I.*, II, 540), but serves more particularly to trivialize the self. Under this general rubric of belittling or minimizing fall those recorded circumstances and remarks that, according to his own statement, prevent him from carrying his head like a holy sacrament.[7] He tells himself aloud that he is about to be fifty, and sings that sentence to a tune of Grétry; he calls himself a "prodigy of ignorance"; he looks down on his work, referring to his autobiography as just a lot of foolishness and nonsense ("galimatias"). He has not the slightest confidence in the posterity of his work: "Where the devil will *Le Rouge* be in 1880? It will have crossed the Styx" (685).

But Stendhal maximizes with the same ironic thrust. It is with deliberately comic amplification that he speaks of his "tyrants" (his family), comparing his struggle for independence with the struggle of the Italian towns in the eighth century. This maximization rests on a whole system of droll parallels. *Comparisons with great men*: his grandfather is likened to a pope founding a library (655); his own taste for quips makes him think of Boccaccio and Vasari; his grief at the death of the manservant Lambert brings to mind Saint John's grief watching his friend and God being crucified (676). *Comparisons with historical events*: young Henry Brulard achieves freedom much as did the communes of the Middle

Ages (711); in 1794, at the age of eleven, he is like the people of Milan in 1835, whom the occupying forces want to prevent from enjoying the beauties of Schiller (745). *Comparisons with works of art* ("I saw myself like Calderón on his military campaigns in Italy"—938): not only have Ariosto and Tasso supposedly shaped his character as a child, and determined his way of seeing a landscape, but the family maid seems to come straight out of a Molière comedy. Stendhal even compares a real person in Grenoble to a fictional character (le père Sorel) in his own novel. A procession of models—Cherubino, Saint-Preux, Tristram Shandy—bridges this tragicomedy of family myths through which the "self-made" Beyle / Stendhal / Brulard tries to establish—*ens causa sui*—the beginning of what he calls his "moral existence" and to create his own origin. The repeated "I am going to be born" ("Je vais naître") proposes a parallel between the meanders of Laurence Sterne's novel and the discontinuities of his own text. It also corresponds to father-hatred and the need for asserting his auto-paternity.

Family breaks and stylistic breaks are also parallel. The principle of discontinuity seems to be omnipresent. A master of disjunction and ellipses, Stendhal imposes *immediacy* at the level of the sentence itself: "I continue this on 23 November 1835!" (534)—"I write when I feel like it"—"But I let myself be carried away, I am getting lost" (538)—"But I anticipate again"—"I should narrate, yet I only jot down *observations*" (547)—"I see a sequence of sharp images" (705). These are the stylistic signals that punctuate the text and establish provocative gaps. The metonymic flow is constantly interrupted, sequentiality is denied, leaving empty spaces which Stendhal himself calls "*les manques.*" The text appears to offer a systematic rejection of any single or unified vision.

Yet the autobiographical quest implicit in the two fictional names Henry Brulard, and in the two initials H.B. belonging to the author who has disappeared in pseudonymity, is doubtless the quest of a consciousness eluding itself in order to seek itself. Temporal discontinuities, as well as the avoidance of sequential narrative order, are paradoxically what allows Beyle / Stendhal to retrieve the underlying psychological and metaphoric structures. The image of the father, projected into lived time, introduces the notion of separation and of a gap; while the image of the mother, an absent presence associated with the interruption that is death, continues to bespeak unity. Stendhal / Brulard insists on chance ("hasard"), on contingency. But chance, by dint of repetitions, also offers an almost Proustian key to significance, and thus denies itself. It is not by chance that young Henry is the only one to have the key to his dead mother's room—a room which becomes for him a refuge, a sanctuary, a place for reverie. It is not by chance that his mother's death corresponds to what he calls his true birth: "There my moral existence truly began" (563). The beginning relates to an end. But more interesting still, the continuity and identity of his psychic life are associated with his mother's death, or rather with his dead mother, precisely because death and desire are linked.

Much has been said and written about the unrepressed Oedipus complex in *Henry Brulard*. But the real interest of the famous passage, where Stendhal recalls his desire as a child to "cover" his naked mother with kisses, is brought out by a remark immediately preceding it concerning a very different woman, Alberthe de Rubempré, who became his mistress some forty years later. The child's erotic model ensures the principle of continuity. Having recourse to one of his favorite images, Stendhal writes: "My manner of hunting happiness [*aller à la chasse du bonheur*] had essentially not at all changed" (556). The permanence and sameness of these erotic patterns, which are also quite Proustian, are metaphorically structured by the coupling of Eros with the death principle. Countess Daru, whom he also loved, and whose identity he conceals under the pseudonym of Mme Petit, died like his mother, he explains, because of an inept obstetrician: "Mme Petit died about the same way in 1814" (562).

As for the metaphoric link between desire and death (or rather, pleasure and death) associated with his father, it is clearly politicized. The overwhelming feature is once again the principle of repetition erasing ironic discontinuities. Stendhal relives that far-distant determining moment, in 1793, in his father's study: they are both seated at a big table (the ten-year-old boy pretending to do his homework, but in reality reading a novel by Prévost) when news of the king's execution arrives. Regicide is immediately perceived as a form of parricide. Young Henry, according to Stendhal, experienced "one of the keenest raptures of joy" he was ever to experience in his life. And he repeats the by now familiar refrain of permanence and sameness: "As I was at the age of ten, so I still am still at the age of fifty-two." And as though to underscore the fact that this continual eroticizing and politicizing characterizes his family myth, Stendhal resorts to his formula of *la chasse du bonheur*, which we have seen associated in a more immediately logical manner with the image of mother and mistress: "in 1793, forty two years ago, I went to hunt for happiness exactly as I do today." And he concludes: "In other words, my character was the same as it is today" (634–635).

But here things become more complicated. For when his Aunt Séra-phie dies, that aunt whom he considers the chief instigator of paternal tyranny, he feels the same raptures of joy he felt upon hearing of the king's death. "I fell on my knees . . . to thank God for this great deliv-erance" (736). The relationship between Eros and politics becomes particularly striking when the legs of this enemy-aunt provoke sexual desire in the young boy, who was later to become such an admirer of Tasso's woman warrior Clorinda: "The legs of my cruelest enemy made a deep impression on me. I would gladly have fallen in love with Séraphie. I imagined the delight of embracing this relentless enemy" (703–705).

What is revealed by this system of repetitions hidden behind apparent textual discontinuities is the specifically Stendhalian association of pol-itics and fiction—an association which at the same time denies irony and exploits its resources. It is both a politicizing of Eros and an erot-icizing of politics: the two faces of Stendhal's fiction are written into the schemes of discontinuities and sameness contained in apparent mu-tual contradiction in the initials H.B. Ultimately even the negation of irony is treated in an ironic mode; the principles of resemblance, iden-tity, and unity (in 1836 he is exactly the same as in 1799) are proposed precisely in relation to irony. "Thus I was in 1799," he writes about his passion for Mozart and his desire to "set down the sounds of [his] soul like musical notes on a printed page" (890). But this musical-literary transfer, which translates writing into an essentially lyric activity, comes right after the passage where "Thus I was in 1799" is intimately bound to the notion of a hidden (though poorly hidden) irony which his friend Di Fiore had no difficulty perceiving (877).

The irony in question could be defined as one that anticipates the irony of the reader—an ironic mask rather than an ironic mechanism, or even an ironic substance. Such irony betrays the fear of irony.[8] Stendhal explains that he was always reluctant to speak of what deeply mattered to him: "the least objection would have pierced my heart" (715). Irony for Stendhal is related to the *unsayable*: the desire to write the score of his inner music ("les sons de mon âme") is exacerbated by the conviction that it remains untranscribable. This stress on musical notation situates Stendhal's sensibility at the frontier of literature, that borderline zone of instability where writing invents itself.

The implicit questioning of literature as act or gesture is not the least ironic aspect of Stendhal's work. The conventional relationship of lived experience and written text is here inverted. Stendhal's autobiographical voice does not define the self; it answers the *what have I been?* by another question, in the present tense of the writing act: *what am I?* The heuristic act of writing creates the self. Stendhal teaches us that the desire to know oneself is first and foremost the desire to construct oneself, that the self is cosubstantial with the act of writing. The writer's consciousness becomes a private stage on which the masquerade of being is constantly rehearsed. Such a theater of self-multiplication and of constant surprises is also the theater of creative irresolution. For the non-ironic unity that irony hides can manifest itself only through an ironic and dynamic instability that remains at the same time a thematic and a structural presence.

T. S. Eliot and the Romantic Heresy

> We condemn the literature of the nineteenth century because it is
> *romantic* . . . —And why is it *romantic?*—Because it is the
> literature of the nineteenth century.
>
> Victor Hugo, 1824 preface to *Odes et Ballades*

"Heresy" is a harsh and uncomfortable word; it implies orthodoxy, smacks of inquisition, points to excommunication. It is a word for which the dogmatic mind shows a permanent fondness. Lifted out of its theological context, it has been made to serve many masters. Literary criticism, not always the most tolerant of avocations, long ago appropriated the term with considerable zest. Baudelaire, inspired by Poe's oft-quoted attack against the "heresy of the didactic," pontificated against the heresy of progress, the heresy of the long poem, the heresy of passion, truth and morality in poetic art. But it remains T. S. Eliot's achievement to have given the term wide circulation in contemporary criticism. *A Primer in Heresy* is the subtitle of a book—originally a series of lectures—in which Eliot not only expresses his aversion to our society worm-eaten with liberalism (he proclaims the undesirability of free-thinking Jews and the dangers of "excessive" tolerance), but also suggests, surreptitiously towing literature in the wake of his admiration for the agrarian South and its homogeneous population, that classicism is to Romanticism what orthodoxy is to heterodoxy.[1] With characteristic humility—perhaps embarrassed by that pontifical solemnity of which he once accused himself—Eliot goes on to concede that heresy is of course appealing, that heretics are frequently endowed with acute perception. Are not most of us heretical to some degree? Yet the term appears to be necessary to distinguish the bad from the good: whether in the early essays of *The Sacred Wood,* or in the later ones of *The Use of Poetry and the Use of Criticism,* we find the term pointing to the Romantic deviators. For sinners and deviators they all are. Coleridge, Goethe, Shelley, Wordsworth, and even D. H. Lawrence—the list is obviously incomplete. "They belong with the numbers of the great heretics of all time."[2] And where there is heresy, there must of course be denunciation. The inevitable excommunication was hurled as early as in *The Sacred Wood* (Methuen, 1920, p. 32): "there may be a good deal to be said for Romanticism in life, there is no place for it in letters."

It has been maliciously suggested that Eliot follows the classical dogma not so much because he cherishes classicism but because he cherishes dogma. In fact, the identification of the religious attitude with classicism (the "sane classical dogma of original sin") goes back to T. E. Hulme, and via Eliot has been taken up, particularly in America, by Allan Tate and the entire group of zealous anti-Romantics known as the New Critics. Enemies of this group have accused Eliot of being responsible for this "new criticism," which by means of a jargon of its own and a forced interpretation of images seeks to view every writer it admires as a dabbler in theology, a preacher of Christian morals, or at the least as a reactionary witness to the collapse of modern civilization.[3] More soberly, Frederick A. Pottle has in a shrewd article exposed the arbitrariness of their method, their strong polemical bias, their misreadings and under-readings of the poets whose reputations they wish to demolish.[4] Certainly dogma is one of their prime concerns. Robert Wooster Stallman, the editor of what amounts to an anthology of "new criticism," defines criticism as "the positing and criticizing of dogmas."[5] It is not surprising that "heresy," applied to Romanticism, should be one of the key words for those critics also. Referring to Cleanth Brooks's *Modern Poetry and the Tradition,* Mr. Stallman describes what he considers a critical synthesis of the modern "revolution" in our conception of poetry: "The revolution, in sum, has consisted chiefly in a return to the Metaphysicals and hence in a repudiation of their *heretical deviators*: the Augustan Neo-Classicists, who regarded metaphor as a decoration of poetic thought-content; and the nineteenth century Romantics, who discredited irony or wit (the essential ingredient of Metaphysical poetry) and regarded poetry as an elevated way of expressing elevated beliefs." It might conceivably be amusing—though I do not believe it would yield any startlingly new observations—to trace the uses of this term in the hands of this body of writers. Thus Cleanth Brooks himself, probably the most gifted among the practicing New Critics, used it with reference to Yvor Winters, whom he accuses of "paraphrastic heresy" in a chapter of *The Well Wrought Urn* appropriately entitled "The Heresy of the Paraphrase." More interesting, no doubt, and more profitable also, would be a study of the New Critics' deep-rooted need to justify art as an independently valid activity. Their flourishing in the Anglo-Saxon world, and particularly in the context of American society, is certainly not a coincidence, and does cast a meaningful light on their repeated affirmation that literature *has* its place, though it is not a substitute for religion, morality, or even thought. Their belief that art is an autotelic activity, or—as Allan Tate has put it—a cognition at least equally valid with that of the scientific method, closely echoes many a pronouncement by T. S. Eliot. Not only their anti-Romanticism, but also these concepts are all to be found in Eliot's body of critical writings.

But what of the anti-Romantic influences to which Eliot himself has been exposed? Three names come to mind: Irving Babbitt, who had been his teacher at Harvard; T. E. Hulme, whom he was to meet in London; Charles Maurras, editor of *L'Action Française,* with whose ideas he presumably became familiar during his stay in Paris in 1910, at the very moment the sterile doctrines of neoclassicism were enjoying prestige in certain literary and political circles of the French capital.

It is Irving Babbitt, the great authority on the will to refrain, who introduced him to the French tradition. From the high priest of "Humanism" he not only learned that expansive emotions are dangerous and that the inner voice is something like whiggery, but also that Romanticism, and particularly Jean-Jacques Rousseau, is to be held responsible for most of our modern ills. According to the author of *Rousseau and Romanticism,* the greatest contribution, and sin, of the nineteenth century was to have seen the supreme good in the supreme thrill, and to have peopled the world of literature with hordes of "glorious rascals." T. S. Eliot was probably a better disciple than Babbitt expected, for very soon he was to move to positions far more extreme than those occupied by his master. He criticized Babbitt's addiction to Confucius, and in general found that Babbitt was not quite narrow enough. "The very width of his culture, his intelligent eclecticism, are themselves symptoms of a narrowness of tradition, in their extreme reaction against narrowness."[6] In a now famous essay on the Humanism of Babbitt, he paradoxically suggested that Babbitt *knew too much.* (One is reminded of Gerontion's complaint: "After such knowledge, what forgiveness?") Eliot still hoped that Babbitt might join forces with the reactionary Charles Maurras, which, one may suppose, enchanted Babbitt even less than the subsequent accusation of being nearer to the view of Rousseau than to the religious view.[7]

In T. E. Hulme, Eliot doubtlessly found a more virulent and a more dogmatic master. The reputation of Hulme as a sort of precocious and oracular genius—a reputation further enhanced by his untimely death and by the fragmentary nature of his writings—is important primarily as a rallying point, and has already become part of English literary history. Hulme was an *excitateur*, and his collected essays, *Speculations*, disappointing though they are, served as an anti-Romantic manifesto for an entire generation of writers and critics who combined a pseudoreligious concept of classicism with a solid contempt for democracy. Hulme proclaimed the superiority of fancy over the imagination, and prophesied the death of "damp" poetry and the coming of a new classical age. From Hulme (himself influenced by Maurras, Lasserre, and the group from *L'Action Française*) Eliot learned that the words "classic" and "Romantic" had a political connotation, and that Romanticism both in England and in France was associated with "certain political views,"[8] particularly with the absurd and wholly negative idea of "liberty" and the laughable notion that progress would come of chaos. Hulme was even more damning than Babbitt: according to him Rousseau had been directly responsible for the French Revolution. On the "spiritual" level, Romanticism meant of course complete failure, or worse: a "spilt religion." The classical view, on the other hand, in harmony with Christian theology, stood for the sane dogma of original sin and regarded man as an "extraordinarily fixed and limited animal whose nature is absolutely constant."[9] Hence the need for tradition, discipline, and institutions: only they can get anything decent out of so thoroughly perverted a being as man. That T. S. Eliot was impressed by Hulme's pronouncements is evidenced by the lengthy quotations he strategically placed in at least three important essays. At the end of his essay on Baudelaire (whom he sees groping his way into Christianity by the back door of satanism), Eliot quotes a paragraph by Hulme dealing with "discipline," "institutions," and "original sin," with the prefatory remark that Baudelaire "would have approved." Similarly, the essay entitled "Second Thoughts about Humanism" ends with another quotation, again about original sin, the wretchedness of man, and the need for dogma—this time with the concluding remark that liberal theologians (and others) "would do well to ponder" Hulme's statement. But though Eliot recognizes Hulme's aptitude for theology, he does not forget that he had also been a poet and a critic. Thus we are regaled with another long quotation from Hulme—this time proclaiming the need for precision—in the concluding chapter of *The Use of Poetry and the Use of Criticism* (p. 149). As for political liberalism and the notion of progress, Eliot never ceased sharing Hulme's contempt for these manifestations of the Romantic heresy.

This brings me to Charles Maurras. Eliot's stay in Paris (1910–

1911)—he was studying philosophy and French literature at the Sorbonne—coincides with the revival of French neoclassicism. In 1908, the *Revue Critique des Idées et des Livres* was founded. *Les Marges* became a regular periodical in 1909. But most of all, *L'Action Française* had recently grown into an important daily paper. It is not clear at what time Eliot began reading Maurras, but thirteen years later, in a "Lettre d'Angleterre" (*Nouvelle Revue Française,* November 1923), Eliot acknowledged his debt to Maurras, referring to *L'Avenir de l'intelligence* as one of the books that had exerted the greatest influence on his intellectual development. *L'Avenir de l'intelligence*, little read today, is a pungent, polemical essay in which Maurras, after some preliminary comments about the degeneration of culture (Jews now attempt to understand Racine!), proceeds to lace into Rousseau (who usurped the attributes of king and priest), and concludes by advocating a holy alliance with the traditional forces of the army and the clergy to ward off further corruption and prepare the way for a counterrevolution. Eliot was sufficiently impressed by Maurras's prose to lift a bit of satiric dialogue from the very first page and use it to conclude with a flourish the first section of his Coriolan ("Et les soldats faisaient la haie? ILS LA FAISAIENT"). As to Maurras's *Prologue d'un essai sur la critique,* first published in 1896 in the *Revue Encyclopédique Larousse* but reprinted later, Eliot certainly read it with great care. The dignity of criticism; the distinction between *real* criticism on the one hand, and descriptive, historical, philological, and moral criticism on the other; the insistence on taste, order, tradition—these ideas are constantly echoed by Eliot. In January 1926, in an editorial for *Criterion,* he defined the "modern tendency" in the following terms: "I believe that the modern tendency is toward something which, for want of a better name, we may call classicism . . . There is a tendency—discernable even in art—toward a higher and clearer conception of Reason, and a more severe and serene control of the emotions by Reason." The passage obviously echoes Maurras's demand for a "sensibilité réfléchie."[10]

Eliot even translated the *Prologue*—though not always faithfully— and printed his translation in *Criterion* (January and March 1928). "We must bring things back to Malherbe" is Maurras's final verdict, and Eliot approved wholeheartedly. As to the political significance of Maurras, Eliot, strangely enough, saw in him a protection against fascism. During the same month that he published the second installment of his translation, he wrote in *Criterion*: "if anything, in another generation or so, is to preserve us from a sentimental Anglo-Fascism, it will be some system of ideas which will have gained much from the study of Maurras."[11] In the light of Maurras's subsequent activities these words are not without irony, though an unbiased reader might, even then, have found them somewhat humorous.

IT WOULD be foolish, of course, to assert that Eliot did not understand Romanticism. He not only understood it, but *felt* it. His account of Romantic sadness—"the fact that no human relations are adequate to human desires, but also . . . the disbelief in any further object for human desires than that which, being human, fails to satisfy them"[12]—is penetrating, and so are his remarks, in his Harvard lectures, concerning the poet's need to transcend beauty and ugliness in order to explore boredom and horror. In an article on George Wyndham, Eliot even made some explicit concessions. Referring to the Ulysses episode in the *Divina Commedia* and to man's yearning for knowledge and adventure—

. . . l'ardore
Ch' i' ebbi a divenir del mondo esperto,
E de li vizi umani e del valore—

he admitted that what is permanent and good in Romanticism is *curiosity*, "a curiosity which recognizes that any life, if accurately and profoundly penetrated, is interesting and always strange."[13] But here the concession ends; the following sentence already implies a retraction: "Romanticism is a short cut to the strangeness without the reality, and it leads its disciples back upon themselves." "Reality" has, it goes without saying, a special meaning in this context which can perhaps best be elucidated by placing beside it this brief statement from *After Strange Gods*: "Hopkins has the dignity of the church behind him, and is consequently in closer contact with reality."[14] Dogma and the need for impersonality in art are the two primary criteria by which Romanticism is tried and condemned.

The call for the depersonalization of the artist is part of what one might call the "literary" condemnation of Romanticism. We all remember the dicta in the early essay "Tradition and the Individual Talent":

The progress of an artist is a continual self-sacrifice, a continual extinction of personality.

The more perfect the artist, the more completely separate in him will be the man who suffers and the mind which creates.

The difference between art and the event is always absolute.

The poet, according to this "impersonal theory" of poetry, does not have a personality to express: he is a *medium*, and his mind perhaps only a catalyst. Art is not the overflow of emotions, and bursts of passion are as disastrous as moral fervor (art is "post-ethical" rather than ethical, as J. C. Ransom later confirmed). These notions are of course not unrelated to Eliot's own moral and religious preoccupations. The cult of individuality is deplored in the "Primer in Heresy" (*After Strange Gods*, p. 35), and so is the idea that passion is what is most *real* in man (again the ambiguous use of the concept of "reality"): "it is by no means self-evident that human beings are most real when most violently excited." Finally, still on the "literary" level, Eliot's militant predilection for Donne and the Metaphysicals, as well as his infatuation with the post-Romantic French poets Baudelaire, Jules Laforgue, Tristan Corbière (whom he considers anti-Romantics), explain why he sees Romanticism as a deviation from the main literary tradition, the most important deviators have been Rousseau, Shelley, Hugo, and Milton before them, who, of course, all deserve to be repudiated and dislodged. England, which has "produced a prodigious number of men of genius and comparatively few works of art,"[15] is in a way even guiltier than France in its glorification of the self-centered Great Man.

The literary criteria for wanting to set the clock back to Donne or Malherbe (since little or nothing could be preserved from the Romantic lumber room) are not unrelated to more strictly dogmatic criteria—social, moral, and religious. The age of Romanticism represents for Eliot the age of political liberalism, "an age of bustle, programmes, platforms, scientific progress, humanitarianism and revolutions which improved nothing, an age of progressive degradation" (*Selected Essays*, p. 342). This is the age into which a Baudelaire had the misfortune to be born! If Eliot is irritated by a Shelley or a Hugo, it is not only because they write imprecise or, as Hulme would have it, damp poetry, but also because the beliefs they hold—pantheism, faith in progress, liberalism—are unpalatable to him, though he prefers not even to discuss these beliefs, but rather to dismiss these poets as "immature." "Maturity," like "reality," thus acquires a very special meaning in Eliot's vocabulary, a meaning which has been preserved by the New Critics, and which makes it possible to apply to any work of literature extra-literary standards without appearing to do so. Most of all, however, Eliot discovers in Romanticism a denial of original sin and views it as a consequence of eighteenth-century Rationalism. In this lumping together of Romanticism with eighteenth-century thought, Eliot again echoes his masters Babbitt and Maurras, though he may also owe a debt to Baudelaire, whose "Eloge du maquillage," with its assertion of the nonnaturalness of virtue, he must have perused with the keenest of interest.

The "dogmatic" and "literary" criteria fail, however, to reveal the more strictly personal and idiosyncratic element in Eliot's aversion to Romantic poetry. Those familiar with Eliot's critical writings must have been struck by the recurrence of the terms "maturity" and "immaturity," terms that have taken their place among the key words of Eliot's vocabulary. The famous definition of classicism and Romanticism (*Selected Essays*, p. 15)—"the difference seems to me rather the difference between the complete and the fragmentary, the adult and the immature, the orderly and the chaotic"—ushers in a whole series of dispersed comments that seek to associate Romanticism with the adolescent mind. In the early essay "Hamlet and his Problems," Eliot had already referred to that "intense feeling, ecstatic or terrible, without an object or exceeding its object" which every person of sensibility has experienced and which, though it often occurs in adolescence, ought nevertheless to be a study for pathologists.[16] Perhaps the greatest insult Eliot ever directed against Shelley was to call him an "intelligent and enthusiastic schoolboy."[17] Poe was likewise accused of "puerile thinking" and of having the intellect of a "highly gifted young person before puberty."[18]

More significant still than these accusations of "immaturity" is the verdict that these poets can be enjoyed only so long as the reader himself remains an adolescent. When Eliot pointed out that *at one period of his life* he did enjoy Swinburne, but now no longer enjoys him—that was about the most devastating comment of which he was capable. Few things are more strongly developed in Eliot than his need for repudiating his early tastes. "I was intoxicated by Shelley's poetry at the age of fifteen," he declared in his Harvard lectures.[19] And not only by Shelley but, so we learn, by Byron, Keats, Rossetti, Swinburne, the border ballads, and Fitzgerald's *Omar*. Yet the intoxication was short-lived. In the pages dealing with the development of taste, he reveals that his twenty-second year marked the end of this "romantic" period, adding with some contempt that this period "is one beyond which I dare say many people never advance" (pp. 33–34). The only legitimate pleasure that Eliot grants the "mature" reader of a Shelley or a Byron is that of sentimentally recapturing the excitement: the memory of an enjoyment. "Shelley has marked an intense period before maturity, but for how many does Shelley remain the companion of age?" (p. 89). Romantic poetry, in other words, belongs to a particular period of life when the interest in poetry has just awakened. Violent, exuberant, ecstatic, full of supernatural wonders, despair, and flights of speculation that delight the preadolescent mentality, Romanticism is comparable to the *âge ingrat* which every healthy boy is expected to outgrow.

But this need to outgrow one's youth (in itself a most non-Romantic notion) is also symptomatic, it seems to me, of a certain more hidden aspect of Eliot's personality. To be sure, the world of childhood, or even of adolescence, is of little interest to the classical mind. Socially, as well as literarily, the child was to a contemporary of Louis XIV little more than a being who had not yet become quite human. "The child is father to the man"—the very thought is hardly conceivable before the late eighteenth century. With Eliot, however, the lack of interest is only the façade: behind it lies hidden what seems to be a very real fear, or at least a deep distrust, of childhood and adolescence. Childhood with its spontaneous, irresponsible, frequently cruel manifestations; puberty and adolescence with their yearnings, perverse curiosity, and sexual awakening seem to be distasteful to Eliot's mind. His imagination, unless it be for satiric or sardonic effects, shuns the very memory of these emotions and seems to endow them with a sense of shame and even guilt. The dirty old waiter's reminiscences of his first sexual awareness at the age of seven, in "Dans le restaurant,"

> Je la chatouillais, pour la faire rire.
> J'éprouvais un instant de puissance et de délire

do not exactly provoke the approbation of the imaginary listener:

> Mais alors, vieux lubrique . . .

and even suggest a sense of guilt:

> Mais alors, tu as ton vautour!

Certainly the glorification of adolescence which is inherent in Romanticism—or at least the analysis of its problems which are *taken seriously* appears to be strongly repugnant to Eliot's sensibility. His young men tend rather to be spiritually empty and carbuncular.

II

Reactions to Eliot's critical ideas have on occasion been violent. Edmund Wilson accused him of pedantry and futile aestheticism.[20] A more bitter and also more superficial critic, Louis Grudin, complained of his "impulsive dogma" and "dialectical irresponsibility."[21] Louis Kronenberger, in an article for *The Nation* (April 1935, pp. 452–453), called him a pedant, a hairsplitter, a snob—and worst of all, a believer in the letter. Norman Foerster, who placed Eliot in the same category with more recent critics such as J. C. Ransom and Cleanth Brooks, accused him of limiting our conception of literature and of going to the other extreme of didactic criticism. In 1943, Yvor Winters stated that Eliot's influence was "the most dangerous and nearly the least defensible of our time."[22] More recently, G. Rostrevor Hamilton, in a suggestive and ingenious book, *The Telltale Article* (Heinemann, 1949), blamed Eliot for seeing man *small* and constantly proposing a depressing and unromantic view of humanity. But the most violent, though also the most disorganized onslaught has come from Albert Mordell, who not only considers Eliot's influence detrimental to culture and literature, but proceeds to compare him with such unflattering models of another day as Gifford of the *Quarterly Review*, Jeffrey of the *Edinburgh Review*, Wilson and Lockart of *Blackwoods*, and Robert Southey.

The very violence of these reactions is partial testimony to Eliot's success as a critic. Bias—in the worst as well as in the best sense of the word—has been his aim and his strength. Certainly he has fulfilled Baudelaire's requirement that criticism be biased, impassioned, and partisan. Remy de Gourmont played a considerable part in confirming Eliot's early notion that criticism is a *sacerdoce*, and the true critic ("rarer still than the great poet") a creator of values.[23] "I was much stimulated and much helped by the writings of Remy de Gourmont. I acknowledge that influence, and am grateful for it," he wrote in the preface to the 1928 edition of *The Sacred Wood*. He particularly admired *Le Problème du style*, in which he discovered the following prefiguration of his own theories on impersonality and "maturity" in art: "Life is a sloughing-off. The aim of man's proper activity is to cleanse his personality, to purge it of all the impurities that education may have left there, to remove all the traces of our adolescent admirations."[24] As a creator of values, Eliot hoped to take his place among the ranks of the English poet-critics: Dryden, Coleridge, Arnold. He felt keenly that since Matthew Arnold the sacerdotal functions had been neglected, that a new creator of values was needed who would speak for his generation and undo the damage done by *Literature and Dogma*. Much of Eliot's anti-Romanticism has to be judged in the light of his *sense of mission*.

To see it in this light does not, however, overcome the reader's irritation and urge to contradict. The entire notion of tradition as expounded by Eliot is flagrantly arbitrary: why leave Romanticism out? Eliot's admiration for certain manifestations of twentieth-century French neoclassicism resembles the infatuation of a neophyte. Few movements have been as out of touch with their time as this revival. One need only read the controversy between Raymond de La Tailhède and Charles Maurras published by Pierre Constans (*Un Débat sur le romantisme*, Flammarion, 1928) to be impressed by the utter futility of the arguments presented. But worse still, no outstanding work, not even of criticism, has come from this revival apparently doomed from the very start to sterility. Moreover, the very satisfaction of having "broken" with the past appears to us now like an illusion. Already in 1928, Gérard Bauër was able to detect how much their political attitudes, their proclamations, the arrogant individualism of their leaders, their seductive appeal owed to Romanticism.[25] Yet they too, in spite of their fierce nationalism, were ready to eradicate without a qualm the two centuries stretching from Rousseau to Bergson. Only on his deathbed was a Jean Moréas willing to concede the stupidity of it all: "Classique, romantique—des bêtises que tout cela."

Eliot's conviction that Romanticism was not concerned with the problem of evil and the sense of sin is equally open to debate. This theory stems partly from a lumping together of Romanticism with the rationalistic thought of the pre-Revolutionary writers. It displays, at any rate, a willful deafness to the clear Pascalian undertones of much that was written by a Vigny, a Leopardi, or a Baudelaire.

On the subject of Baudelaire, Charles Maurras was unquestionably more perspicacious than Eliot. "I believe that I can and must maintain that Baudelaire is a disease of our sensibility,"[26] meaning thereby that he was a Romantic, or, as Sainte-Beuve put it, the author of a bizarre and artificial work at the extreme outpost of a Romantic Kamchatka. Eliot, on the other hand, fascinated by *Les Fleurs du mal* and perhaps even more by the intimate writings of Baudelaire, has heroically attempted to rescue him from his period, perhaps even from himself. He has tried to suggest that Baudelaire, though inevitably the offspring of Romanticism and doomed to work with the materials on hand, was a classicist by nature, and the first counter-Romantic in poetry. His prostitutes, cats, Jewesses, and corpses were merely props: the *real* Baudelaire is to be found in his acedia "arising from the unsuccessful struggle towards the spiritual life" (*Selected Essays,* p. 339). The attempt to demonstrate that Baudelaire was "essentially Christian" (not because he practiced Christianity, but because he asserted its necessity) once again points to the inveterate habit of identifying the religious attitude with classicism.

To be sure, Baudelaire scorned the "gigantic absurdity" of the idea of progress, abused the sentimental materialism of a Heine, and proclaimed the natural *méchanceté* or perversity of man. As an artist, he abhorred rhetoric, shunned the mere tour de force, preferred simple language, displayed a talent for axiomatic lines, and frequently recaptured the transparency and musicality of Racinian verse. His quasi-theological concept of the nonnaturalness of virtue, as well as his Poe-insired notion of the impersonality of great poetry, contributed to endear him to Eliot. And yet he was far more of a Romantic than Eliot is willing to grant.

First as poet: the erotic exoticism, the urge to escape "anywhere out of the world," the debauches of the imagination, the sense of victimhood and the prophetic affirmation of the poet's destiny and suffering, the taste for the perverse, the dolorism and mania to blacken himself, the curiosity stretching to the point of wishing to be both the tortured and the torturer—these are not exactly classical virtues, nor do they express the serenity that we have come to associate with the Olympian mind. Sartre's cruel dissection of Baudelaire's brand of "immaturity" (his need for judges, his notion of evil as a luxury, his onanistic attitude toward love) constitutes a valuable corrective to Eliot's vision of the author of *Fusées* as a discarnate spirit groping for a back door to Christianity. Baudelaire's debt to Romanticism is not merely a matter of props!

Can we ignore Baudelaire's explicit statements? "My heart is filled with gratitude and love for the famous men who have surrounded me with their friendship and advice," he wrote in an impassioned letter to *Le Figaro* (June 1858), leaving no doubt as to who had been the masters of his youth. Did he not proclaim elsewhere that Romanticism was a celestial (or infernal) grace to which we all owed eternal stigmata? Who but an admirer of Stendhal could bluntly have stated that Romanticism is "the most recent, the most up-to-date expression of the beautiful," adding (this being even more Romantic than Stendhal) that this new conception of beauty implied "intimacy, spirituality, color, longing for the infinite."[27] And how well he spoke of Balzac, in whom he unerringly admired precisely that which is most admirable: "Oh, Honoré de Balzac, you the most heroic, the strangest, the most romantic, and the most poetic among all the creatures that you have begotten!" How many *implicit* Romantic views clutter his prose! Like Balzac, he perceived the wonder of city life: Paris was to him pregnant with poetry and strangeness. "Le merveilleux nous enveloppe et nous abreuve," he wrote in the *Salon de 1846*. Yet in the midst of this pulsating city, he dreamt of the arrogant loneliness of the pariah. "When I will have inspired universal horror and contempt, I will have achieved loneliness" (*Fusées*). Wagner's ardent and "despotic" music revealed itself to him as a dizzying dream world more potent than a drug: "les vertigineuses conceptions de l'opium." To artists, he attributed the *fatality* of genius; male beauty he endowed with sadness, mystery, and satanic grandeur; modern life—equalitarian, desolate, and grimacing—impressed him with its as yet unexploited epic proportions. But above all, he conceived of greatness striding alone. Even in pleasure. "Le vrai héros s'amuse tout seul" (*Mon Cœur mis à nu*).

Eliot's astigmatic approach to Baudelaire is a typical case of dilution and willful misreading. Only it is ironic that, after blaming Goethe and Coleridge for having metamorphosed Hamlet into a flattering image of themselves, he should in turn have succumbed to the temptation of rescuing Baudelaire from the sinful aberrations of his Romantic milieu, and proceeded to endow Baudelaire's work with virtues that we are more willing to read into his own.

To CHALLENGE the neoclassical view of literature should merely be the first step toward a fairer reassessment of the Romantic writers. There is indeed a more permanent and "finer" Romanticism than the one we frequently choose to hold up as an example. The need for reevaluation is particularly felt in the field of French letters, where the first wave of poets, at the beginning of the nineteenth century, was handicapped by its schooling in rhetoric and the necessity to imitate prose writers.[28] Without sharing Alex Comfort's extreme enthusiasm for the Romantic ideology of "responsible disobedience," we can, I believe, affirm—or reaffirm—the *moral* contents of Romanticism, the awareness of the tragic and one-sided struggle between the physical world in which man exists and the particular qualities which make up humaneness: mind, purpose, consciousness, will, and personality.[29] Cocteau's quip that the heart no longer is fashionable ("le cœur ne se porte plus") applies only to the sentimental and probably most vulnerable aspect of Romanticism. There has been not only a continuity, but a revival and exploitation in depth of much that is Romantic in the best sense of the word: the feeling of anguish and instability, the awareness of the absurd, the view of man as a creator of values. Except that Romanticism has become more cerebral, and in the process more self-critical, too. We blush more easily and prefer ambiguities. We disavow our heritage and rebel against ourselves. A bond links us with the great Romantics: we communicate with them through anguish and irony. Were not the very neoclassicists fervent admirers of Stendhal? The most fervent, perhaps. There is something paradoxical, but also highly revealing, in their learning *Le Rouge et le Noir* by heart.

Notes
Credits
Index

Notes

Approaches

1. Marcel Proust, *A la Recherche du temps perdu* (Paris: Pléiade, 1954), III, p. 911. Montaigne, *Essais* (Paris: Pléiade, 1933), p. 647.
2. Max Frisch, *Stiller* (Frankfurt and Hamburg: Fischer Bücherei, 1966), p. 249.
3. T. S. Eliot, "Tradition and the Individual Talent," in *Selected Essays: 1917–1932* (New York: Harcourt, Brace, 1932), p. 9.
4. Virginia Woolf, *A Room of One's Own* (New York: Harcourt Brace Jovanovich, 1957), p. 83.
5. Jorge Luis Borges, "Pierre Menard, Author of the *Quixote*," in *Labyrinths* (New York: New Directions, 1964), p. 44.
6. Charles Baudelaire, "Richard Wagner et 'Tannhäuser' à Paris," in *Oeuvres complètes* (Paris: Pléiade, 1961), p. 1215. André Malraux, *L'Espoir* (Paris: Gallimard, 1937), p. 284.
7. T. S. Eliot, *Four Quartets* (New York: Harcourt, Brace, 1943), p. 7.
8. Borges, "Tlön, Uqbar, Orbis Tertius," in *Labyrinths*, pp. 17–18.

Opening Signals in Narrative

1. The text, now out of print, was published with amusing illustrations, some of which were by Aragon himself, in the attractive collection *Les Sentiers de la création* (Geneva: Albert Skira, 1969).
2. Frank Kermode, *The Sense of an Ending: Studies in the Theory of Fiction* (New York: Oxford University Press, 1967), pp. 6, 8, 53, 67, 133, 140.
3. Jean-Paul Sartre, *La Nausée* (Paris: Gallimard, 1938), pp. 60–63.
4. See Joseph Frank's presentation of Lessing's views and his own brilliant discussion of spatialization in "Spatial Form in Modern Literature," in *The Widening Gyre: Crisis and Mastery in Modern Literature* (New Brunswick, N.J.: Rutgers University Press, 1963).
5. This paragraph and the following lean heavily on my preface to Michael Issacharoff, *L'Espace et la nouvelle* (Paris: Corti, 1976).
6. "Pour une socio-critique ou variations sur un Incipit," *Littérature* 1 (February 1971): 5–14.
7. "Commencements romanesques," in *Le Roman contemporain* (Paris: Klincksieck, 1971).
8. "Modalités de la narration dans 'La Route des Flandres,'" *Poétique* 14 (1973): 234–249.
9. "Novels: Recognition and Deception," *Critical Inquiry* 1 (September 1974): 103–122. Mention should also be made of Ian Watt, "The First Paragraph of *The Ambassadors:* An Explication," *Essays in Criticism* 10 (1960):

250–274. See also Steven G. Kellman, "Grand Openings and Plain: The Poetics of First Lines," *SubStance* 17 (1977): 139–147.

10. "Muse und Helios: "Über epische Anfangsnöte und -weise," in *Romananfänge,* ed. Norbert Miller (Berlin: Literarisches Colloquium, 1965).

11. "Die Rolle des Erzählers: Zum Problem des Romananfangs im 18. Jahrhundert," in Miller, *Romananfänge,* pp. 37–91.

12. "Structures narratives du mythe," *Poétique* 1 (1970): 25–34.

13. *S/Z* (Paris: Seuil, 1970), pp. 24–29.

14. *Beginnings* (New York: Basic Books, 1975).

15. *Les Travailleurs de la mer* (Paris: Club Français du Livre, 1969), XII, 685.

16. *Le Mythe de l'éternel retour* (Paris: Gallimard, 1949), pp. 12–19, 209, 216–220, 240.

17. "Littérature, générativité de la phrase," in *La Place de la madeleine* (Paris: Mercure de France, 1974). See also Gaëtan Picon's interesting comments on the first sentence, in *Lecture de Proust* (Paris: Mercure de France, 1963), pp. 22–25.

18. "Discours du récit," in *Figures III* (Paris: Seuil, 1972).

19. Genette refers here to Günther Müller, "Erzählzeit und Erzählte Zeit," in *Festschrift für Kluckhorn* (1948), reprinted in Günther Müller, *Morphologische Poetik* (Tübingen: M. Niemeyer), 1968.

20. Kellman, "Grand Openings and Plain."

21. I borrow this expression from Michael Riffaterre.

22. See the note by Pierre-Georges Castex in his edition of *Le Père Goriot* (Paris: Garnier, 1963), pp. 6–7.

Natalie, or Balzac's Hidden Reader

1. The page numbers in parentheses refer to *Le Lys dans la vallée* (Paris: Garnier, 1966). Italics are mine, except when otherwise indicated.

2. For a presentation of the genesis of the text, see Moïse le Yaouanc in the Garnier edition, 1966.

3. Roland Barthes has shown how, in certain cases, *comme* may refer to the specific concerns of the reader, signaling a displaced voice which the reader attributes to the discourse by proxy. *S/Z* (Paris: Seuil, 1970), p. 157.

La Peau de chagrin

1. *La Peau de chagrin,* ed. Maurice Allem (Paris: Garnier, 1955, p. 102).

2. *Le Père Goriot,* ed. Pierre-Georges Castex (Paris: Garnier, 1960), p. 309.

3. *La Peau de chagrin,* pp. 6, 9.

4. *Ibid.,* p. 6.

5. Erich Auerbach, "In the Hôtel de la Mole," in *Mimesis: The Representation of Reality in Western Literature* (New York: Doubleday Anchor, 1957). See in particular the section dealing with *Le Père Goriot,* pp. 413–425.

6. *La Peau de chagrin,* p. 29.

7. *Illusions perdues* (Paris: Garnier-Flammarion, 1966), pp. 362, 224.

8. "Des Artistes," in Balzac, *Oeuvres complètes* (Paris: Conard, 1912–1940),

XXXVIII, 351–360. *Lettres à l'Etrangère* (Paris: Calmann-Lévy, 1899–1950), I, 202, 355–356.

9. *La Peau de chagrin,* p. 77.

10. *Ibid.,* p. 41.

Hugo's *William Shakespeare*

1. All page numbers in parentheses refer to Victor Hugo, *Oeuvres complètes,* ed. Jean Massin, XII (Paris: Club Français du Livre, 1967–1970).

2. See the "Prospectus" for *William Shakespeare* prepared by his Belgian publishers, Lacroix and Verboeckhoven, with important changes made by Hugo. *Oeuvres complètes,* XII, 358.

3. See Henri Peyre, *Qu'est-ce que le symbolisme?* (Paris: Presses Universitaires de France, 1974), pp. 10, 117.

4. On the theological echoes of the word "immanent" in Hugo's vocabulary, see Yves Gohin, *Sur l'emploi des mots immanent et immanence chez Victor Hugo* (Paris: Archives des Lettres Modernes, 1968).

5. The difficult relationship between aesthetic and political theory in this text has been intelligently discussed by Jacques Seebacher in "Esthétique et politique chez Victor Hugo: L'Utilité du Beau," *Cahiers de l'Association Internationale des Etudes Françaises* (March 19, 1967): 233–246.

6. The association of Jesus and the artist-genius is part of the Romantic tradition. See Balzac's "Des Artistes," first published in 1830. Balzac, *Oeuvres complètes* (Paris: Conard, 1912–1940), XXXVIII, 351–360. For a development of these ideas, see Victor Brombert, *Victor Hugo and the Visionary Novel* (Cambridge, Mass.: Harvard University Press, 1984), esp. pp. 165–168.

7. Charles Baudelaire, *Oeuvres complètes* (Paris: Pléiade, 1963), p. 705.

8. The image is explicit. Hugo writes in *William Shakespeare:* "Votre intelligence, ils la dépassent, votre imagination, ils lui font mal aux yeux." *Oeuvres complètes,* XII, 262.

9. See "Pasteurs et troupeaux" and "Magnitudo Parvi" in *Les Contemplations,* in *Oeuvres complètes,* IX, 287, 196–214.

10. Baudelaire, it is interesting to note, thought that excess was Hugo's natural domain: "L'excessif, l'immense, sont le domaine naturel de Victor Hugo; il s'y meut comme dans son atmosphère natale." Baudelaire, *Oeuvres complètes,* p. 709.

11. See Jean Gaudon, "Vers une rhétorique de la démesure: *William Shakespeare,*" *Romantisme* 3 (1972): 78–85. Hugo's text "Sur Mirabeau" (1834) appears in Hugo, *Oeuvres complètes,* V, 192–221.

The Edifice of the Book

1. Throughout this chapter, volume and page numbers given in parentheses refer to Victor Hugo, *Oeuvres complètes,* ed. Jean Massin, 18 vols. (Paris: Club Français du Livre, 1967–1970).

2. This paragraph follows closely Victor Brombert, *Victor Hugo and the Visionary Novel* (Cambridge, Mass.: Harvard University Press, 1984), p. 58.

3. G. W. F. Hegel, *Aesthetik,* 2 vols. (Frankfurt: Europäische Verlagsan-

stalt, n. d.), Part 2, Section 2, Chapter 3c. See in particular II, 452.

4. Jean Gaudon, *Le Temps de la contemplation* (Paris: Flammarion, 1969), p. 202.

5. For a development on the auctorial status in *Les Travailleurs de la mer,* see Brombert, *Victor Hugo and the Visionary Novel,* pp. 165ff.

6. See Jacques Derrida, *De la Grammatologie* (Paris: Editions de Minuit, 1967), p. 65. See also Shira Wolosky, "Derrida, Jabès, Levinas: Sign-Theory as Ethical Discourse," *Prooftexts* 2 (1982): 283–302.

7. See Pierre Albouy's critical edition of *L'Ane* (Paris: Flammarion, 1966), p. 83.

8. On the relation of the mask to the monster, see Jean-Pierre Reynaud, "Carnaval de Dieu: La Dé-monstration selon Hugo," *Revue des Sciences Humaines* 188 (October–December 1982): 33–59.

9. *L'Ane,* pp. 73–76, 89–95.

V.H.: The Effaced Author or the "I" of Infinity

1. Pierre Albouy, "Hugo, ou le *Je* éclaté," in Albouy, *Mythographies* (Paris: Corti, 1976), p. 74.

2. *Ibid.,* pp. 66–81.

3. Alfred Glauser, *La Poétique de Hugo* (Paris: Nizet, 1978), pp. 245–261.

4. *Promontorium somnii,* in *Oeuvres complètes,* ed. Jean Massin (Paris: Club Français du Livre, 1967–1970), XII, 465. In the following notes, this edition is referred to as *O.C.* Volume and page numbers given in parentheses in the text refer to this edition.

5. Georges Poulet has very aptly spoken of the absence of "altérité" in Hugo's work. Poulet, *La Distance intérieure* (Paris: Plon, 1952), pp. 194–230.

6. Victor Hugo, *Les Voix intérieures* (Paris: Garnier, 1950), p. 300.

7. See Suzanne Nash, *Les Contemplations of Victor Hugo: An Allegory of the Creative Process* (Princeton: Princeton University Press, 1976).

8. The expression is from Jean-Bertrand Barrère, *La Fantaisie de Victor Hugo* (Paris: Klincksieck, 1972), II, 420.

9. "Sur Mirabeau," *O.C.,* V, 214–215.

10. Charles Baudelaire, *Exposition universelle de 1856,* in *Oeuvres complètes* (Paris: Pléiade, 1963), p. 959.

11. On this question, see Victor Brombert, *Victor Hugo and the Visionary Novel* (Cambridge, Mass.: Harvard University Press, 1984), pp. 239–240.

12. See the important pages of Roger Dragonetti, "La Littérature et la lettre," *Lingua e stile* 4, no. 2 (1969): 205–222. The passage in question from the *Convivio* is IV, vi, 3–6.

13. See Michael Riffaterre, "La Poésie métaphysique de Victor Hugo: Style, symboles, et thèmes de *Dieu,*" *Romanic Review* (December 1960): 268–276.

14. See my chapter "Victor Hugo: The Spaceless Prison," in Victor Brombert, *The Romantic Prison* (Princeton: Princeton University Press, 1978), pp. 88–119.

15. Albert Béguin, *L'Ame romantique et les rêves* (Paris: Corti, 1939), p. 374.

16. Anne Ubersfeld, *Le Roi et le Bouffon* (Paris: Corti, 1974), p. 473.

17. Sartre speaks of Hugo as "l'interviewer favori de Dieu." Sartre, *L'Idiot de la famille* (Paris: Gallimard, 1971), I, 841.

18. On the latter, see Michel Grimaud, "De Victor Hugo à Homère-Hogu: L'Onomastique des *Misérables*," *L'Esprit créateur* (Fall 1976): 220–230.

19. See the very enlightening observations by Pierre Albouy in "La Préface philosophique des *Misérables*," in Albouy *Mythologies* (Paris: Corti, 1976), pp. 121–137.

20. The expression is from Ubersfeld, *Le Roi et le Bouffon*, p. 474.

21. See principally the section entitled "Souls" ("Les Ames") in *William Shakespeare, O.C.*, XII, 222–228.

Sartre, Hugo, a Grandfather

1. Jeffrey Mehlman appropriately speaks of Hugo's role in the French nineteenth century as "metonym of Literature itself," as "Literature incarnate." Mehlman, *Revolution and Repetition: Marx, Hugo, Balzac* (Berkeley: University of California Press, 1977), pp. 44–46.

2. *L'Idiot de la famille* (Paris: Gallimard, 1972), III, 383.

3. "Le Rhin," *Oeuvres complètes* (Paris: Club Français du Livre, 1967–1970), VI, 535.

4. *William Shakespeare*, ibid., XII, 170, 242.

5. Ibid., XII, 294–295.

6. *L'Idiot de la famille*, III, 162–163.

7. *Les Mots* (Paris: Gallimard, 1964), pp. 15–16.

8. Ibid., p. 49.

9. *L'Idiot de la famille*, I, 841.

10. *Oeuvres complètes*, X, 300, 308, 320.

11. *Les Mots*, pp. 50, 145.

12. *L'Idiot de la famille*, III, 203, 382–383.

13. *Situations* 2 (Paris: Gallimard, 1948), pp. 12–13, 246–250.

14. *Oeuvres complètes*, V, 38.

15. *L'Idiot de la famille*, III, 203.

16. *Situations* 2, p. 10.

17. *Les Mots*, p. 47.

18. Ibid., p. 208.

19. Ibid., p. 146.

20. Jean-Paul Sartre, "Avant-propos," in Paul Nizan, *Aden Arabie* (Paris: François Maspero, 1960), p. 33.

21. This is the final line of the poem "Suite," which follows the well-known "Réponse à un acte d'accusation," *Oeuvres complètes*, IX, 81.

The Will to Ecstasy

1. "Du Vin et du hachish," *Oeuvres complètes* (Paris: Pléiade, 1961), p. 325. Throughout this chapter, page numbers in parentheses refer to this edition of the complete works.

2. "Théodore de Banville," *Oeuvres complètes*, p. 740.

3. For an intelligent discussion of "Le Beau Navire" as a poem about the

poetic control over desire, see Jean Prévost, "De l'émotion poétique," in Prévost, *Baudelaire* (Paris: Mercure de France, 1953), pp. 340–356.

4. "Fusées," *Oeuvres complètes*, p. 1256.

"Le Cygne"

1. For a study of the Virgilian echoes in "Le Cygne," see Lowry Nelson, "Baudelaire and Virgil: A Reading of 'Le Cygne,'" *Comparative Literature* 13, no. 4 (1961): 332–345.

2. Baudelaire writes: "tout pour moi devient allégorie." Perhaps, as Paul de Man suggests, one should speak of repetition, of "Wiederholung," in a Kierkegaardian sense. "The Rhetoric of Temporality," in Paul de Man, *Blindness and Insight*, 2nd ed., rev. (Minneapolis: University of Minnesota Press, 1983), pp. 187–228.

3. For a study of the explosion of the first-person singular in "personal" poetry, see Pierre Albouy's important essay, "Hugo, ou le *Je* éclaté," in *Mythographies* (Paris: Corti, 1976) pp. 66–81.

4. Walter Benjamin, "Paris, die Hauptstadt des XIX. Jahrhunderts," and "Über einige Motive bei Baudelaire," in *Illuminationen* (Frankfurt: 1955), translated as *Illuminations* (New York: Harcourt, Brace, and World, 1968).

5. "La noire majesté de la plus inquiétante des capitales." Baudelaire, *Salon de 1859*, in *Oeuvres complètes* (Paris: Pléiade, 1961), p. 1084.

Lyricism and Impersonality

1. Charles Baudelaire, *Correspondance générale* (Paris: Conard, 1947), II, 256. Idem, *Oeuvres complètes* (Paris: Pléiade, 1963), pp. 343, 1099.

2. The following is a fairly literal prose translation of the poem: "Pluviôse, angry with the entire city, pours from his urn a flood of shadowy gloom on the pale inhabitants of the nearby cemetery, and mortality on the foggy suburbs.

My cat, looking for a place to bed down on the flooring, restlessly moves its thin mangy body. The soul of an old poet wanders in the gutter with the sad voice of a ghost sensitive to the cold.

A church bell is wailing, and the smoky log accompanies in a falsetto the clock's catarrh, while in a deck of cards filled with rank perfumes—fatal inheritance of a dropsical old woman—the handsome knave of hearts and the queen of spades chat in a sinister fashion of their dead love affairs."

3. On the neoclassical elements of the first quatrain, see Judd D. Hubert's excellent remarks in *L'Esthétique des "Fleurs du Mal"* (Geneva: Pierre Cailler, 1953), p. 107.

4. *Oeuvres complètes*, pp. 229, 243–244, 1160, 1248.

5. On the relation between the third person and the "absent" one, see Emile Benvéniste, *Problèmes de linguistique générale* (Paris: Gallimard, 1966), p. 228.

6. See in particular Marie Malkiewicz-Strzalko, "Baudelaire, Gresset et Saint-Amant," *Revue d'Histoire Littéraire de la France* 49 (October–December 1949): 364–369.

7. See the poems "Les Visions (lines 20–32), and "La Petarrade aux rondeaux" (lines 55–60).

8. Jean Prévost, *Baudelaire* (Paris: Mercure de France, 1953), p. 233.

9. "Les Foules," *Oeuvres complètes*, p. 244.

10. See "Les Petites vieilles" and "Déjà." Jean Prévost makes some fine comments on the "retour du poète sur lui-même," the inevitable return to the self. Prévost, *Baudelaire*, pp. 158, 160.

11. See the already mentioned essay by Pierre Albouy, "Hugo, ou le *Je* éclaté," in *Mythographies* (Paris: Corti, 1976), pp. 66–81.

12. *Oeuvres complètes*, pp. 1294, 1273, 1276, 288, 244. *Correspondance générale*, I, 365.

13. T. S. Eliot, "Tradition and the Individual Talent," in *Selected Essays, 1917–1932* (New York: Harcourt, Brace and Company, 1932), pp. 3–11.

14. See the prose poem "Les Tentations ou Eros, Plutus et la Gloire," *Oeuvres complètes*, pp. 259–262.

15. *Oeuvres complètes*, pp. 240. 288, 372, 1161, 1271.

16. Ibid., p. 1247.

17. Ibid., pp. 339, 365, 346, 343.

18. Ibid., pp. 736, 757. Eliot, "Tradition and the Individual Talent," p. 10.

Erosion and Discontinuity in Flaubert's *Novembre*

1. Jean-Paul Sartre, *L'Idiot de la famille* (Paris: Gallimard, 1971), I, 721, 952.

2. Gustave Flaubert, *Correspondance*, ed. Jean Bruneau (Paris: Pléiade, 1973), I, 410.

3. Ibid., I, 708.

4. "Le Problème de Wittgenstein," in *L'Entretien infini* (Paris: Gallimard, 1969), pp. 487–497.

5. Pierre Bergounioux, "Flaubert et l'autre," *Communications* 19 (1972): 40–50.

6. *Flaubert: The Uses of Uncertainty* (Ithaca, N.Y.: Cornell University Press, 1974), pp. 14, 48.

7. Gérard Genette quite rightly speaks of silence in the plural. "Silences de Flaubert," in Genette, *Figures* (Paris: Seuil, 1966).

From *Novembre* to *L'Education sentimentale*

1. Throughout this chapter, volume and page numbers given in parentheses refer to Gustave Flaubert, *Oeuvres complètes* (Paris: Conard, 1926–1933), 22 vols.

2. *L'Education sentimentale* (Paris: Garnier-Flammarion, 1969), p. 278.

3. *Correspondance*, ed. Jean Bruneau (Paris: Pléiade, 1973), I, 106.

4. Ibid., I, 100.

5. *L'Education sentimentale*, pp. 73, 98.

6. Ibid., pp. 307, 301, 319, 316.

7. *Correspondance*, (Paris: Conard, 1926–1933), III, 150–151.

8. *L'Education sentimentale*, p. 120.

9. *Correspondance*, (Paris: Pléiade, 1980), II, 340.

10. Ibid, I p. 410.

11. *Madame Bovary* (Paris: Garnier-Flammarion, 1966), p. 73.

12. Jean-Paul Sartre, *L'Idiot de la famille* (Paris: Gallimard, 1971), II, 1281, 1771–1882.

13. *Correspondance*, (Paris: Pléiade, 1973), I, 655.

14. *L'Education sentimentale*, pp. 38, 137, 236.

15. Ibid., p. 218.

16. Ibid., pp. 434–435.

17. Ibid., p. 272.

18. Ibid., pp. 438–439.

19. Bernard Masson, "L'Eau et les rêves dans *L'Education sentimentale*," *Europe* 485–487 (September–November 1969): 86; Albert Thibaudet, *Gustave Flaubert* (Paris: Gallimard, 1935), p. 143.

20. *L'Education sentimentale*, pp. 82, 98, 135, 356.

21. Ibid., pp. 109–110.

22. Ibid., p. 84.

23. *Correspondance* (Paris: Pléiade, 1980), II, 24.

24. *Correspondance* (Paris: Conard, 1926–1933), III, 268; IV, 464.

25. Ibid., III, 263.

26. Ibid., I, 410.

Idyll and Upheaval in L'Education Sentimentale

1. *Madame Bovary* (Paris: Garnier-Flammarion, 1966), p. 43.

2. Ibid., p. 287.

3. L'Education sentimentale (Paris: Garnier-Flammarion, 1969), p. 43.

4. Ibid., p. 134.

5. See in particular, ibid., pp. 344–348.

Flaubert and the Articulations of Polyvalence

1. Henry James, "Gustave Flaubert," in James, *Notes on Novelists* (New York: Scribners, 1914), p. 84.

2. Gustave Flaubert, *Correspondance: Supplément* (Paris: Conard, 1954), II, 65. Idem, *Correspondance* (Paris: Conard, 1926–1933), V, 363.

3. *L'Education sentimentale* (Paris: Garnier-Flammarion, 1969), p. 398.

4. Quoted in *L'Education sentimentale* (Paris: Conard, 1910), pp. 693–695, 703.

5. See in particular Georg Lukács, *Theory of the Novel* (Cambridge, Mass.: MIT Press, 1971), pp. 124–125.

6. *Correspondance*, II, 76, 88. Kierkegaard proposed "infinite absolute negativity" as the definition of the ultimate ironic outlook on life. Kierke-

gaard, *The Concept of Irony* (New York: Harper and Row, 1965), p. 278.

7. *Correspondance*, II, 88.

8. *Correspondance: Supplément*, II, 100, 175–176. *Lettres inédites à Tourgueneff* (Monaco: Editions du Rocher, 1946), p. 206.

9. See *The Sense of an Ending: Studies in the Theory of Fiction* (New York: Oxford University Press, 1967), esp. pp. 67–89.

10. This sentence appears in the letter of 14 January 1857 to Mme Schlésinger. Albert Thibaudet, keenly aware of the retrospective beauty of this scene, makes the far-reaching comment that Mme Arnoux (but the same could be said of Frédéric) now *possesses* her dream "instead of being possessed by it." Thibaudet, *Gustave Flaubert* (Paris: Gallimard, 1935), p. 150.

11. See Sarah Kofman, *L'Enfance de l'art: Une Interprétation de l'esthétique freudienne* (Paris: Payot, 1970), pp. 82–95.

12. *Correspondance*, VII, 369.

The Temptation of the Subject

1. Gustave Flaubert, *Correspondance*, ed. Jean Bruneau (Paris: Pléiade, 1973), I, 708. Henceforth referred to as Pléiade.

2. *Correspondance* (Paris: Conard, 1926–1933), VI, 2.

3. Charles Baudelaire, *Oeuvres complètes* (Paris: Pléiade, 1963), 657.

4. Pléiade, I, 708.

5. For a reaction to some of these overstatements, see P. M. Wetherill, "Flaubert et les distortions de la critique moderne," *Symposium* 25 (Fall 1971): 271–279; and Louis Fournier, "Flaubert et le 'Nouveau Roman': Un Cas de paternité douteuse," *Amis de Flaubert* 52 (May 1978).

6. *Correspondance*, II, 345; III, 249, 248; IIIa, 96.

7. Maurice Blanchot, *L'Entretien infini* (Paris: Gallimard, 1969), 492; Pierre Bergounioux, "Flaubert et l'autre" *Communications* 19 (1972): 40–50; Claude Burgelin "La Flaubertolâtrie," *Littérature* 15 (October 1974): 5–16; Jonathan Culler, *Flaubert: The Uses of Uncertainty* (Ithaca, N.Y.: Cornell University Press, 1974), p. 13; Jean-Paul Sartre, *L'Idiot de la famille* (Paris: Gallimard, 1971), I and II, passim. For perspectives on Flaubert's modernity, see also Jean Rousset, "*Madame Bovary* ou le 'livre sur rien,' " in Rousset, *Forme et Signification* (Paris: Corti, 1962); Nathalie Sarraute, "Flaubert le précurseur," *Preuves* 168 (February 1965): 3–11; Jeanne Bem, "Sur le sens d'un discours circulaire," *Littérature* 15 (October 1974): 95–109.

8. *Correspondance*, IV, 164; Baudelaire, *Oeuvres complètes*, p. 652.

9. *Correspondance*, VII, 322; III, 249; II, 345; VII, 294; II, 345.

10. *Correspondance*, IV, 225; II, 345; VIII, 207.

11. *Correspondance*, III, 322; VIII, 175, Pléiade, I, 679.

12. *Correspondance*, VII, 281; III, 330, 355.

13. For a short and useful theoretical discussion of satire, see Alvin Kernan's fine chapter "A Theory of Satire," in Kernan, *The Cankered Muse* (New Haven, Conn.: Yale University Press, 1959).

14. *Correspondance*, III, 45, 351; V, 91; IV, 356.

15. Sartre, in *L'Idiot de la famille*, has given complex analyses of the fundamental (and willful) misunderstanding.

16. *Correspondance: Supplément* (Paris: Conard, 1954), IV, 52; V, 26. The hierarchy of the arts was obviously a conviction of Flaubert's. See his letter to Turgenev: "Je vous soupçonne de vouloir . . . entendre de la musique ou voir de la peinture, *arts inférieurs.*" *Correspondance: Supplément*, IV, 59.

17. *Correspondance*, II, 364; *Oeuvres de jeunesse inédites* (Paris: Conard, 1910), II, 184. *L'Education sentimentale* (Paris: Garnier-Flammarion, 1969), p. 59; *Correspondance*, II, 279.

18. *La Première Education sentimentale* (Paris: Seuil, 1963), 244. *Correspondance*, I, 302; VIII, 300; II, 353. For a concise discussion by Sartre of the "posthumous" stance of both Flaubert and Baudelaire, see his "Introduction" to Baudelaire's *Ecrits intimes* (Paris: Point du Jour, 1946).

19. *Correspondance*, II, 343, IV, 5: VII, 285. *La Première Education sentimentale*, p. 237. *Correspondance*, VII, 351; VIII, 309.

20. Pléiade, I, 652, 637. *Oeuvres de jeunesse inédites*, I, 526, 540.

21. *Oeuvres de jeunesse inédites*, I, 496; II, 164.

22. *Correspondance*, III, 157, 66. *La Première Education sentimentale*, p. 246.

23. *Correspondance*, II, 439; Pléiade, I, 627–628.

24. *Correspondance*, IV, 464; III, 268: IV, 215, 463, 212. *L'Education sentimentale*, p. 81.

25. Pléiade, I, 37. *La Première Education sentimentale*, pp. 246–251. Pléiade, I, 680, 679.

26. *Correspondance: Supplément*, II, 92; *Correspondance*, III, 100; II, 157; IV, 3. Alain Robbe-Grillet, "Une voie pour le roman futur," *Nouvelle Nouvelle Revue Française* (July 1956): 77–84.

27. "L'Aqueduc et le piédestal," *Tel Quel* 18 (Summer 1964): 18, 87–88.

28. *Correspondance*, I, 385; V, 111; II, 343; III, 269; VII, 331.

29. *Correspondance*, I, 192, 178; II, 343. Roland Barthes, *"L'Effet de réel,"* *Communications* 11 (1968): 84–89.

30. *Correspondance*, II, 169; III, 210; I, 339; III, 384; IX, 3; *Correspondance: Supplément*, II, 95–96.

31. *Correspondance*, III, 21; V, 338; *Correspondance: Supplément*, II, 118; *Correspondance*, VII, 230; IV, 249; IV, 52. Pléiade, I, 495.

32. *Correspondance*, III, 388, 344, 161; VIII, 374. Raymonde Debray-Genette, "Flaubert: Science et Ecriture," *Littérature* 15 (October 1974): 41–51. *Correspondance*, III, 138.

33. *Correspondance*, III, 317, 320; IV, 18.

34. Raymonde Debray-Genette, "Du Mode narratif dans les 'Trois Contes,' " *Littérature* 2 (May 1971): 39–62.

35. *Correspondance*, IV, 357; II, 461.

36. *Correspondance*, II, 38; VI, 441; II, 461.

37. *Oeuvres complètes*, p. 654. Albert Thibaudet, *Gustave Flaubert* (Paris: Gallimard, 1935), p. 150.

38. *La Première Education sentimentale*, pp. 262, 237. *Correspondance*, III,

45. I wish to express my debt to Charles Carlut's most useful concordance and repertory *La Correspondance de Flaubert: Etude et répertoire critique* (Columbus: Ohio State University Press, 1968).

Stendhal, Reader of Rousseau

1. Paul Arbelet, *La Jeunesse de Stendhal* (Paris: Champion, 1919), I, 190.
2. Jules Alciatore's studies on the influence of the Idéologues are particularly valuable. See his *Stendhal et Helvétius* (Geneva: Droz, 1952), which contains a bibliography of his articles on the relations between Stendhal and Destutt de Tracy, Pinel, and Lancelin. See also Alciatore's *Stendhal et Maine de Biran* (Geneva: Droz, 1954), and his article "Stendhal, Hobbes, le courage et la colère," *French Review* 30 (January 1957): 211–217.
3. Francine Marill has written some subtle pages on the influence of Rousseau in *Le Naturel chez Stendhal* (Paris: Nizet, 1956), pp. 184–191.
4. *Journal,* in *Oeuvres intimes,* 2 vols. (Paris: Pléiade, 1982), I, 325. For most of the quotations, I have used *Oeuvres complètes* (Paris: Le Divan, 1927–1937). However, for the *Journal, Vie de Henry Brulard,* and *Souvenirs d'égotisme,* I have used *Oeuvres intimes* (Paris: Pléiade, 1982), 2 vols. The edition of the *Correspondance* used is likewise the Pléiade edition, 1968, 3 vols. The references to *Promenades dans Rome* are to the Pléiade, edition of *Voyages en Italie* (1973).
5. *Oeuvres intimes,* II, 596, 701, 780. The letter cannot, however, be trusted completely. Beyle was writing to Edouard Mounier in order to pay court to Mounier's sister. If he claims to read Virgil and Jean-Jacques, it is no doubt to display his "tender" soul. But even that deserves to be noted.
6. *Oeuvres intimes,* II, 936, 940, 944.
7. Ibid., II, 716, 908.
8. *Correspondance,* I, 2, 161–162.
9. Ibid., I, 175. Stendhal's Italian spelling is somewhat capricious.
10. Ibid., I, 176, 240.
11. *Pensées: Filosofia Nova,* 2 vols. (Paris: Divan, 1931), I, 149; *Oeuvres intimes,* II, 777–778. See Henri Martineau's comments in his critical edition of *Vie de Henry Brulard* (Paris: Divan, 1949), II, 245.
12. *Oeuvres intimes,* II, 951; *Histoire de la peinture en Italie* (Paris: Divan, 1929), II, 78–79; *Correspondance,* I, 659; *Pensées: Filosofia Nova,* I, 187.
13. *Pensées: Filosofia Nova,* I, 40, 67; *Mémoires d'un touriste* (Paris: Divan, 1929), III, 71.
14. *Oeuvres intimes,* II, 833–834. This does not prevent him from speaking of "our father Walter Scott" in his letter to Balzac. *Correspondance,* 3 vols. (Paris: Pléiade, 1982), III, 398.
15. *Mélanges de littérature* (Paris: Divan, 1933), III, 114; *Mélanges intimes et marginalia* (Paris: Divan, 1936), II, 287; *Oeuvres intimes,* II, 935.
16. *Oeuvres intimes,* I, 821; *Mélanges de littérature,* III, 125.
17. *Correspondance,* III, 395.
18. *Pensées: Filosofia Nova,* I, 94; *Correspondance,* I, 570; *Oeuvres intimes,* I, 590; *Correspondance,* I, 659.

19. Proust, *Contre Sainte-Beuve* (Paris: Gallimard, 1954), p. 413. I have tried to show, however, how Stendhal uses this irony for fictional purposes. Victor Brombert, *Stendhal et la voie oblique* (Paris: Presses Universitaires de France, 1954).

20. *Oeuvres intimes*, II, 818.

21. *Mémoires d'un touriste*, III, 37; *Promenades dans Rome*, in *Voyages en Italie* (Paris: Pléiade, 1973), p. 917. *Mémoires d'un touriste*, III, 98; *Pensées: Filosofia Nova*, II, 33.

22. *Pensées: Filosofia Nova*, I, 157; II, 9; *De l'Amour* (Paris: Divan, 1927), II, 155–156.

23. *Courrier anglais* (Paris: Divan, 1935), I, 187; *Mémoires d'un touriste*, III, 12; *Oeuvres intimes*, II, 939.

24. *Histoire de la peinture en Italie*, I, 21; *Mélanges intimes et marginalia*, II, 99; *De l'Amour*, II, 124; *Mémoires d'un touriste*, III, 70 *Mélanges de littérature*, III, 96; *Oeuvres intimes*, I, 591; *Mélanges intimes et marginalia*, I, 339; *Napoléon* (Paris: Divan, 1930), I, 311; *Mélanges de littérature*, III, 107, 111.

25. *Mémoires d'un touriste*, III, 127; *Oeuvres intimes*, II, 460, 473. Julien Sorel, too, reacts to Valenod's vulgarity by uttering three times in succession the word *canaille*. Henri Martineau sees in this triple exclamation an echo of Rousseau's triple exclamation *carnifex*.

26. *Oeuvres intimes*, I, 170.

27. Charles Monselet, preface to *Armance*, 2nd ed. (Paris: D. Giraud, 1853), p. vii; P. Brun, *Henry Beyle, Stendhal* (Grenoble: Gratier, 1900), p. 58.

28. *Mélanges de littérature*, II, 358.

29. *Romans et nouvelles* (Paris: Divan, 1928), I, 171, 189; *Mélanges de littérature*, I, 63.

30. Jean-Jacques Rousseau, *Les Confessions*, in *Oeuvres complètes* (Paris: Pléiade, 1959), p. 518; Stendhal, *Le Rouge et le Noir* (Paris: Garnier-Flammarion, 1964), p. 49; *Les Confessions*, 117, 97, 314.

31. *Les Confessions*, 30, 108.

32. *Les Confessions*, 45, 158, 283, 290; Stendhal, *Oeuvres intimes*, II, 869.

33. *Les Confessions*, 325, 157, 38, 301; Charles Baudelaire, "L'Oeuvre et la vie de Delacroix," *Curiosités esthétiques* (Paris: Pléiade, 1963), p. 1140.

34. *Les Confessions*, 77, 320–322. Zulietta's famous words "Lascia le donne e studia la matematica" are repeated in M. Leuwen's letter to his son Lucien.

35. *Oeuvres intimes*, II, 541.

36. Albert Bazaillias, "Rousseau et les femmes," *La Revue de Paris* (January 15, 1914): 367–405.

37. *Correspondance*, I, 967.

38. *Les Confessions*, 34, 278, 292, 513, 354; *Oeuvres intimes*, II, 957, 640–641.

39. *Les Confessions*, 52, 95, 444.

40. *Les Confessions*, 172, 646; Stendhal, *La Chartreuse de Parme* (Paris: Garnier, 1942), p. 319.

41. *Les Confessions*, 636; *Correspondance*, III, 140.

Vie de Henry Brulard

1. Throughout this chapter the page numbers in parentheses refer to *Vie de Henry Brulard*, in *Oeuvres intimes*, ed. Victor Del Litto (Paris: Pléiade, 1982), vol. II.

2. *Souvenirs d'égotisme*, in *Oeuvres intimes*, ed. Victor Del Litto (Paris: Pléiade, 1982), vol. II, 434.

3. Ibid., II, 453.

4. Harald Weinrich, *Linguistik der Lüge* [Linguistics of the Lie] (Heidelberg: Verlag Lambert Schneider, 1966).

5. Vladimir Jankélévitch, *L'Ironie ou la bonne conscience* (Paris: Presses Universitaires de France, 1950).

6. Georg Lukács, *The Theory of the Novel* (Cambridge, Mass.: MIT Press, 1971), p. 124.

7. *Oeuvres intimes*, II, 878.

8. For a study of this type of irony, see Victor Brombert, *Stendhal et la voie oblique* (Paris: Presses Universitaires de France, 1954).

T. S. Eliot and the Romantic Heresy

1. T. S. Eliot, *After Strange Gods: A Primer in Heresy* (New York: Harcourt, Brace, 1934), p. 22.

2. T. S. Eliot, *The Use of Poetry and the Use of Criticism* (London: Faber & Faber, 1933), p. 100.

3. See Albert Mordell's rather disheveled and unfair pamphlet, *T. S. Eliot's Deficiencies as a Social Critic* (Girard, Kansas: Haldeman-Julius Publications, 1951), p. 32.

4. "The New Critics and the Historical Method," *The Yale Review* 43, no. 1 (Autumn 1953): 14–23.

5. "The New Critics," in Stallman, *Critiques and Essays in Criticism* (New York: Ronald Press, 1949), pp. 488–506.

6. Eliot, *After Strange Gods*, p. 42.

7. Eliot, *Selected Essays*, (New York: Harcourt, Brace, 1932), pp. 391–392, 401.

8. T. E. Hulme, *Speculations* (New York: Harcourt, Brace, 1924), p. 115.

9. Ibid., p. 116.

10. *Prologue d'un essai sur la critique* (Paris: La Porte Etroite, 1932), p. 55.

11. "The *Action Française*, M. Maurras and Mr. Ward," *Criterion* 7 (March 1928): 195–203.

12. *Selected Essays*, p. 343.

13. *The Sacred Wood*, p. 31.

14. Eliot, *After Strange Gods*, p. 53. For a further dogmatic use of the word "reality," see Eliot's discussion of the *Vita Nuova* (*Selected Essays*, p. 235), where he describes a "practical sense of realities" (the belief in an afterlife) as anti-Romantic.

15. *The Sacred Wood*, p. 140.

16. Ibid., p. 102. It is in this essay that we first find the definition of the "objective correlative."

17. *The Use of Poetry and the Use of Criticism,* p. 88.

18. "From Poe to Valéry," *The Hudson Review* 2, no. 3 (Autumn 1949): 327–342.

19. *The Use of Poetry and the Use of Criticism,* p. 96.

20. *Axel's Castle* (New York: Scribners, 1931), pp. 93–131.

21. *Mr. Eliot among the Nightingales* (Paris: L. Drake, 1932), pp. 4–9.

22. See Mordell, *T. S. Eliot's Deficiencies as a Social Critic.*

23. "Sainte-Beuve créateur de valeurs," in *Promenades philosophiques* (Paris: Mercure de France, 1905), pp. 33–44. A similar thought had been voiced earlier by Charles Maurras: "A Sainte-Beuve and a Renan stand a good chance of some day eclipsing Flaubert, Leconte, perhaps even Hugo." *Prologue d'un essai sur la critique,* p. 21.

24. Quoted in *The Sacred Wood,* p. 139.

25. *Les Métamorphoses du Romantisme* (Paris: Cahiers de la Quinzaine, 2e cahier, 19e série, 1928), p. 11.

26. Quoted by Pierre Constans in his avant-propos to Charles Maurras, *Un Débat sur le Romantisme,* Paris: Flammarion, 1928), p. 203.

27. Baudelaire, "Qu'est-ce que le Romantisme?" in *Salon de 1846, Oeuvres complètes* (Paris: Pléiade, 1963), pp. 878–880.

28. See Margaret Gilman, "Revival and Revolution in English and French Romantic Poetry," *Yale French Studies* 6 (1950): 14–26.

29. *Art and Social Responsibility* (London: Falcon Press, 1946), p. 17.

Credits

A number of essays included in this volume have appeared in an earlier form, in some cases with a slightly different title: "Opening Signals in Narrative," *New Literary History* 11 (Spring 1980); "Introduction" to Balzac's *La Peau de chagrin* (New York: Dell 1962); "Hugo's *William Shakespeare:* The Promontory and the Infinite," *Hudson Review* 34 (Summer 1981); "Sartre, Hugo, a Grandfather," *Yale French Studies* 68 (1985); "The Will to Ecstasy: The Example of Baudelaire's 'La Chevelure,'" *Yale French Studies* 50 (1974); "Flaubert and the Temptation of the Subject," *Nineteenth-Century French Studies* 12 (Spring 1984); "T. S. Eliot and the Romantic Heresy," *Yale French Studies* 13 (1954). For permission to reprint these pieces in a revised form I wish to thank the respective editors.

Other essays originally appeared in French, in a considerably different form: "Natalie ou le lecteur caché de Balzac," in *Mouvements Premiers: Etudes critiques offertes à Georges Poulet* (Paris: Corti, 1972); "Hugo: L'Edifice du livre," *Romantisme* 44 (1984); "V.H.: L'Auteur effacé ou le moi de l'infini," *Poétique* 52 (November 1982); " 'Le Cygne' de Baudelaire: Douleur, Souvenir, Travail," in *Etudes Baudelairiennes,* III (Neuchatel: La Baconnière, 1973); "Lyrisme et dépersonnalisation: l'exemple de Baudelaire," *Romantisme* 6 (1973); "Usure et rupture chez Flaubert: l'exemple de *Novembre*," *Contrepoint* 28 (1978); "De *Novembre* à *L'Education:* Communication et voie publique," *Revue d'Histoire Littéraire de la France* 81 (Fall 1981); "Lieu de l'idylle et lieu du bouleversement dans *L'Education sentimentale*," *Cahiers de l'Association Internationale des Etudes Françaises* 23 (1971); *L'Education sentimentale:* Articulations et polyvalence," in *La Production du sens chez Flaubert* (Paris: 10/18, 1975); "Stendhal lecteur de Rousseau," *Revue des Sciences Humaines* 92 (October–December 1958).

Two essays—"Approaches" and *"Vie de Henry Brulard:* Irony and Continuity"—appear here for the first time.

Index